# EMPLOYMENT EQUITY:
# MAKING IT WORK

# EMPLOYMENT EQUITY: MAKING IT WORK

Nan Weiner, Ph.D.

**Butterworths**
Toronto and Vancouver

**Employment Equity: Making It Work**

© Butterworths Canada Ltd. 1993
 Published September, 1993

**The Butterworth Group of Companies**

| | |
|---|---|
| *Canada* | Butterworths Canada Ltd., 75 Clegg Road, MARKHAM, Ontario, L6G 1A1 and 409 Granville St., Ste. 1455, VANCOUVER, B.C. V6C 1T2 |
| *Australia* | Butterworths, SYDNEY, MELBOURNE, BRISBANE, ADELAIDE, PERTH, CANBERRA and HOBART |
| *Ireland* | Butterworths (Ireland) Ltd., DUBLIN |
| *New Zealand* | Butterworths of New Zealand Ltd., WELLINGTON and AUCKLAND |
| *Puerto Rico* | Butterworth of Puerto Rico, Inc., SAN JUAN |
| *Singapore* | Butterworths Asia, SINGAPORE |
| *United Kingdom* | Butterworth & Co. (Publishers) Ltd., LONDON and EDINBURGH |
| *United States* | Butterworth Legal Publishers, AUSTIN, Texas; CLEARWATER, Florida; ORFORD, New Hampshire; ST. PAUL, Minnesota; SALEM, New Hampshire |

Readers wishing further information on excerpts provided through the co-operation of Statistics Canada may obtain copies of related publications by mail from Publications Sales, Statistics Canada, Ottawa, Ontario, K1A 0T6, or by calling 1-613-951-7277 or national toll-free 1-800-267-6677. Readers may also facsimile their order by dialing 1-613-951-1584.

**Canadian Cataloguing in Publication Data**

Weiner, Nan
 Employment equity: making it work

Includes bibliographical references and index.
ISBN 0-409-91176-3

1. Discrimination in employment – Law and legislation – Ontario. I. Title.

KE0659.W45 1993   344.713'01133   C93-094051-2
KF3464.W45 1993

To my best friends over the decades

*Max(ine) Davis*
*Pam Nichols*
*Mary Jane Rotheram*
*Myra Schiff*

To two special guys

*Richard Kenneth*
*Dana Nathaniel*

# Preface
# and
# Acknowledgments

No one ever writes a book on their own. Help and support come from many sources. I want to thank Cathy Fantauzzi who proofread the manuscript over and over and over and over again. To Angela D'Origo who tracked down obscure facts, verified dates and data, challenged me and made the book better. To Elizabeth Perry, Vicki Skelton and Bruce Pearce, librarians at the University of Toronto's Centre for Industrial Relations, who are not only extremely helpful and resourceful, but are wonderfully pleasant to work with. To the memory of my father, Sam Weiner, who always had faith in me.

To all those working in the field of employment equity from whom I have learned so much – to those in unions and in work organizations, to those who advocate for employment equity, to those in government, and especially to my clients and students.

The field of employment equity is developing and changing. By the time this book is printed some parts will be out of date, some will be old-hat, and some will be politically incorrect. May those who use this book do so with two axioms – a desire to increase equality within employment and a sense of humour.

# Contents

# List Of Boxes

# List of Figures

# List of Tables

# CHAPTER 1

# Introduction

*What is employment equity?*

Employment equity (hereafter EE) is a set of activities designed to ensure that an organization has equality for all its employees in all aspects of employment such as recruiting, hiring, compensation, training, and so on. The goal of EE is to have organizations' work-forces mirror or reflect the composition of the labour market from which each recruits, for employment policies and practices to work well for all employees, and for all employees to be able to progress to the full extent of their ability (given opportunities).

*Why is EE needed?*

Employment equity is needed to remove systemic discrimination to ensure that those who have traditionally been disadvantaged are no longer disadvantaged.

The disadvantaged groups are referred to as designated groups or target groups; they include:

- Women
- Aboriginal Peoples or First Nations people
- Persons with disabilities, and
- Visible or racial minorities.

Employment equity is not about giving these groups an advantage, but to provide them with their fair share of employment opportunities by overcoming the effects of past and present discrimination.

*What is systemic discrimination?*

Systemic discrimination is a particular kind of discrimination. It differs from the common perception of discrimination. The more common kind of discrimination is referred to as direct or intentional discrimination. It is easier to define systemic discrimination by contrasting it to direct discrimination. Direct discrimination is typically presumed to involve the behaviour of a bigoted or prejudiced individual. Such a person, it is believed, knowingly and intentionally discriminates against others. Sometimes such discrimination is clearly meant to do someone harm – "I will not hire Aboriginal People because I do not want them around." Sometimes the discrimination is motivated by concern – "I will not hire women because they are likely to get hurt doing the heavy lifting required." Either kind of behaviour is discriminatory because a decision is being made for an individual which is not based on characteristics of personal skill. Rather, such decisions are based on the presumed characteristics of a group to which the individual belongs. Employment equity addresses direct and systemic discrimination. Systemic discrimination is more pervasive than direct discrimination.

Systemic discrimination is unintentional; it is not typically a conscious decision to discriminate. In fact, systemic discrimination tends to occur through the normal operation of employment practices, policies and systems which are often subtle in the way they discriminate. The systems which may systemically discriminate include recruitment, selection, compensation, training and other employment systems. These systems are designed to accomplish some objective – to recruit, to identify the most qualified person, to pay people fairly, and so on. They discriminate because they adversely effect one or more of the designated groups. For example, one community college found that its educational assistance program worked against women in lower paid jobs – unintentionally. The program was designed like most: employees could take any course they wanted and they would be reimbursed upon successful completion of the course. The problem was that many of the women in lower paid jobs could not manage the cash flow of paying for a course ahead of time and being reimbursed months later. So, a program designed to help employees develop and move up within the organization was adversely affecting one of the groups it was specifically designed to help.

Another example of systemic discrimination is word-of-mouth recruiting. This recruiting technique tends to be low cost and highly effective. Current employees screen their friends, neighbours and relatives and tell only those they feel would work well for the organization about job openings. Further, they give these individuals a realistic picture of what it is like to work for the organization. So how is this discriminatory? An organization with a predominately white work-force is going to find that the friends, neighbours and relatives of its current employees are also likely to be white. So, word-of-mouth recruiting is unlikely to result in racial minority candidates applying. The same can be said about an organization which primarily employs people of Chinese ancestry and relies on word-of-mouth recruiting. It is not likely to provide employment opportunities for non-Chinese minority groups or for Whites.

### How does systemic discrimination differ from direct discrimination?

The difference between direct and systemic discrimination is outlined in Table 1-1. With direct discrimination there tends to be a specific event

TABLE 1–1

COMPARISON BETWEEN DIRECT AND SYSTEMIC DISCRIMINATION

| DIRECT | SYSTEMIC |
|---|---|
| **View of discrimination** | |
| Exceptional or aberrant incident. | Systemic discrimination results from the operation of a policy, procedure or system which is designed to serve the organization but which, in addition to its intended purpose, has an unintentional adverse impact on (discrimination against) women, Aboriginal Peoples, persons with disabilities and/or visible minorities. |
| **Awareness of discrimination** | |
| Discrimination is known or suspected. Complaint can be filed. | Subtle and difficult to see unless looking for it. |
| **Scope of remedy** | |
| Purpose of remedy is to "make one whole". | Usually more than one possible way to change system(s). |
| **Liability timeframe** | |
| Liability begins at time of complaint. Retroactivity is often required. | A reasonable period to correct the system(s) is needed. Remedy often phased-in. |
| **Orientation of remedy** | |
| Remedy looks to past. | Remedy looks to future. |
| **Approach** | |
| Complaint-based approach. | Pro-active, problem-solving approach is best. Still learning about how systemic discrimination operates. |
| **Issue of guilt** | |
| Blame is relevant. | Typically impersonal and unintentional; issue of blame is irrelevant. |

which is discriminatory – for example, the decision not to hire a black person, not to promote a person with a disability, not to pay a woman the same as a man with identical qualifications, or not to send an Aboriginal person to a supervisory training program. This event is usually seen as an aberration, not the normal way of doing things. Systemic discrimination results from the on-going operation of established procedures and systems. None of these systems were designed to discriminate. Systemic discrimination occurs when some aspects of employment systems unintentionally have an adverse impact against one or more of the designated groups. For example, the typical terms and conditions of employment, such as hours of work, were established when the workforce was primarily comprised of able-bodied men. So, the hours of work are based on the assumption that there would be a division of labour within the family, that men would work outside the home (be employed) and women would work within the home. Even where a wife worked, it was presumed that her husband's job was more important (and, in all likelihood, paid more than her's). Today, these traditional hours of work operate against many women with family responsibilities, some of whom may have problems getting to work during rush hour, persons with disabilities and some white able-bodied men. One reason employment systems have unintentional negative effects on some groups is because times change. For instance, today only 16 per cent of Canadian families have an employed husband with a wife staying at home to care for the children and the household. So, traditional hours of work cannot meet the needs of the majority of today's workers – including men with young children, and those in dual career relationship.

Systemic discrimination often results from practices which rely on outdated assumptions and beliefs. For instance, in one organization a man and a woman with similar qualifications were hired to begin the same job on the same day. Within a few of weeks their starting date, the woman discovered that she was being paid $2,000 per year less than her male co-worker. When she asked why, she was told it was because men have families to support. The realities were that his family consisted of himself and a working spouse. She, on the other hand, was widowed and supporting seven children!

As you can see from the above examples systemic discrimination is often subtle. This means it is difficult to see unless one is looking for it. Direct discrimination, on the other hand, is often suspected and, where it exists, the individual who feels wronged can file a complaint. If direct discrimination is found to exist, then a remedy can be applied. The goal of this remedy is to make the person discriminated against "whole". That is, to ensure that the person is in the position they would have been in if the discrimination had not occurred. So, if someone has been denied a promotion because they are of East Indian ancestry, the remedy involves back pay to the date on which the person should have been promoted. Finding a remedy for systemic discrimination is typically more complex. The remedy requires change to an employment system. However, the system has a purpose (to recruit, to hire) which must continue, though without the adverse impact. Further, changes in one system may necessitate changes in other systems because they are interrelated. To further complicate things, there is usually more than one way to change an employment system to remove systemic discrimination.

Because of the time needed to identify systemic discrimination and the complexity of addressing it, a period of time is required before a remedy can be put into place. Thus, remedies to systemic discrimination have a future focus. On the other hand, a remedy for direct discrimination looks to the past (did discrimination occur and, if so, what is needed to "make the person whole", as if it had not occurred). So a complaint-based system (such as human rights) is a sufficient means of addressing direct discrimination, but not systemic discrimination. Correction of systemic discrimination requires a pro-active, problem-solving approach. Only a pro-active, problem-solving approach recognizes that systematic discrimination

- is subtle and its identification often requires specifically examining employment systems looking for such discrimination,
- may be complex to remedy, and
- requires on-going monitoring and adjustments because identification of systemic discrimination involves an on-going learning process since, until some such discrimination is identified and remedied, other, more subtle discrimination is unlikely to be seen.

The on-going process to remedy systemic discrimination in employment is EE. Employment Equity involves looking for employment barriers which are systemically discriminating and correcting them. It does not mean waiting for a complaint to see if there is a problem. Rather, EE is pro-active.

A final difference between direct discrimination and systemic discrimination concerns the issue of blame. Because direct discrimination is about conscious, deliberate behaviours there is the issue of guilt. Blame and guilt are irrelevant when addressing systemic discrimination. Systems were designed for a particular purpose, not to discriminate. The fact that they do discriminate, means that there is an obligation to correct such discrimination as quickly as possible once it is recognized. In EE one is saying "we can see a better way to do things", rather than saying "we have made a mistake". For instance, one does not feel guilty when a better way is found to market a product or service, to train salespeople, or to structure an organization. The same can be said about EE. It involves finding a better way – one which does not adversely affect certain groups – First Nations peoples, persons with disabilities, racial minorities and women. Another way to say this is that systems must work for all people in the labour force: men and women; Whites, racial minorities and Aboriginal Peoples; people who are able-bodied and people who are disabled.

An important similarity between dealing with direct and systemic discrimination is that the issue of intent is not of relevance in either kind of discrimination. The Supreme Court of Canada has ruled that it is the effect, not intent, which defines a practice as discriminatory.

### Why are Aboriginal Peoples, persons with disabilities, racial minorities and women targeted for EE consideration?

These four groups are disadvantaged in terms of employment. Employment equity is concerned about group rights. That is, the groups as a whole are disadvantaged in terms of:

- higher levels of unemployment and underemployment,
- lower pay for equal qualifications, and
- lower participation in positions of authority (*e.g.*, management).

For those interested, Appendix A provides the statistical evidence for these different aspects of disadvantage.

### What exactly does EE involve?

A wide range of activities are part of EE – everything, from putting four bricks under a desk so that it will accommodate a person using a wheelchair to establishing an on-site day care centre. Anything that helps identify and remove employment barriers for the designated groups. A partial listing of EE initiatives is provided in Box 1-1. Implementation of such initiatives is discussed in Chapter 7.

It is important to remember that while the ultimate goal of EE is to have a representative work-force, there are still many EE activities which can (and should) be done, even though your organization is not hiring. For example, one major EE activity is to ensure that job requirements and qualifications are totally job related. Reviewing job qualifications is best done when the organization is *not* hiring. When a position is vacant there is pressure to fill it as quickly as possible; a careful review (and questioning) of the job requirements will slow down the process. Reviewing job requirements months before any possible hiring is likely to result in a more thorough assessment of all the possible ways future employees could obtain the qualifications they need to do the job.

**Box 1-1**

Sample of Employment Equity Initiatives
(See Chapter 7 for a more complete list)

**General**
- Negotiating employment equity into labour contracts.
- Communication strategy (jointly for unionized employees).
- Providing mechanism for managers, staff, union representatives, etc., to provide input on potential barriers.

**Recruitment**
- Contacts and development of on-going relationship with First Nations peoples, persons with disabilities, racial minorities and women.
- Advertising in other than English and mainstream papers (*i.e.*, ethnic papers) and locations.
- Up-to-date skills inventories.
- Avoidance of informal practices (*e.g.*, old boys network) for filling of permanent jobs or casual, part-time or secondment which leads to permanent jobs.

**Hiring and promotion**
- Review of job descriptions to determine qualifications truly needed to do the job.
- Physical demands analysis for all jobs.

**Training and orientation**
- Review of how decisions are made as to whom to send to training programs.
- Integrating employment equity into on-going supervisory and other training programs.

**Work climate and environment**
- Orientation for non-traditional employees.
- Are dress codes able to make reasonable accommodation for individual religious observances and dress requirements?

**Interaction between work and other aspects of life**
- Facilitate persons with disabilities getting to your location and accessibility within and around work site.
- Work scheduling to facilitate caring for family members.

**Lay-offs and recall**
- Are seniority systems designed so that designated groups are not unduly affected by lay-offs?

### Doesn't EE mean hiring unqualified people?

No. One should never hire unqualified people. Employment equity should broaden the pool from which the organization recruits and result in the hiring of a more diverse work-force in the future. But it never means hiring unqualified people.

People assume that their employer always hires the best qualified person for the job. In reality the most any organization can do is hire the most qualified person *from those who apply.* Employment equity activities include increasing the pool from which hires are made.

It is not enough for candidates to apply. In order for them to be hired they must be qualified *and* be perceived to be qualified. Most of us tend to have a mental picture of the kind of person who should be performing certain kinds of jobs. Think of a *nurse.* Virtually everyone thinks of a women in a white uniform. Think of a *manager.* How tall is *he*? Most of us picture tall men as managers. Think of a hotel maid, a construction worker, a librarian, a secretary, a computer programmer, or an engineer. Each of these jobs brings a picture to our minds. When someone unlike our mental picture applies for a job it may be difficult for us to see them as qualified. We sometimes unintentionally ignore factual information in order to maintain consistency between the people hired and the picture of who should be doing a particular job. For instance, researchers sent out six resumes to a group of human resource professionals along with a job description for a junior management position. Five of the resumes were identical. For the sixth resume, half of the human resource professionals were given a resume for a *John* Smith. The other half received an identical resume, except that the first name was changed to *Joan*, indicating a female candidate. The human resource professionals were asked to rank the six candidates in terms of their qualifications compared to those set out in the job description. Both female and male human resource professionals tended to rank the resume of Joan Smith lower than the identical resume of John Smith. So the gender of the candidate, not the education and years of experience, influenced judgments about the candidate's qualifications.

In another study, a black and a white "candidate" applied for over 200 jobs advertised in *The Globe and Mail* and *The Toronto Star.* These "candidates" were really actors who played the role necessary for the various jobs for which they were applying. Both black and a white person applied for each of the jobs. The researchers supplied each pair applying for the same job with an equivalent (rather than an identical) resume. So the qualifications of the black candidate were equal to those of the white candidate. Yet, the black candidate was treated worse than the white candidate three times more often. That is, when the black candidate went in to submit the resume he or she was told the job was filled; the application of the white candidate was accepted. Or, if both resumes were accepted, the white candidate was called in for an interview while the black candidate was not, and so on.

Another way interviewers may miss identifying qualified people is because ethnic groups handle themselves differently in an interview than one might expect. Canada is a multi-cultural country and different ethnic groups may express the same characteristics differently. For example, most North Americans equate a firm handshake, eye contact and a particular style of dress as appropriate behaviour for an employment interview. Other cultures may express respect differently. For example, in many Aboriginal cultures and some Asian cultures avoiding eye contact with a person of higher status (the interviewer) is the way to show respect.

In summary, there may be many reasons why designated group members have not traditionally been hired into work organizations, or have not been hired into decision-making jobs *which have nothing to do with their qualifications*. So, rather than hiring unqualified people, EE is about ensuring that job qualifications are truly job-related, the largest pool of applicants possible is generated, and everything is done to ensure that talent and qualifications are recognized, even when they are "packaged" differently.

### Why is EE needed – isn't it just more government interference?

Employment equity initiatives are consistent with the future labour market conditions. For many, it is impossible to conceive of a time when there are not going to be a multitude of job seekers for every opening. However, the long-term forecasts are for a very different kind of world. One reason is simple demographics. Traditionally, a society has the greatest number of young people with increasingly fewer people in each higher age group. This classic pattern has a triangle shape. However, this pattern is changing and will affect the supply of labour for decades to come. Figure 1-1a shows the Canadian population as of 1981. The figure has a basic triangular shape, though, already, there is a slight under-cutting at the bottom. The shape of the figure begins to resemble a diamond if one looks at the population projections for 2006 in Figure 1-1b. Assuming that most people enter the labour force at about age 20, the 20-year-olds who will be available in 2006 were born in 1986, so this number is known. The third Figure 1-1c, shows the demographic projections for the year 2031. Again the pattern has changed, now it resembles an up-side down triangle. This means there are more older people – in the 40 to 70 year range – than there are young people. There will be a labour shortage. Today the Canadian birthrate is 1.5. This means that couples are not replacing themselves and if it were not for immigration the Canadian

FIGURE 1–1A

## POPULATION BY AGE AND SEX
Canada, 1981 (Census)

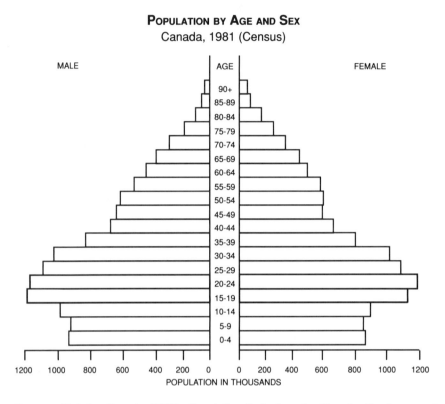

SOURCE:  Statistics Canada (1985), *Population Projections for Canada, Provinces and Territories, 1984-2006.* Cat. No. 91-520. Reproduced with the permission of the Minister of Industry, Science and Technology, 1993.

population would decrease in the future even faster than it will. Canada has been a country of immigrants since the 1700s. Immigrants have always come to Canada because they felt they could gain a better life here than in their country of origin. What has changed over time is the countries from which immigrants come. Once it was primarily Northern Europe, then Southern Europe. In 1961, 90 per cent of immigrants were from Europe and tended to be white. Now immigrants are more likely to come from developing countries and from groups which are racial minorities in Canada. In 1988, 43 per cent of immigrants were Asian and 18 per cent were black. By 2006, 140,000 visible minority persons will be immigrating to Canada each year.

Immigration is needed to deal not only with future labour shortages but also with skill shortages. A labour shortage means that there will not be enough people to do all the work which needs to be done. A skill

FIGURE 1–1B

POPULATION BY AGE AND SEX
Canada, 2006

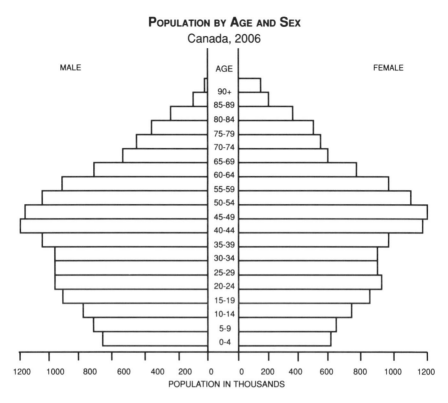

MALE · AGE · FEMALE

SOURCE: Statistics Canada (1985), *Population Projections for Canada, Provinces and Territories, 1984-2006*. Cat. No. 91-520. Reproduced with the permission of the Minister of Industry, Science and Technology, 1993.

shortage means that the people available to work do not have the skills required to do the work. This skill shortage will exist even though it is predicted that Canadian unemployment will remain at about 11 per cent until 1997. High unemployment and skill shortage can exist at the same time because the economy is going through a structural change. That is, the kinds of skills required in the past (and held by many who are unemployed such as those needed on assembly line) are not the skills needed for the future (e.g., computer skills).

Educational levels for racial minorities, either recent immigrants or Canadian born, are higher than for the mainstream population. Canada's immigration policies give preference to educated and skilled individuals to enter the country. Immigration has always been a traditional way for employers to recruit people with needed skills. Educational levels are increasing for Aboriginal Peoples, people with disabilities and women.

FIGURE 1–1c

POPULATION BY AGE AND SEX
Canada, 2031

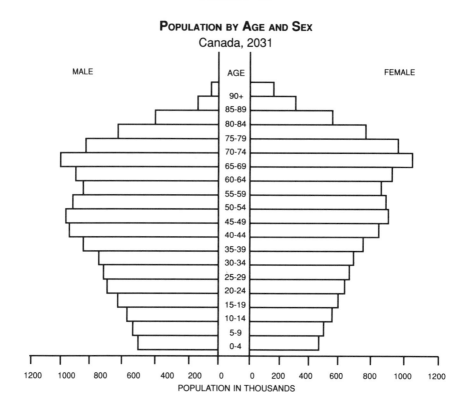

SOURCE:   Statistics Canada (1985). *Population Projections for Canada, Provinces and Territories, 1984-2006.* Cat. No. 91-520. Reproduced with the permission of the Minister of Industry, Science and Technology, 1993.

Figures 1-2a and 1-2b show the enrolment of men and women for community colleges and universities (undergraduate) spanning 1972 to 1988. The numbers of both men and women have increased dramatically over this time. However, the number of women receiving post-secondary education has surpassed that of men since the late 1970s.

The composition of the Canadian labour force has changed. Figure 1-3 shows the composition of the Canadian labour force based on data from the 1986 census. At that time just under half (48 per cent) of the labour force was comprised of white, able-bodied men. This contrasts with our image and history that white, able-bodied men almost totally comprise the Canadian work-force. Because able-bodied men have always been in the labour force, it is not surprising that a changing work-force means the inclusion of those who have not traditionally been employed, par-

FIGURE 1–2A

COMMUNITY COLLEGE ENROLMENT
Comparing men and women

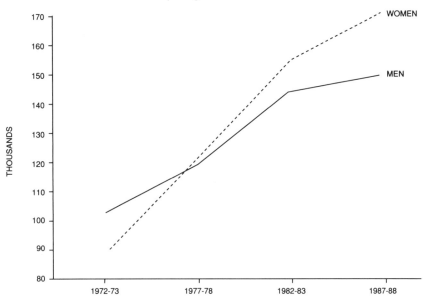

SOURCE: Statistics Canada (1990), "Women in Canada: A Statistical Report," 2nd ed., Cat. No. 89-503E, Table 8, p. 158. Reproduced with the permission of the Minister of Industry, Science and Technology, 1993.

ticularly women and persons with disabilities. In addition, because of changes in the countries of origin of immigrants there will be more members of racial minority groups in Canada and in the labour force. Further, labour force participation of Aboriginal Peoples has increased from 50 per cent to 60 per cent between 1981 to 1986.

Figure 1-3 shows that among the 52 per cent of the labour force in 1986 which is comprised of designated groups, 44 per cent are women (1 per cent Aboriginal women, 2 per cent women with disabilities, 3 per cent women who belong to visible minorities and 38 per cent white, able-bodied women). Male designated group members comprise approximately 8 per cent of the labour force (1.2 per cent Aboriginal men, 3.2 per cent men with disabilities, and 3.4 per cent visible minority men).

It is expected that the proportion of each of the designated groups in the labour force will increase over time. Designated group members will dominate the new entrants into the labour force. Eighty-five per cent of the new entrants to the labour force between 1985 and 2000 will be from

**FIGURE 1–2B**

**UNDERGRADUATE UNIVERSITY ENROLMENT**
Comparing men and women

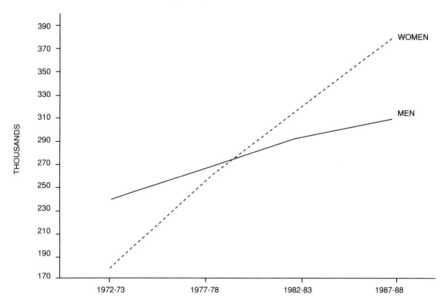

SOURCE:    Statistics Canada (1990), "Women in Canada: A Statistical Report," 2nd ed., Cat. No.
           89-503E, Table 1, p. 52. Reproduced with the permission of the Minister of Industry,
           Science and Technology, 1993.

among these groups.[1] Figure 1-4 provides support for this prediction.
Figure 1-4 shows the composition of the Canadian *population of working
age*. This differs from Figure 1-3 showing the Canadian labour force. The
labour force are those people, ages 15 to 64, who are in the labour force,
including those who are employed and unemployed. The working age
population, in contrast, includes all individuals between the ages of 15
and 64 (employed, unemployd and those not in the labour force) and
provides an indication of the potential available labour supply.

A clear indication of the changing labour force demographics is shown
in Figure 1-5 which shows the proportion of men and women in the
labour force between 1951 and 1991. The proportion of men has dropped
slightly, and seems to have stabilized at about 75 per cent. (That is 75 per
cent of men between the ages of 15 and 64 are in the labour force.) The
dramatic story shown in this graph is the rapid increase in the proportion of women in the labour force – from about 22 per cent in 1951 to 58
per cent in 1991. Women have accounted for 94 per cent of employment
growth between 1981 to 1986.

FIGURE 1–3

COMPOSITION OF THE LABOUR FORCE
Canada, 1986

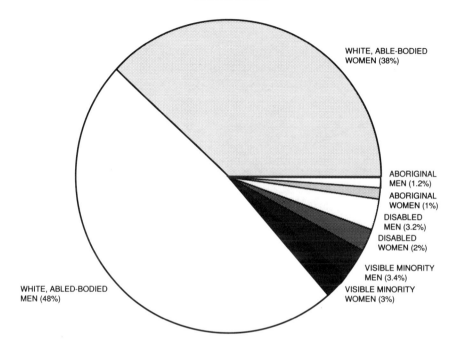

SOURCE:  Adapted from Statistics Canada, 1986 data. Combination of information from Employment Equity Availability Data Report, Tables 6 & 13 and Health and Activities Limitation Survey.

Even more surprising is that women with the largest increased involvement in the labour force are mothers with children under three years of age. The reason? Economics. One U.S. study found that 66 per cent of men indicated that they work because they need the money; almost as high a proportion of women, 63 per cent, gave the same reason. Wives working full-time contribute about 40 per cent to the family income. Because of these trends by the year 2000 it is predicted that half the labour force will be women.

*What are the steps involved in EE?*

While many activities can be part of overcoming systemic discrimination, EE should be carried out as a program. Steps for achieving EE are:

**FIGURE 1–4**

**COMPOSITION OF THE WORKING AGE POPULATION**
Canada, 1986

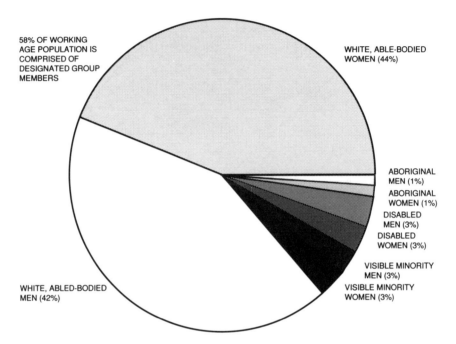

58% OF WORKING AGE POPULATION IS COMPRISED OF DESIGNATED GROUP MEMBERS

WHITE, ABLE-BODIED WOMEN (44%)

ABORIGINAL MEN (1%)
ABORIGINAL WOMEN (1%)
DISABLED MEN (3%)
DISABLED WOMEN (3%)
VISIBLE MINORITY MEN (3%)
VISIBLE MINORITY WOMEN (3%)

WHITE, ABLED-BODIED MEN (42%)

Source: Adapted from Statistics Canada, 1986 data. Combination of information from Employment Equity Availability Data Report, Tables 8 & 14 and Health and Activities Limitation Survey.

1. Organizational Preparation
   a. Commitment
   b. Communication
   c. Accountability

2. Data collection and analysis
   a. Data collection and analysis of the organization's current workforce in terms of designated group members
   b. Systems review

3. Implementation
   a. Setting goals and timetables
   b. Special measures

4. Monitoring and evaluating

FIGURE 1–5

**PROPORTION OF MEN AND WOMEN IN THE CANADIAN LABOUR FORCE
1951 TO 1991**

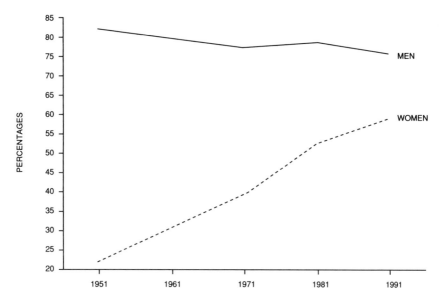

SOURCE: Adapted from Historical Labour Force Statistics, Statistics Canada, Cat. No. 71–201.

How to carry out each of these steps is discussed in detail in this book.

Employment equity says that the *status quo* is not fair to everyone and so there must be changes. It is based on the premise that the *status quo* involves making certain kinds of mistakes – this is the loss of talented designated group members. Further, EE is based on the principles that:

- Equality does not mean treating everyone the same.
- Notions of equity evolve as more is learned about how certain groups are disadvantaged.
- For a period of time, there is a need to explicitly focus on characteristics (*e.g.*, race and gender) which should not influence employment decisions, but do.
- The goal of a representative work-force assumes that talent is found among all kinds of people, but our pre-set notions prevent us from seeing it.
- Those who have been advantaged must share with those who have been disadvantaged. So whites must share with people of colour; men must share with women, and so on.

### What are the benefits of EE?

While EE will require some blood, sweat and tears it also is likely to have the following benefits:

- Improved human resource policies and practices.
- Access to a broader pool of qualified candidates for jobs.
- Creativity which comes from diversity.
- Reduced risk of legal action from unintended discriminatory practices.
- Knowing the organization is operating in a fair and equitable manner.

# NOTES

1. Johnston, William B., *Work Force 2000: Work and Workers for the 21st Century*, Indianapolis, Indiana: Hudson Institute, 1987, p. 95.

# REFERENCES

William W. Black,
  *Employment Equity: A Systemic Approach*, Ottawa, Human Rights Research and Education Centre, University of Ottawa, 1985.

William B. Johnston, *Work Force 2000: Work and Workers for the 21st Century*, Indianapolis, Indiana: Hudson Institute, 1987.

# CHAPTER 2

# Workplace Equality Legislation

At the time this book is being written the legislative environment is evolving. Legislative requirements are important but the focus of this book is on EE as good human resource practices. Many EE activities will not be specifically mentioned in legislation (*e.g.*, work and family policy). So, while compliance with legislation is one component of EE, ensuring EE principles are incorporated into good human resource practices is more important.

This chapter provides a basic overview of the various pieces of legislation related to workplace equality. Since the subject of this book is EE, the majority of this chapter is devoted to employment equity legislation and contractors' programs. However, related legislation such as human rights, the *Canadian Charter of Rights and Freedoms*[1] and pay equity are also discussed so that the reader can understand the interrelationships. The first section of this chapter discusses which organizations are covered by federal and provincial legislation and how court decisions made under one piece of legislation can influence the interpretation of legislation in other jurisdictions.

## FEDERAL AND PROVINCIAL LEGISLATION

With a few exceptions, an organization is covered by either federal or provincial legislation. Federal legislation covers:

- Federally regulated industries;
- Federal Crown corporations; and
- Federal public service.

Federally regulated industries can be described as those whose product or service "flows" across provincial boundaries. For example, radio waves cannot be regulated by different laws in different provinces. While interprovincial trucking could be regulated by different provincial laws it would needlessly complicate the trucking industry. Rather, it is easier to have the same trucking regulations in place from St. John's to Victoria. The industries which are federally regulated include:

- Atomic energy (nuclear research and manufacturing and uranium mining)

- Banking
- Communication (interprovincial postal and courier services, telecommunication and telephone, radio and television broadcasting and cable companies)
- Milling (flour and feed milling and grain storage)
- Resource extraction (coal mining, oil and gas exploration which crosses provincial boundaries)
- Transportation (interprovincial air, bus, rail, trucking, water and pipeline)

Many, but not all, federally regulated industries are comprised of private sector, profit-making organizations. While the industries which are federally regulated tend to make some sense there are some inconsistencies. For examples, banks are federally regulated while trust companies are provincially regulated.

Any organization which is not federally regulated is provincially regulated. These include:

- Private sector companies not in federally regulated industries. Organizations must obey the legislation in each of the provinces in which they operate.
- Provincial Crown corporations (*e.g.*, Manitoba Hydro)
- Provincial public service
- Broader public sector organizations (*e.g.*, municipalities, hospitals, universities).

At the present time there are three pieces of EE legislation (which are discussed in detail later in this Chapter). The federal *Employment Equity Act*[2] covers federally regulated industries and federal Crown corporations. It does not cover the federal public service; rather, the government, as an employer, has committed to EE outside of a legislative framework. The Quebec *Charter of Human Rights and Freedoms*,[3] the provincial human rights legislation, has both voluntary and required EE components. This legislation covers all public and private sector organizations typically covered by Quebec legislation. The Ontario *Employment Equity Act*[4] will cover both public and private sector employers.

The federal government, and Ontario and Quebec provincial governments also have contractors' programs which require EE of some organizations not covered by that jurisdiction's legislation. A contractors' program is not legislation. Rather, it sets out that a condition of doing business with a provincial or the federal government is the implementation of an EE program. More is said about contractors' programs later.

While federal legislation and each province's legislation are separate from each other, it is possible for court cases in one jurisdiction to affect the interpretation of legislation in another jurisdiction. This is because the Supreme Court of Canada hears cases related to legislation from all the jurisdictions. For example, a human rights case in Manitoba in 1989 *Brooks v. Canada Safeway Ltd.*[5] raised the issue of whether discrimination on the basis of pregnancy constituted sex discrimination covered under the Manitoba *Human Rights Code.*[6] The Supreme Court decided that discrimination on the basis of pregnancy is discrimination on the basis of sex. Every Canadian jurisdiction includes sex as a prohibited ground of discrimination in its human rights legislation. So even though this particular case involved the Manitoba *Human Rights Code* it had relevance for the interpretation of every piece of human rights legislation in the country.

Alternatively, sometimes differences in legislation in different jurisdictions results in different interpretations. A set of human rights cases illustrates this point. In 1985, the Supreme Court issued two decisions on the same day dealing with the issue of accommodation for religious beliefs. One case, *Bhinder v. C.N.R.,*[7] was under federal legislation while the second case, *O'Malley v. Simpsons-Sears,*[8] was under the Ontario *Human Rights Code.*[9] The Supreme Court said that Simpsons-Sears had to accommodate Ms. O'Malley because of the accommodation requirements in the Ontario *Human Rights Code.* On the other hand, C.N.R. was not required to accommodate Mr. Bhinder because of the way the *Canadian Human Rights Act*[10] was written. [In 1990, the Supreme Court over-turned its ruling in the *Bhinder* case when it ruled in *Central Alberta Dairy Pool v. Alberta (Human Rights Commn.).*[11] More is said about this case in Chapter 8 on the duty to accommodate.]

## WORKPLACE EQUALITY LEGISLATION

Table 2-1 summarizes workplace equity legislation across Canadian jurisdictions. The federal government, the ten provinces and the two territories all have human rights legislation. The actions of governments (*e.g.,* federal, provincial) are also covered by the *Canadian Charter of Rights and Freedoms.* The federal government, eight of the provinces and the territories all have some requirement for pay equity, at least for their public sector. Private sector organizations are covered by pay equity legislation in Quebec, Ontario, Yukon and those in federally regulated industries (regardless of which province(s) they operate in). Employment equity is required by legislation and via contractors' programs in Ontario and Quebec and for those doing business with the federal government. Each of these laws is discussed in more detail later in this chapter.

TABLE 2–1
## WORKPLACE EQUITY LEGISLATION IN CANADIAN JURISDICTIONS

| Legislation Jurisdictions | Human Rights (public & private sectors) | Pay Equity Public sector | Pay Equity Private sector | Employment Equity Public sector | Employment Equity Private sector | Contractor's Program (public & private sectors) |
|---|---|---|---|---|---|---|
| Federal Government | Yes | In Human Rights legislation | | Yes | Yes | Yes |
| Alberta | Yes | No | No | No | No | No |
| British Columbia | Yes | Yes | No | No | No | No |
| Quebec | Yes | In Human Rights legislation | | In Human Rights legislation | | Yes |
| Manitoba | Yes | Yes | No | No | No | No |
| Newfoundland | Yes | Yes | No | No | No | No |
| New Brunswick | Yes | Yes | No | No | No | No |
| Northwest Territories | Covered under federal Human Rights legislation | Under federal Human Rights legislation | | No | No | No |
| Nova Scotia | Yes | Yes | No | No | No | No |
| Ontario | Yes | Yes | Yes | Yes | Yes | Yes |
| Prince Edward Island | Yes | Yes | No | No | No | No |
| Saskatchewan | Yes | No | No | No | No | No |
| Yukon | Yes | In Human Rights legislation | | No | No | No |

All governments, municipal, provincial, territorial and federal are covered by the *Canadian Charter of Rights and Freedoms*; private sector organizations are not.

### Employment equity legislation: Federal

The federal *Employment Equity Act* was passed in 1986 in response to recommendations in the 1984 Abella Commission *Report on Equality in Employment*. The Act covers federally regulated employers with at least 100 employees. About 5 per cent of the Canadian labour force is covered by this piece of legislation.

The purpose of the Act, stated in section 2, is "to achieve equality in the work place so that no person shall be denied employment opportunities or benefits for reasons unrelated to ability and ... to correct the conditions of disadvantage in employment experienced [by the four designated groups]." The Act states that EE does not mean treating everyone the same and requires special measures and the accommodation of differences.

The federal law allows unions to obtain information, to ask questions and make suggestions with respect to EE initiatives. Employers are required to:

- Identify and eliminate employment barriers;
- Institute positive policies and practices and reasonable accommodation to ensure representation of qualified designated group members;
- Collect and report on data showing number and proportion of designated group members within the organization; and
- Develop EE plans which set out goals and timetables for achieving EE.

Data collection requires each employer to submit an annual report on its work-force indicating the number (and proportion) of designated group members within the organization, their number (and proportion) in each occupational group and at various salary levels, and the number of employees hired, promoted and terminated by designated group status. The first report was to be made in June 1988.

The reports are made available to the public and tabulated and reported by Canada Employment and Immigration. In this way, the groups representing the various target groups are involved in "enforcing" the Act. That is, such advocacy groups can use public pressure to ensure greater adherence to EE principles.

The reports are also sent to the Canadian Human Rights Commission. The Human Rights Commission handles any complaints filed against a company for not fulfilling their EE requirements. Further, the Commission can initiate complaints against employers who, based on a statistical analysis of their EE reports, are not achieving representation of designated group members. It is, however, not totally clear if the Canadian Human Rights Commission has jurisdiction to do this.

In reality, the focus of the federal *Employment Equity Act* has been on data collection, even though the Act requires special measures to achieve representation of designated group members. For instance, employers can be fined up to $50,000 for failing to report their data, whereas there is only the potential of a penalty if they fail to achieve equality in employment.

Typical of legislation in the equality area, the *Employment Equity Act* required a review of the legislation after five years. In May 1992, a parliamentary committee released its report, *A Matter of Fairness: Report of the Special Parliamentary Committee on the Review of the Employment Equity Act*. The proposed changes to the Act are presented below.

**Coverage**: Extend coverage to

- Federal public service, R.C.M.P., Armed Forces, Parliament itself (*e.g.*, the House of Commons, the Senate and the Library of Parliament), and all federal agencies, boards and commissions.
- Unions certified by federal tribunals to be required, as employers, to sign a certificate of compliance with the principles of EE.
- Those doing business with the federal government with 75 employees (rather than the current cut-off of 100 currently in the federal contractors' program).
- Federal licensees to sign a certificate of compliance.

**Employment equity plans**: All EE programs have achievable plans, goals and timetables setting out both quantitative and qualitative goals. While it is recommended that workplace parties continue to have discretion in the development of their plans, it is proposed that new regulations to the *Employment Equity Act* set out requirements and standards for EE programs. Further, such programs should be approved by a monitoring agency prior to implementation and thereafter become binding on the employer.

**Unions**: The Act would require that bargaining agents or employee representatives be consulted (not negotiated with) and have input into the preparation and implementation of the plan.

**Reporting requirements**: While the reporting requirements will remain unchanged, there are recommendations to refine the definitions of designated groups so that they are acceptable to all parties. Standardized data collection, allowing for identification of persons who are members of more than one designated group, and further refining of the data used to reflect the labour force availability of the four designated groups are other recommendations found in the Report.

In recognition of the different data collection requirements in the different jurisdictions, it is recommended that the federal government exercise leadership to ensure that data collected for the purposes of EE be standardized and harmonized.

**Enforcement of the Act**: Canada Employment and Immigration should be the monitoring agency and the Canadian Human Rights Commission should be the enforcement agency. Further, Canada Employment and Immigration should undertake regular on-site reviews of employers' progress.

Also recommended is the application of a $50,000 fine in cases of violations, not just for failure to provide an annual report.

A better means of assessing the qualitative efforts of employers towards achievement of EE should be established.

Additionally, powers should be given to the enforcement agency to deal with seniority when it is a barrier.

**Establish a national EE strategy**: A strategy should be developed and made public by November 1993. The strategy should include:

- teamwork among interested parties;
- public education;
- ensuring members of designated groups are prepared for the labour market;
- help for employers in locating designated group members.

### Employment equity legislation: Ontario

Ontario's EE legislation is scheduled to become effective in 1994. Seventy-five per cent of Ontario employees will be covered by the legislation, over 10,000 employers. Wise employers will begin EE activities before the legislation becomes effective because

- More time than is set out in the legislation will be useful to develope an EE plan. (What is required in an EE plan is noted shortly.)
- Those organizations which get a head start on EE will be better able to attract the best designated group members.

- The organization's commitment to EE can be demonstrated by beginning EE activities before being forced by legislation.

Unlike some other pieces of legislation (*e.g.*, pay equity), EE, with a couple of exceptions, can be started before the legislation is finalized. This is because there are numerous EE activities an organization can undertake which will clearly be consistent with the legislation. Some of these activities are discussed in Chapters 7 to 10. One clear exception is the data collection required for the work-force analysis (discussed in Chapter 5). It is likely that there will be clear legislative directions on how to implement the work-force analysis, so this process may be delayed until the regulations are finalized.

The purpose of the *Employment Equity Act* is to ameliorate the employment disadvantage experienced by the four designated groups. The following is a discussion of the Act after first reading.

**Coverage**:

- Ontario Public Service.
- Broader public sector with at least ten employees. (Employers with fewer than 50 employees have less stringent requirements.)
- Private sector with 50 or more employees. (Employers with fewer than 100 employees – who continue to have fewer than 100 employees – have less stringent requirements.)

**Requirements**: Implement and maintain EE by

- Staff awareness: Staff (*e.g.*, supervisory, human resource) responsible for or involved in recruiting, hiring, supervising, evaluating or promoting employees must be fully informed about the employer's EE plan and follow EE principles. (Section 8(1) and (2))
- Collection of work-force information: Conduct a self-report survey of current employees to determine their status in terms of gender, race and disability status. (Sections 9(1) and 17(2))
- Review of employment policies: Identify systemic barriers in hiring, retention, promotion, and terms and conditions of employment. (Section 10)
- Preparation of EE plan.

There is to be one plan per organization, though it may have many chapters. That is, the required parts of the plan (noted below) may be based on different geographical areas, and different bargaining units. The plan is to run for three years and must include (as per the draft regulations):

1. Qualitative measures to eliminate barriers, achieve and maintain representation of members of the designated groups within each

occupational group, and incorporate EE principles into the work environment. Specific measures could include those which:

- Aid in the hiring, retention and promotion of designated group members;
- Eliminate barriers;
- Accommodate the special needs of members of the designated groups; and
- Eliminate discrimination and harassment in the workplace.

2. Numerical goals are required of all but small employers. These goals are to achieve representation in each occupational grouping of each designated group based on the working age population in the relevant geographic area (geographic area is defined in the glossary). A numerical goal is the proportion of hirings/promotions into each occupational group which will be filled by members of the designated groups.
3. Goals and timetables for qualitative and numerical goals.
4. Monitoring process for the development and implementation of goals and timetables and identification of those responsible for carrying out the monitoring.

In addition, the plan must describe the consultation that took place with employees not represented by a bargaining agent. A summary of the comments that the employer received and how they were addressed should be included. (Consultation is discussed further in Chapter 4.) Also to be included in the plan is the procedure for accommodating employees and applicants with disabilities.

**Communication to EE Commission**: Employers will be required to inform the government that they have developed their EE plan via a certificate which provides baseline data of the number of employees and the number of designated group members. The Employment Equity Commission *may* require the employer to file a copy of the plan with the Commission. (Section 11(2) and (3)) Progress reports will be required on the composition of the employer's work-force and the development, implementation, review and revision of the employer's EE plan. (Section 18)

**Standard against which EE efforts will be judged**: Reasonable efforts will be the standard against which an organization's EE efforts will be judged. (Section 12).

**Joint union/management responsibility: Union involvement (Section 14)**: The following must be done jointly:

- Collection of work-force data;
- Review of employment policies within the collective agreement;
- Development of the EE plan (including establishment of goals and timetables);

- Revisions to the EE plan.

If the employees within an organization are represented by more than one bargaining agent, the employer and the bargaining agents shall establish a committee to co-ordinate and carry out their joint responsibilities. The committee shall be composed of one representative of each bargaining agent and up to the same number of employer representatives.

Employment equity should be carried out in good faith, separately from normal collective bargaining. However, collective bargaining contracts must be compatible with EE.

**Regulations**: Draft Regulations were released in June 1993 which set out the following:

- Designated groups: Definition of Aboriginal Peoples, persons with disabilities and racial minorities. (See Table 2-2)
- What work-force information must be collected.
- How to review employment policies (systems review). (Discussed in Chapter 6.)
- How joint responsibilities are to be carried out between the employer and bargaining agent(s) and what information the employer must share with the bargaining agent(s) in order to implement EE. (Discussed in Chapter 4.)
- How non-union employees will be involved in the EE process. (Section 15) (Discussed in Chapter 4.)
- What information must be posted about EE for all employees. (Section 16) (Discussed in Chapter 4.)

**Timetable for implementation (Section 20)**: The collection of work-force information, the review of employment policies and the development of the EE plan must be completed within the following schedule (the time is measured from the effective date of the legislation):

- Ontario Public Service: 12 months
- Broader public sector: 18 months
- Private sector:
     With 500 or more employees: 18 months
     With 100 to 499 employees: 24 months
     With 50 to 99 employees: 36 months

**Seniority**: Seniority rights with respect to lay-off or recall are specifically allowed. (Section 5(2)) The Employment Equity Commission is charged with working with employers and bargaining agents to ensure that existing seniority systems will not be a barrier to EE. (Section 41(1)5.) Seniority and its implications for EE is discussed in Chapter 4.

TABLE 2–2

DEFINITIONS OF DESIGNATED GROUPS UNDER DIFFERENT LEGISLATION

|  | Federal | Quebec | Ontario |
|---|---|---|---|
| Women | Not defined | Not defined | Not defined |
| Aboriginal Peoples | Indians, Inuit or Métis and those who identify themselves as Indians, Inuit or Métis. | Status Indians, non-status Indians, Métis | Person who is member of the Indian, Inuit, Métis peoples of Canada. |
| Persons with disabilities | (i) have any persistent physical, mental, psychiatric, sensory or learning impairment, (ii) consider themselves to be, or believe that an employer or a potential employer would be likely to consider them to be, disadvantaged in employment by reason of an impairment referred to in subparagraph (i), and (iii) identify themselves to an employer, or agree to be identified by an employer, as persons with disabilities. All three regulatory requirements mentioned above must be adhered to before a person can be reported as "a person with disabilities". | Persons with a persistent physical, mental, psychological or sensory disability, or persons with a persistent learning disability, and who think they are disadvantaged with regard to employment as a result of their disability, or an employer considers them as such. | Person who has a persistant physical, mental, psychiatric, sensory or learning impairment and, (a) who considers her/himself to be disadvantaged in employment by reason of that impairment, or (b) who believes that an employer or potential employer is likely to consider her or him to be disadvantaged in employment by reason of that impairment. |
| Visible/ racial minorities | Persons, other than Aboriginal Peoples, who are, because of their race or colour, a visible minority in Canada are considered to be persons who are non-Caucasian in race or non-white in colour and who identify themselves as such. | Persons who are non-white by race or non-white by colour. | Person who, because of her or his race or colour, is in a visible minority in Ontario. |

**Compatibility with other legislation:** Employment equity is deemed to be a special program under the Ontario *Human Rights Code*. Special programs are initiatives which help ameliorate the effects of past discrimination, remove current discrimination and work toward representation of persons from the designated groups. By stating that EE efforts outlined in an EE plan constitute special programs, human rights complaints filed by non-designated group members because of EE are not valid. In addition the Human Rights Commission will pass onto the Employment Equity Commission any complaints relevant to an employer with an EE plan. This prevents organizations from facing the double jeopardy of carrying out EE while being vulnerable to complaints of reverse discrimination.

The draft regulations recognize that some Ontario employers are subject to contractors' programs in other jurisdictions or have voluntarily begun EE. If a work-force audit and/or an employment systems review has been completed which would achieve results consistent with those required by the Ontario Act and regulations then the employer does not have to re-do these. If there is any question the Employment Equity Commission will determine if the audit and/or survey are sufficient.

**Enforcement:** The Employment Equity Commission may audit employers to determine if they have developed and are implementing their EE plan(s). If the Commission feels that an employer is not complying with the principles of EE, the Commission may endeavour to affect a settlement. The Commission may order, without a hearing, an employer to take specific steps to achieve EE (*e.g.*, work-force survey, systems review, development and/or implementation of EE plan, consultation with employees). (Section 24)

An employer or bargaining agent may be brought before the Employment Equity Tribunal by:

- The Employment Equity Commission (Section 25);
- The other party for failure to resolve any matter that is their joint responsibility (Section 27);
- An employee (Section 28); or
- Any other person (Section 26(1)).

The Tribunal has the power to (Section 33):

- Establish or amend an EE plan.
- Create an EE fund, financed by the employer, to be used for the purposes specified.
- Appoint an administrator who, at the expense of the employer, is responsible for developing, implementing, reviewing and revising the employer's EE plan.

### Employment equity legislation: Quebec

Section 86 of the Quebec *Charter of Human Rights and Freedoms*[12] defines an affirmative action program as designed to "remedy the situation of persons belonging to groups discriminated against in employment". This section of the *Charter* came into force in mid-1985. An EE program is deemed non-discriminatory if it is established in conformity with the *Charter*. Guidelines have been issued to help workplace parties. Because the Quebec *Charter* is, primarily, human rights legislation it lists a multitude of categories such as sex, race, etc. In terms of sex, human rights legislation protects both men and women. However, an affirmative action program is specifically designed to protect those systemically discriminated against in employment, that is, women, not men. Material published by the Quebec Human Rights Commission (des droits de la personne) on EE programs refers to women, visible and ethnic minorities, Aboriginal Peoples and persons with disabilities as the disadvantaged groups.

The purpose of EE programs is to implement "corrective measures that temporarily give preferential treatment to members of groups that are discriminated against."[13] Corrective measures (the same as positive measures in Ontario jargon) and equal opportunity measures (barrier elimination measures) are used to create and then maintain EE (*i.e.*, a representative work-force).

Employment equity programs can be voluntarily undertaken, are required of some governmental organizations, or can be required by the Human Rights Commission following the investigation of a complaint. Further, there is a contractors' program for those doing business with the Quebec government (discussed later). Departments and agencies of the provincial government are required to implement programs. Voluntary EE programs can be undertaken by private sector organizations and public sector organizations not required to have a program. The program may be jointly agreed to by the employer and union and members of designated groups. The program is legal inasmuch as it is set up in accordance with *Guidelines Concerning the Validity of Voluntary Affirmative Action Programs In the Field of Employment* issued in 1986. The Commission's unit, Direction des programmes d'acces a l'egalite, provides assistance to workplace parties who request it. Alternatively, the Commission can order that a public or private sector organization establish an EE program based on the Commission's findings when it investigates a complaint.

The procedure outlined by Quebec guidelines for developing and implementing an EE program is as follows:

1. Assess need
   - Assess under-utilization of designated group members via analysis of staff and compare with availability data;
   - Analyze the employment process to identify any rules and practices that may have a discriminatory effect.

2.  Devise the program
    - Establish goals and timetables;
    - Devise corrective measures (eliminate the effects of discrimination against a group by temporarily according them certain preferences); and
    - Devise equal opportunity measures (ensure equality in the exercise of a right by eliminating discriminatory practices in the management of an undertaking);
    - May devise support measures (aimed at solving certain employment problems for target group members but that may also be beneficial to all personnel);
    - Devise evaluation mechanisms.
3.  Implement program
    - Implement measures to achieve goals according to the timetable established.
4.  Evaluate program
    - Periodically evaluate results;
    - Based on evaluation, adapt program to ensure achievement of EE.

When an EE program is required by the Quebec Human Rights Commission there are requirements to make all employees aware of the measures used within the EE program and to file an annual report with the Commission. This report must include: (1) all activities initiated during the year to implement the program; (2) progress made toward reaching the objectives, compared to the timetables; (3) problems encountered in reaching program objectives and any steps planned to resolve them; and (4) any changes to the program.

Table 2-2 provides the definitions of the four designated groups found in various legislation.

## EMPLOYMENT EQUITY THROUGH CONTRACT COMPLIANCE PROGRAMS

In addition to legislation, organizations may become involved in EE through contract compliance programs. Contract compliance programs cover organizations which supply goods or services to a government which has a contractors' program in place. For example, the federal government established its contractors' program in 1986, the Quebec government in 1987 and the Ontario government is establishing its program in its *Employment Equity Act*,[14] to become effective in 1994.

A contractors' program in one jurisdiction can cover organizations which are not covered by that jurisdiction's legislation. For example, the businesses that sell paper clips to Supply and Services, Canada, or the car company that sells jeeps to the Department of Defense, or the pharmaceutical company selling drugs to federal psychiatric hospitals are all covered by provincial legislation. But, if these companies want to do business with the federal government, as a condition of winning the contract with the federal government they must agree to implement an EE program. The difference between being regulated by legislation versus a contractors' program is one of choice. Legislation regulates all organizations within a jurisdiction, whereas contractors' programs regulate only those organizations that do business with a government.

The parameters of the contractors' programs differ between the federal, Quebec and Ontario programs.

## Federal Contractors' Program

Only firms with at least 100 employees, providing goods or services to the federal government in a contract of at least $200,000, are covered by the federal contractors' program. When such a firm bids on a federal contract they must promise that if they are awarded the contract they will implement EE. The organization that wins the contract can then be monitored to ensure that they have, in fact, carried out EE. If a federal contractor is found not to have implemented EE they can be prevented from bidding on future contracts.

The steps in the federal contractors' program are:

1. Commitment to EE by the signing of a certificate promising to implement EE if awarded the contract.

Upon winning the contract:

2. Appointment of a senior person to be accountable for EE.
3. Communicate EE to all employees.
4. Data collection and analysis of the work-force compared to the availability of designated group members in areas from which the organization recruits.
5. Review of human resource policies and practices for systemic discrimination.
6. Setting of goals and timetables based on EE needs identified through data analysis and systems review.
7. Implementation of special programs.
8. Monitoring and evaluation.

## Quebec Contractors' Program

Under the Quebec contractors' program, organizations with at least 100 employees which bid for a government contract or grant valued at $100,000 or more must be willing, if they win the contract, to implement an EE program. Subcontractors are also covered if they have at least 100 employees and a subcontract worth at least $100,000. Quebec firms that implement an EE plan under the Federal Contractors' Program must ensure that their program is in accordance with the Quebec *Charter of Human Rights and Freedoms.*

The EE program may extend beyond the term of the contract. That is, the contractor or grant recipient commits to achieving EE regardless of how long it takes. The EE program must:

- Communicate to all employees a commitment to implement EE.
- Appoint a senior manager to be accountable for EE.
- Assess the situation of designated group members in the organization within nine months of the award of the contract or grant by comparing the work-force analysis to availability data.
- Develop an EE program within four months after assessing the situation. Establish quantitative goals, timetables and means of addressing underutilization.
- Implement a program and report annually.

Failure to comply can result in *Attestation d'engagement* being cancelled, being prohibited from participating in any tender or applying for a grant for a minimum period of two years.

### Ontario Contractors' Program

The Ontario *Employment Equity Act* provides for a contractors' program. The provincial program is much more inclusive than the federal program. First, there are no restrictions as to the size of the contract nor the number of employees. The Ontario contractors' program also applies to subcontractors. Those receiving grants, contributions or loans from the Ontario government must also implement and maintain EE. So, all organizations doing business with the Ontario government or receiving grants or loans must agree to EE. That is, create staff awareness, collect work-force data, review employment policies, prepare an EE plan including barrier elimination, positive and accommodation measures and setting of goals and timetables.

If the Employment Equity Tribunal finds that EE is not being implemented and maintained then the contract, subcontract, grant, contribution or loan can be cancelled or the organization can be prevented from future contracts, grants, contributions or loans.

# HUMAN RIGHTS LEGISLATION AND EMPLOYMENT EQUITY

Human rights legislation is designed to recognize the dignity and worth of every person. Employment equity will be needed only until the designated groups are no longer disadvantaged in terms of high unemployment, low pay and underrepresentation in decision-making positions. Human rights protection will be needed forever. Human rights legislation protects everyone from being discriminated against. For example, all human rights laws cover race – this means that Whites and all peoples of colour are protected under such legislation.

Typically, categories protected by human rights legislation include the following:

- Race, ancestry, place of origin, colour, ethnic origin, citizenship
- Sex
- Disability status
- Religion
- Age
- Marital status
- Political belief
- Pardoned conviction
- Sexual orientation
- Family status

The need for human rights legislation was first recognized following World War II when legislation requiring fair employment practices became prevalent. However, this legislation put the full responsibility on those feeling victimized to gain a resolution. The courts, at that time, generally were not sympathetic to human rights issues. In the 1960s and 1970s human rights legislation was passed in all Canadian jurisdictions. Such legislation included the establishment of human rights commissions which worked with those alleging discrimination and those perceived to be discriminating to promote greater equality. Human rights protection has increased over time. On one front human rights protection has been extended to additional groups, for instance, protection for persons with disabilities was first added to the New Brunswick *Human Rights Act*[15] in 1974, and subsequently to all other human rights acts. Further, human rights legislation has been strengthened by remedies which have moved from apologies to financial remuneration.

Still, human rights legislation, for the most part, assumes that discrimination, whether malicious or not, is the result of the intentional behaviour of one person toward another. Unlike EE laws, human rights legislation is not based on the fact that help is needed to overcome employment disadvantages faced by an entire group. Rather, human rights law is meant to help individuals who are discriminated against because they are members of a particular group. For example, Jewish men are not a group characterized by high unemployment nor by low pay. Yet, it is possible for a particular man to be discriminated against because he is Jewish. Such discrimination can be addressed by human rights legislation.

There is some concern that human rights legislation and EE legislation are in conflict since positive measures seems to "give privilege" to designated group members. The *Canadian Charter of Rights and Freedoms* and some human rights legislation, such as Ontario's, deal with this potential conflict. Section 15(2) of the *Canadian Charter of Rights and Freedoms* reads:

[The guarantee of equality] does not preclude any law, program or activity that has as its objective the *amelioration of conditions of disadvantaged individuals or groups* including those that are disadvantaged because of race, national or ethnic origin, colour, religion, sex, age or mental or physical disability. [Emphasis added]

That is, positive measures which are designed to correct the employment disadvantage of designated groups are legal under human rights legislation. Section 15(2) expedites the removal of such disadvantage. Once such disadvantage is removed, then positive measures will cease to exist.

With passage of the Ontario *Employment Equity Act*, the Ontario *Human Rights Code* and *Employment Equity Act* will be made compatible by clarifying that EE plans which fulfil the requirements of the Ontario *Employment Equity Act* are considered special programs under the Code. This means that employers and unions are guaranteed that their EE plans are protected from human rights complaints of reverse discrimination from nondesignated group members.

## THE CANADIAN CHARTER OF RIGHTS AND FREEDOMS AND EMPLOYMENT EQUITY

The *Canadian Charter of Rights and Freedoms* (hereafter the *Charter*) is part of the constitution. It limits governmental powers so as not to infringe on the rights of individuals. Governments include the federal, provincial and territories governments (excluding Quebec which replaced the Canadian *Charter* with its own), municipal governments and bodies which receive their powers from statutes, such as Police Commissions. The *Charter* covers a wide range of issues:

- Fundamental freedoms (*e.g.*, of thought, belief and expression, of peaceful assembly, of association);
- Democratic rights (*e.g.*, to vote and to run for political office);
- Mobility rights (including the right to live and to seek employment anywhere in Canada);
- Legal rights (to life, liberty and security of the person);
- Equality rights for all individuals;
- Official languages of Canada (English and French are the official languages of Canada);
- Minority language education rights (regardless of whether English or French is the majority language in a province, those who speak the other official language have the right to have their children educated in that language);
- Canada's multicultural heritage;
- Native peoples' rights.

The section of the *Charter* known as the equality section (section 15) is the most relevant to EE issues. Section 15(1) reads:

> Every individual is equal before and under the law and has the right to the equal protection and equal benefit of the law without discrimination and, in particular, without discrimination based on race, national or ethnic origin, colour, religion, sex, age or mental or physical disability.

Though section 15(1) lists protected groups, much like human rights legislation, there is one important difference. In human rights legislation the list of protected groups is exhaustive. That is, if a group is not listed in a human rights act then it is not protected. In the *Charter*, the listing of protected classes is illustrative, not exhaustive. So the courts can decide that other groups need protection under the *Charter*.

Section 15(1) also refers to protection "before ... the law," "under the law" and "equal protection and equal benefit of the law". The exact meanings of each of these goes beyond the purpose of this book. However, it is sufficient to say that the *Charter* added new protection by ensuring that equality means more than just the same application of a law to everyone. Rather, it requires a court to determine if the same application of a law creates inequities for protected groups. For example, there used to be a law that if an Aboriginal woman married a non-Aboriginal man she lost her "Indian" status. An Aboriginal man who married a non-Aboriginal woman retained his status. Before the *Charter* existed this was not seen as discriminatory since the law was applied equally to all Aboriginal women and equally to all Aboriginal men. The requirements of the *Charter* recognize the discriminatory aspect of treating Aboriginal women differently from Aboriginal men.

As noted, the second subsection of the equality section allows special programs or positive measures which may seem to favour some groups over others. These programs or measures are allowed where

- They are directed at disadvantaged individuals or groups; and
- Their purpose is the amelioration of such disadvantage.

Therefore, EE efforts directed at the four designated groups are allowed under the *Charter*.

The *Charter* does set a limit on equality. The limitation is found in Section 1 which notes that rights and freedom are subject to "reasonable limits ... as can be demonstrably justified in a free and democratic society". An example of this limit was *McKinney v. University of Guelph*, a decision by the Supreme Court in 1990,[16] on mandatory retirement. The Court said that mandatory retirement at age 65 is discrimination on the basis of age but it is reasonable in a free and democratic society.

## PAY EQUITY LEGISLATION AND EMPLOYMENT EQUITY

Pay equity focuses on women, one of the designated groups addressed by EE. It is, however, limited to a particular employment issue, compensation, specifically, the determination of salaries/wages for jobs. Wage determination is an area with its own specialized methodology (including job evaluation and wage lines) which is unrelated to other employment issues. The purpose of pay equity is to bring about equal pay for work traditionally performed by women when it is equal in value to work traditionally performed by men. Most occupations have either been traditionally associated with women (*e.g.*, health care, elementary school teaching, secretarial, service) or men (*e.g.*, construction, law, management). Women's work has been undervalued because of general societal values which assign less value to whatever women do, because of the assumption that men are providers for their families and women are dependents, and because of presumed lower attachment to the labour force on the part of women.

A comparison of the basics of pay and EE are shown in Table 2-3.

The purpose of EE is to have a representative work-force while the intent of pay equity is to ensure fairness in compensation to those working in traditionally female jobs. The means of achieving each objective differs. For example, EE uses statistical data to identify the kinds of people employed in various occupations and at various salary levels. Pay equity assesses job information against a set of criteria to determine job value and compares the salaries for female and male jobs of equal value.

Pay equity involves a particular technology – job evaluation. Achieve-

TABLE 2-3

COMPARISON BETWEEN PAY AND EMPLOYMENT EQUITY

|  | Pay Equity | Employment Equity |
|---|---|---|
| Objective | Equal pay for work of equal value | Removal of systemic barriers to ensure a work-force representative of the labour market from which an organization recruits |
| Concern | Compensation | All aspects of employment |
| Focus | Jobs; compensation system | All human resource systems; Individuals |
| Who is covered | Men and women working in female-dominated jobs | Women; Visible minorities; Persons with disabilities; Aboriginal Peoples |
| Implementation | Gender neutral evaluation of female and male jobs; and equal compensation for comparatively valued jobs | Identification and removal of barriers via data collection and analysis; policy and systems review; goals and timetables; and implementation of special programs. |

SOURCE: Adapted from Nan Weiner, "Employment Equity and Pay Equity: Similarities, Differences and Integration" (June, 1993) C.L.L.J., Vol. 2, No. 1.

ment of EE is not tied to any particular technology since some employers may bring it about by outreach recruiting, while others may concentrate on training to prevent harassment, or sponsor English as a second language courses. Employment equity addresses a multitude of barriers while pay equity focuses on those within the wage determination process.

The most obvious difference between pay and EE is the scope. Pay

equity is concerned with compensation and the work historically performed by women. Employment equity is concerned with all aspects of
employment and involves four designated groups. It should not be assumed, however, that pay equity is concerned only with white women.
As in other employment areas, women of colour, women who are disabled and Aboriginal women often experience double jeopardy in terms
of pay. Tables 2-4, 2-5 and 2-6 show this double jeopardy in pay. These
tables show the difference in pay equity for men and women who are
members of a designated group and those who are not. From these tables
one can see the salary differential associated with being a woman, with
being a member of another designated group, and with being both a
woman and a member of another designated group. In all cases being
both a woman and a member of another designated group results in a
lower salary than that due to being a woman or to being a member of
another designated group only.

Pay and EE are both linked to occupational segregation. Occupational
segregation is the association, both stereotypically and in practice, of
certain kinds of work with certain groups. For example, certain jobs are
thought of as primarily performed by and appropriate to visible minority women while others are thought of as inappropriate for Aboriginal
men, and so on. However, no occupational segregation is as pervasive as
that based on sex. In fact, one U.S. study[17] found that since the 1940s,
occupational segregation based on race has been reduced substantially,
and that based on gender only slightly.

Despite some change, it is still true that most jobs are perceived to be
either "men's work" or "women's work". This is a consistent fact about
North American workplaces, even though there has been some change in
the occupations associated with each gender. Teaching and secretarial
work were initially "male jobs" which have become "female jobs". Police
dispatching and school-bus driving were originally "male jobs" which
have become predominantly female. Few jobs are gender neutral. Jobs
are more likely to shift from being associated with one gender to the
other, rather than being associated with both. The vast majority of jobs
are gender specific (*e.g.*, engineers, labourers, librarians, managers, nurses,
sales clerks, social workers).

Both pay equity and EE are concerned with occupational segregation
based on gender, although they differ in what they attempt to do about
it. Pay equity is directed at redressing the underpayment of women's
work. But it is not directed at reducing occupational segregation. Rather,
the goal of pay equity is to ensure that what has historically been wom-
en's jobs are paid fairly for their value. Employment equity, on the other
hand, is designed to reduce occupational segregation among traditionally male jobs by removing the barriers which have kept women out.
This difference, however, does not make the two incompatible, rather

## TABLE 2-4

### COMPARISON OF MEDIAN INCOME FOR WOMEN AND MEN
### WHO ARE OF ABORIGINAL ORIGINS AND NOT OF ABORIGINAL ORIGINS

|  | Women | Men | Lower salary due to being a woman |
|---|---|---|---|
| Aboriginal origins | $ 6,817 | $ 8,533 | $ 1,716 |
| Non-Aboriginal origins | $ 9,601 | $20,001 | $ 10,400 |
| Lower salary due to being Aboriginal | $ 2,784 | $11,468 | Lower salary due to being a woman and of Aboriginal origins: $13,184 |

SOURCE: Adapted from Aboriginal Peoples Output Program, A Data Book on Canada's Aboriginal Population, 1986, Census of Canada, Statistics Canada.

## TABLE 2-5

### COMPARISON OF MEDIAN EMPLOYMENT INCOME FOR WOMEN AND MEN
### WITH DISABILITIES AND WITHOUT DISABILITIES

|  | Women | Men | Lower salary due to being a woman |
|---|---|---|---|
| Persons with disabilities | $ 8,360 | $19,250 | $10,890 |
| Persons without disabilities | $10,000 | $21,000 | $11,000 |
| Lower salary due to having disability | $ 1,640 | $ 1,750 | Lower salary due to being a woman and having disability: $12,640 |

SOURCE: Adapted from Health and Activity Limitation Survey, Statistics Canada, 1986.

they provide equality for different groups. Pay equity provides equality in compensation for men and women who have the talent and interest to perform traditionally female jobs. These people will continue to work in

## TABLE 2-6

### COMPARISON OF MEDIAN SALARY
### FOR WOMEN AND MEN WHO ARE BLACK AND WHITE

|  | Women | Men | Lower salary due to being a woman |
|---|---|---|---|
| Black | $12,126 | $15,125 | $ 2,999 |
| White | $13,961 | $22,390 | $ 8,429 |
| Lower salary due to being black | $ 1,835 | $ 7,265 | Lower salary due to being a women and black $10,264 |

SOURCE:   Adapted from Statistics Canada, 1986 data.

female jobs because they do not want to change or cannot change be-cause of lack of training, skills or awareness of the opportunities. As a generalization, this group will disproportionately be older women. Em-ployment equity will aid those women who have the talent and interest to work in jobs which have traditionally been done by men. One study found that affirmative action in the United States helped younger women because they had not yet made educational and other training decisions nor amassed years of experience which closed, rather than opened, doors for them. Older women, on the other hand, had fewer choices. These women can benefit from pay equity but are unlikely to benefit from EE. Thus, EE can impact on occupational segregation and reduce it over time. It cannot help men or women currently working in jobs which have been, and without pay equity would continue to be, underpaid because the jobs have been historically female.

While pay and EE are totally compatible they address different equity problems. There could be some conflict in implementation if one tries to resolve an EE issue with a pay equity solution, or vice versa. One should have a clear idea of how the two relate in order to facilitate the accom-plishment of both. A potential conflict relates to data analysis. Look at the case of more women moving into senior management positions within banks, for example. It is possible that because of this employment equity success the gender wage gap[18] within the bank might increase rather than decrease in the short run. As women move into management there will be a smaller proportion of men in the managerial ranks. However, these men are likely to be in the most senior jobs and, thus, will be more highly paid than the women who have more recently moved into management positions. It is likely that the average pay for men within the bank will increase more than the average pay for women. The gap between average male and average female salaries could therefore increase because of EE success.

Another potential conflict may result if a strict percentage definition of gender predominance (*e.g.*, 70 per cent male incumbents defines job as "male") is used to identify female and male jobs for pay equity purposes. In this case, EE success might lead to jobs which have historically been gender specific being excluded from the pay equity process (*i.e.*, now only 68 per cent male dominated). These jobs would no longer meet the percentage cut-off, even though the salaries attached to them have been affected by the gender of those who have traditionally performed the work. This can be avoided by including a criterion of "historical incumbency," as is done in Ontario's pay equity legislation.

A third example, is the criticism of some job evaluation systems because they have factors which are management oriented. This is a fair criticism when the factor can only measure aspects of management jobs (*e.g.*, managerial know-how) rather than a characteristic found in all jobs (*e.g.*, process know-how). However, sometimes the criticism is based on the reasoning that measuring job aspects found predominantly in management jobs (*e.g.*, planning responsibility) is gender biased because there are no women in managerial jobs. This is confusing an EE problem with a pay equity problem. Employment equity is needed to increase the representation of women in managerial positions. But the lack of women in a job does mot make the measurement of skill, effort, responsibility and working conditions found in the job, gender biased.

## NOTES

1. *Constitution Act, 1982*, Pt. I of Schedule B, enacted by the *Canada Act, 1982* (U.K.) 1982, c. 11.
2. R.S.C. 1985, c. 23 (2nd Supp.).
3. S.Q. 1975, c. 6.
4. Bill 79, introduced for 2nd reading July 12, 1993.
5. [1989] 1 S.C.R. 1219, 59 D.L.R. (4th) 321.
6. S.M. 1974, c. 65 [now *The Human Rights Code*, S.M. 1987-88, c. 45].
7. [1985] 2 S.C.R. 561, 23 D.L.R. (4th) 481.
8. *Ontario (Human Rights Commission) and O'Malley v. Simpson Sears Ltd.*, [1985] 2 S.C.R. 536, [1985] 7 C.H.R.R. D/3102, 23 D.L.R (4th) 321.
9. R.S.O. 1990, c. H.19.
10. R.S.C. 1985, c. H-6.
11. [1990] 2 S.C.R. 489, 72 D.L.R. (4th) 417.
12. S.Q. 1982, c. 61 [am. 1989, c. 51, s.11].
13. "L'accès à l'égalité dans l'emploi: Guide d'élaboration d'un programme volontaire." Quebec Human Rights Commission, November, 1988, p. 6.
14. Prior to this the City of Toronto had a contractors' program which covered about 8,000 employers. The program was in existence from 1989 until 1992 when it was eliminated for private sector organizations because of the introduction of the Ontario *Employment Equity Act*. The city's contractors' program for grant recipients began in 1987 and is on-going as is its program for civic agencies (begun in 1986).
15. R.S.N.B. 1973, c. H-11.
16. [1987] 9 C.H.R.R. D./4573, 46 D.L.R. (4th) 193; affd [1990] 3 S.C.R. 229.
17. Donald J. Treiman and Kermit Terrell, "Women, Work and Wages – Trends in the Female Occupational Structure Since 1940", in *Social Indicator Models*, K.C. Land and S. Spilerman, eds., New York: Russell Sage Foundation, 1975.
18. The wage gap is the difference in the average salary of women versus men compared to the average salary of men:

$$\text{Wage} = \frac{\text{Average male salary} - \text{Average female salary}}{\text{Gap average male salary}}$$

# REFERENCES

Denise Reaume, *The Law Review Seminar: Race, Culture, and the Law: Law in a Pluralistic Society*, Toronto: Faculty of Law, University of Toronto, 1992.

Donald J. Treiman and Kermit Terrell, "Women, Work and Wages – Trends in the Female Occupational Structure Since 1940," in *Social Indicator Models*, K.C. Land and S. Spilerman, (eds.), New York: Russell Sage Foundation, 1975.

# CHAPTER 3

# Designated Groups

The four designated groups are discussed in this chapter. Questions which are addressed include: Why are certain groups targeted for EE assistance? What are the employment barriers that each group faces? How is each designated group defined? While statistics showing how the four groups are disadvantaged are provided in Appendix A, this chapter characterizes the experiences for some of the sub-groups comprising the designated groups to give the reader an understanding of why EE is needed.

*Why are certain groups targeted under EE?*

Employment equity is designed to assist members of *groups* which have traditionally been disadvantaged in employment. Disadvantaged groups tend to have:.

- Higher unemployment;
- Lower paying jobs;
- Higher underemployment; and
- Lower representation in positions of authority.

**Higher unemployment:** The unemployed are those who are willing and able to work and are looking for work but have not been hired. Members of the four designated groups, Aboriginal Peoples, persons with disabilities, racial minorities and women, tend to have consistently higher rates of unemployment than do those who are not members of the designated groups. That is, persons of colour have higher unemployment than Whites; women have higher unemployment than men, and so on. (Statistics are provided in Appendix A)

**Lower paying jobs:** It is true that some white, able-bodied men hold low paying jobs while others hold high paying jobs. However, many members of designated groups are employed in lower paying jobs for inappropriate reasons. For instance, jobs traditionally associated with women (such as nursing and secretarial work) have been paid less than comparably valued male jobs (see Chapter 2 section on pay equity).

**Higher underemployment:** To be underemployed means that one cannot find a job which uses one's full range of skills and abilities and so one is forced to take a job requiring lower skills than one possesses. For instance, many people of colour who are recent immigrants are often underemployed and consequently paid less than their skills should command because they lack "Canadian experience". People of colour may also be prevented from taking supervisory positions, even though they are qualified, because of a perceptions that "Whites should be the bosses". In the past when college graduates were interviewed the women were asked if they could type, while the men were asked if they wanted to be management trainees. Women still face a glass ceiling which keeps them from senior management jobs.

**Lower representation in positions of authority:** Those in positions of authority design the rules which govern organizations. There is a natural tendency for persons in authority to design systems which work best for persons and groups who are most similar to themselves. This is not because people mean to do others harm. Rather, it is because it is so easy to assume that one's perspective is the only one and what is best for oneself is best for all. So if white, able-bodied men, are in positions of authority they will design systems which work well for them. Just as when women, Aboriginal Peoples, persons with disabilities or racial minorities are in positions of authority they will design systems which work well for them. There is a general need for greater sensitivity to others' perspectives and the best way to achieve this is to have diversity among those in positions of authority.

The four designated groups – Aboriginal Peoples, persons with disabilities, racial minorities and women – have in common higher levels of unemployment, inappropriately being in lower paying jobs, more underemployment, and lower representation in positions of authority. Two additional points need to be made about the disadvantaged groups at this time. First is that the focus is on the group. That is, there are individuals within the four designated groups who may not experience any of the characteristics of disadvantage. But statistics show that when each of the designated groups is compared to the corresponding non-designated group (*e.g.*, women to men, Whites to people of colour, etc.) the designated groups – as groups – are disadvantaged.

Second, over time, with EE efforts, it is intended that the groups will cease to be disadvantaged. Once Aboriginal Peoples, persons with disabilities, racial minorities or women are no longer disadvantaged then EE efforts will no longer be needed for these groups.

*How are the designated groups defined?*

Different agencies define the designated groups slightly differently, as noted in Chapters 2 and 5. A basic definition for each designated group, the basic subgroups comprising each and the preferred terminology for each group is provided below (though it must be noted that the language in this area is still developing.)

**Aboriginal Peoples:** Essentially, Aboriginal Peoples are defined racially as those who are descendants of the original or Native peoples who, when the Europeans arrived, lived on the lands which have become Canada. Aboriginal Peoples include:

- Canadian or North American "Indians" who have status[1] under the *Indian Act* of 1876,[2] as amended in 1985;
- Non-status "Indians" under the *Indian Act*;
- The Métis, descendants of French-Indian heritage or other European-Aboriginal heritage; and
- The Inuit and Denes and other Aboriginal Peoples who were not included in the *Indian Act*.
- Those whose ancestry is partially Aboriginal and consider themselves as such.

According to the 1986 census there are 712,000 status and non-status Natives in Canada, but this figure is a clear under-estimation. It is known that over 45,000 Natives boycotted the census. Since 1986 a change in the *Indian Act* has led to approximately 100,000 people receiving status. Further, there are 40,000 Inuit. So a more realistic figure is a million people of Aboriginal ancestry.

While the phrase "Indian" has been used to describe the original peoples of Canada, preferred terminology includes Native peoples, First Nations or Aboriginal Peoples. Aboriginal is the best collective term for all the groups noted above since Métis and some Inuit do not consider themselves "Native". These terms emphasize that Aboriginal Peoples are descendants of different nations who have been in Canada for thousands of years, rather than the few hundreds of years which characterize those of European ancestry. Using the term "Indian" for Aboriginal Peoples continues the confusion of Christopher Columbus that his expedition had landed in India. Further, since those from the country of India (East Indians) are a visible minority in Canada it can be confusing to continue to refer to Aboriginal Peoples as "Indians".

**Persons with disabilities:** This designated group is the most difficult to define. First, it is important to remember that there is no clear dividing line between being able-bodied and having a disability. The definition is:

A person who has persistent physical, mental, psychiatric, sensory or learning impairment which is perceived to disadvantage the person with respect to employment.

Because persons with disabilities is the most difficult group to define, those covered by EE legislation should be sure to examine its exact wording and any interpretations. It is possible for human rights and EE legislation to have somewhat different terminology or definitions covering persons with disabilities.

As a designated group, persons with disabilities differ from all the others in one important way. While sex and race are determined at birth, disability status can change at any point in time. Anyone could become a person with a disability. In other words, there are persons with disabilities and those who are temporarily able-bodied.

Currently the term "persons with disability" is the preferred terminology since it emphasizes the person, not the disability. The term "handicapped" is old fashioned. "Handicap" comes from the notion of someone begging "cap-in-hand". It is likely that over time the phrase "persons with disability" may change since it still contains an emphasis on *dis*ability. "Differently abled" is also being used. Table 3-1 provides some preferred terminology for persons with various disabilities.

Disabilities may be categorized as follows:

- Physical disabilities
  (Mobility impairments, visual impairments, hearing impairments, speech impairments, muscular impairments, disfigurement, hidden disabilities related to heart or respiratory systems, arthritis, diabetes, or epilepsy)
- Psychiatric or mental disabilities
  (Emotional or psychological impairments)
- Learning disabilities
- Developmentally disabled (Low intelligence)

The diversity among persons with disabilities cannot be over-emphasized. It is impossible to accommodate (see Chapter 8), or to make many generalizations about hiring persons with disabilities without knowing the specific person, the person's abilities and any special needs related to her or his disability. The need to emphasize this diversity among persons

## Table 3-1

### Preferred Terminology for Persons with Disabilities

NOTE: Language changes, so some phrases below may become out-dated.

| Instead of | Use |
|---|---|
| Blind | A person with almost no vision, or none at all, is blind. Persons with some sight are partially sighted, visually impaired or have low vision, not partially blind |
| Brain-damaged | Brain-injured |
| In, or confined to, a wheelchair | Person who uses a wheelchair. (This emphasizes the wheelchair as a mobility aid.) |
| Crazy, insane | Mentally ill |
| Crippled | Person with a disability |
| Deaf | Deaf. Person with severe hearing loss who uses sign language to communicate |
| Fits, spells | Seizures |
| Hearing impaired | Hard of hearing (person with any degree of hearing loss who communicates primarily by speech) |
| Mongolism | Down's Syndrome |
| Normal | Not to be used as contrast to disabled. Non-disabled, or able-bodied are preferred, as are specific terms, e.g., sighted, ambulatory |
| Physically challenged | Physically disabled |
| Mentally retarded | Developmentally disabled, or having developmental disabilities. |
| Stutterer | Person having a speech impairment |
| The disabled | Persons with disabilities |

with disabilities is heightened because typically when one refers to "a person with a disability" most people think of someone who is using a wheelchair. This may, in part, be a function of the symbol sometimes used to refer to persons with disabilities, as shown above.

The use of this symbol on parking spaces and washrooms is consistent with the needs of those using wheelchairs and others who have another mobility disability. However, it could be totally irrelevant for someone who is blind, deaf, learning or developmentally disabled or who has diabetes. Further, those having the same disability are not the same. Each person's abilities and any special needs will be individualistic. For employment purposes issues of abilities and special needs cannot be considered in a vacuum but must be related to the specific job being filled.

In addition to the diversity of kinds of disabilities found among members of this designated group, it should be remembered that persons with disabilities also vary across the other designated groups — gender, race and being of Aboriginal ancestry. This, of course, is true for all the designated groups so there are individuals who are members of two, three or four of the designated groups.

Table 3-2 shows the numbers and proportion of people with various disabilities. The 1991 data indicates that 15.5 per cent of the Canadian population are persons with disabilities, 12.9 per cent of the population are persons of working age with disabilities and 12.6 per cent of the population are working age disabled persons who are not institutionalized.

**Racial or visible minorities:** In Canada, reference to "race" is often about skin colour. Visible minorities can be defined as those who are non-Caucasian by race or non-white by colour. Anthropologists think in terms of three races, Caucasian (White), Mongoloid (Aboriginal and Asian) and Negroid (Black). People of colour in Canada include East Indians (those from the Indian sub-continent) who are of the Caucasian

**TABLE 3-2**

**DISABLED PERSONS 15 YEARS OF AGE AND OVER IN HOUSEHOLDS**

| Physical disability | Women | Men | Total |
|---|---|---|---|
| Mobility | 1,075,000 18.7%** | 726,000 12.6%** | 1,801,000 31.4%** |
| Agility | 875,000 15.2% | 663,000 11.5% | 1,538,000 26.8% |
| Seeing | 274,000 4.8% | 172,000 3.0% | 446,000 7.8% |
| Hearing | 373,000 6.5% | 488,00 8.5% | 861,000 15.0% |
| Speaking | 72,000 1.3% | 89,000 1.5% | 161,000 2.8% |
| Other | 399,000 6.9% | 364,000 6.4% | 763,000 13.3% |
| Unknown | 74,000 1.3% | 100,000 1.7% | 174,000 3.0% |
| Total | 1,468,000* 52.5%† | 1,326,000* 47.5%† | 2,794,000 100% |

\*　Components include persons reporting multiple disabilities, and therefore add to more than the totals shown.

\*\*　Proportion of total number of disabilities, 5,744,000.

†　Proportion of total number of people.

SOURCE:　Adapted from Health and Activity Limitation Survey, Statistics Canada, 1986.

race but are non-white in colour. Since those who are non-Caucasian have "coloured" as opposed to "white" skin tone, people of colour comprise visible (racial) minorities in Canada. (Four-fifths of the world's population are people of colour.)

Race does *not* refer to country of birth or citizenship. For instance Blacks have come to Canada directly from Africa, by way of the United States, the Caribbean, Europe and other parts of the world. Someone immigrating to Canada from Jamaica could be a Black, Chinese, White, East Indian or of mixed ancestry.

Visible minorities or racial minorities are acceptable terms for this designated group as is people (or persons) of colour. Since the term "non-white" emphasizes what people are not, rather than what they are, it is a less effective term.

Basic visible minority groups are:

- Black Canadians (those whose ancestors originated from Africa).
- Asians or East-Asian-Canadians (for example, those whose ancestors originated from China, Japan, Korea).
- South-Asian-Canadians (for example, those whose ancestors originated from India, Sri Lanka, Pakistan, Bangladesh).
- Southeast-Asian-Canadians (for example, those whose ancestors originated from Vietnam, Laos, Cambodia, Philippines).
- Amer-Indian-Canadians (First Nations people from Central and South America).
- Arabs or West-Asian-Canadians (for example, those whose ancestors originated from Egypt, Jordan, Syria, Saudi Arabia, Iraq).

Table 3-3 provides some respectful language related to race.

**Women:** While women do not need to be defined, it should be pointed out that the preferred terminology for the female population should always correspond to that used for the male population. For example, if the term "girls" is used, then use "boys", "guys"[3] corresponds to "gals", "ladies" corresponds to "gentlemen", and "women" corrsponds to "men". Table 3-4 provides a listing for non-sexist language.

A distinction can be made between "sex" and "gender". "Sex" technically refers to the biological differences between men and women. "Gender" technically refers to the socially defined differences between feminine and masculine (female and male). What is considered feminine and masculine changes over time. For example, today it is acceptable for women to take aerobics classes and be physically fit while in the past it was not considered ladylike to sweat. In Shakespeare's time fashionable men of the English court wore tights while women's legs were fully covered.

While a specific definition of each designated group is needed in order to implement EE, remember that there is a great deal of heterogeneity within each of the designated groups. For example, a person who is blind shares the label "person with a disability" with a paraplegic and with a person who has epilepsy, but that may be all they share. While an African-Canadian, Asian-Canadian and an East Indian-Canadian are all considered members of racial minorities, a black person may have the same

## TABLE 3-3
### RESPECTFUL LANGUAGE RELATED TO RACE

NOTE: Language changes, so some of the phrases in this table may have become out-dated.

| For | Use |
|---|---|
| Those of Negroid stock | Black, African-Canadian, African-American, people of colour |
| Those of Mongoloid stock | Asian, rather than Oriental, or hyphenated phrases such as Japanese-Canadian, "those of Korean ancestry" or people of colour |
| "Indians" or descendants of Aboriginal Peoples | Aboriginal Peoples, First Nations, First Nations people |
| Those of Caucasian stock | White or mainstream (which is better than dominant culture) |

stereotypes about an Asian or East Indian person as a white person. Further, the experiences of a fourth generation Chinese-Canadian and a new immigrant from Hong Kong are likely to be different. There are similarities and differences between Aboriginal Peoples who have been raised on a reserve rather than an urban setting. Women who are found in all the other designated groups often experience double or triple jeopardy – for instance, a Japanese woman faces employment barriers because of race *and* sex.

### What are *employment barriers?*

Employment barriers inappropriately restrict or prevent full equality of opportunity, and/or results, for members of designated groups versus those who are not members of designated groups. An obvious barrier is requiring unnecessary qualifications which members of one or more of the designated groups are less likely to have. For example, requiring that work experience be acquired in Canada when this is irrelevant, or requiring people be of a certain height, when it is not job related. Other barriers are subtle. For example, if co-workers are cold and unhelpful to the first East Indian hired into the work unit then this individual is less likely to succeed because he or she will not receive the informal orientation and training required.

Part of EE is about removing barriers. Such barriers may be found in

## TABLE 3-4

### PREFERRED NON-SEXIST LANGUAGE

NOTE: Language changes, so some of the phrases in this table may have become out-dated.

| Instead of | Use |
|---|---|
| Gender specific titles (*e.g.*, policeman, mailman or fireman) | Use generic titles (*e.g.*, police officer, letter carrier or firefighter) |
| Do not always put the masculine first (*e.g.*, his and her) | Either put them in alphabetical order (female and male) or alternate the order in different sentences. |
| Do not use feminine or diminutive endings such as "ette" or "ess" | Poet (not poetess), actor (not actress), waiter or server (not waitress) |
| Do not use physical descriptions of women unless pertinent to the topic. | Use the test: Would I include this reference if I were writing about a man? |
| Man the phones | Staff the phones |
| Brotherhood | Society, kinship. community |
| Cameraman | Camera operator, photographer |
| Draftsman | Drafting technician or Draftperson |
| Layman | Layperson |
| Chairman | Chair or chairperson |
| Manpower | Human resources |
| Old wives' tale | Superstitious beliefs |
| Workmanship | Handiwork |
| Man-made | Manufactured, artificial |
| Man hours | Staff hours, employee hours, person hours |
| Maiden name | Birth name |

SOURCE: Adapted from "Equality in Language" Ontario Ministry of the Environment, January 1992.

any employment system such as recruiting, establishing job requirements, orientation, work scheduling, compensation. Barriers are often present because of a lack of adequate recognition of the diversity existing among employees. That is, polices and procedures are based on the erroneous assumption that most employees face the work environment typically associated with white, able-bodied men.

All of the designated groups face employment barriers. However, the barriers faced by each group differ. Further, because of the heterogeneity within each designated group, barriers will differ for sub-groups within each designated group. Therefore, in reading the sections on the specific barriers faced by each of the designated groups keep in mind that some generalizations have been made and the full diversity found among the members of the various designated groups cannot be reflected.

### What barriers are faced by all of the designated groups?

One of the more subtle barriers is the image we all have about the kind of people who should do certain kinds of work. Think of nursing. Look at the image which comes to mind. Usually, it is a woman dressed from head to toe in white. Think of a computer programmer. For most people the image is that of a man, for many it is a man of Chinese ancestry. Images affect those making hiring decisions in subtle ways. An applicant for a managerial job who is a petite, soft-spoken, Japanese woman will not fit with the image most of us have of a tall, white, man in a suit. The fact that designated group members do not look like those who traditionally perform certain work blocks their entry into jobs in which they are underrepresented. This barrier, while subtle, is pervasive because designated group members are not hired for jobs not traditionally held because they do not "look the part" and they do not look the part because they are not hired for such jobs. This spiral must be broken by removing the images people hold about who should do what kind of work. This can be done by making the images explicit, having job requirements which are truly relevant to the job, and accurately assessing job candidates' qualifications, even when their appearance differs from those one usually sees.

Another danger of these images is that they are also held by designated group members too. Consequently, members of the designated groups do not always explore non-traditional jobs because they cannot "see" themselves in those jobs. This barrier can be overcome by outreach recruiting and the use of role models. Seeing others like oneself performing a job, or simply seeing others like oneself employed within the organization communicates an important message. It is sometimes difficult for those in mainstream groups – men, Whites and the able-bodied – to understand these subtle barriers. Members of the mainstream see others like themselves in virtually all work situations. They do not know what it is like to feel out-of-place on a daily basis because of their gender, race or disability.

As noted earlier, each designated group faces unique barriers. Some of these are discussed below.

## What has been the history of Aboriginal Peoples in Canada?

Aboriginal Peoples lived on the lands that would become Canada when the British and the French arrived in North America. The Aboriginal communities were critical in the early economic activity of the Europeans – the fur trade. Over time the Europeans switched from trading to farming. Farming required land. So, the English made treaties with some of the First Nations regarding land. These treaties were recognized by Canada when the constitution was repatriated in 1982. The *Indian Act* was passed in 1876 and affected and controlled virtually every aspect of life for Aboriginal Peoples. The Act ensured that Aboriginal Peoples settled where the government wanted them (on reserves), controlled movement off the reserves, and provided a commitment from the government for education, health and welfare systems. In effect, the enforcement of the *Indian Act* worked toward the abolishment of Aboriginal traditions. This was justified in terms of assimilating with the majority, white culture. Whether assimilation is perceived as an appropriate goal or not, isolation on the reserves could not facilitate this goal; nor could such practices as denying Aboriginal Peoples living on reserves the right to vote until 1960.

The system of "Indian" reserves formalized in the *Indian Act* began in the 1850s. The reserves system was partly an attempt to encourage members of First Nations to become farmers, despite their desire to continue the traditional hunting and fishing way of life. The reserves limited mobility and segregated Aboriginal Peoples and were counter to traditional Aboriginal culture in many ways. First, reserves were counter to the nomadic culture of many First Nations peoples. The elimination of this nomadic tradition was one of the primary reasons for the creation of the reserve system. The reserves served the Europeans by making it easier for white farmers to move west. A key difference between Aboriginal culture and European culture is a differing view of private property with respect to land. Within Aboriginal culture, land is seen as belonging to everyone to use collectively, not as something which some people own and keep for their exclusive use. This orientation fits with that of nomadic peoples. The reserve system is counter to this.

While it is impossible to fully capture the basic tenets of such diverse people as are found among the First Nations, a basic listing of traditional cultural norms is provided by Rupert Ross in his book on Aboriginal justice:[4]

- Ethics of Non-interference. Letting others learn in their own way and through their own mistakes. (Contrasted with the Canadian

contradictory values of: "minding one's own business" and "being one's brother's keeper".)
- Ethics that anger not be shown (Contrasted with the Canadian value system that anger is the one emotion which men are allowed to show.)
- Ethic of not praising or showing gratitude. (Appreciation can be shown by asking the other person to continue with her or his contribution.)
- Ethic of thinking things through before acting. (Contrasted to the Canadian culture where action is valued.)
- Notion that the "time must be right". Hunting and agricultural cultures are more dependent on "things in season". (Contrasted with the Canadian business notion of getting the most out of time, controlling time, not wasting time.)

In summary, Ross states (p. 65):

Euro-Canadian society has come to prize as virtues aggressiveness and a dogged determination to prevail regardless of the odds. Native people, by contrast value quiet accommodation instead. One group sees itself as properly the master of all creation; the other as a component and dependent *part* of all creation. In turn, the two groups cannot help but characterize each other in negative terms: [Euro-Canadians] decry [Aboriginal] caution and passivity as apathy, while [Aboriginals] see [Euro-Canadian] aggressiveness as arrogant and wilfully wrong.

### What kind of employment barriers do Aboriginal Peoples face?

Aboriginal Peoples face many of the same barriers as those faced by other people of colour (racial minorities), but there are some unique differences that only this group faces, such as being treated as a conquered people. For example, while multiculturalism has been Canadian policy since 1971, the stance toward Aboriginal Peoples has been one of assimilation, isolation, and a denial of Native peoples' languages and heritages. The specific employment barriers discussed are:

- Lack of recognition of diversity
- Lack of employment opportunities on reserves
- Lack of support within organizations
- Stereotypes and racism
- Harassment

**Lack of recognition of diversity:** None of the designated groups are homogeneous, yet this seems hardest to keep in mind when addressing issues related to Aboriginal Peoples. One assumes that the employment barriers will be different for Blacks than for Asians. (If for no other rea-

son than the stereotypes are different.) One intuitively knows that employment barriers for a person with a mobility disability will differ from
those for a person with a hearing loss. Yet typically, the mainstream
cultures assume all Aboriginal persons are the same, a single set of stereotypes apply. Not only are there important cultural differences among
the various peoples (*e.g.*, Cree, Ojibway)[5] but there are some key geographic differences. As Figure 3-1 shows, in terms of geographic background there are at least five basic groups for whom barriers will differ.

These geographic differences have implications for employment barriers. About 75 per cent of the Canadian Aboriginal population live off
reserves.[6] One difference between Aboriginal Peoples on and off reserves
is that the latter have a labour force participation rate which is virtually
the same as the Canadian population as a whole (65 per cent compared
to 67 per cent). On-reserve Aboriginal Peoples have a participation rate
of 43 per cent. In terms of income the proportion of those earning an
income below $10,000 is 68 per cent for those on-reserve, 51 per cent for
those off-reserve compared to 39 per cent for the Canadian population as
a whole. As a generalization, off-reserve Aboriginals have employment
characteristics which are between mainstream culture and on-reserve
Aboriginals. Those on reserves in isolated areas will face different barriers than those on reserves close to cities.

**Lack of employment opportunities on reserves:** Only about 25 per cent
of the Aboriginal population lives on reserve. However, the statistics noted
above show that they have the least favourable employment situation. Many
reserves are located in areas with poor employment opportunities. As a
result there is especially high unemployment on reserves. This is further
complicated by the lack of opportunities for training and education on reserves. Leaving the reserve to obtain training and education can be more
difficult for Aboriginal Peoples who have lived on the reserve. The Aboriginal culture is a particularly supportive one. The non-Aboriginal environment is often very hostile. So there is a great discrepancy between the reserve and the city where training and education is available.

**Lack of support within organizations:** The lack of support within
organizations is a barrier which both on-reserve and off-reserve Aboriginal Peoples face. Aboriginal communities are highly supportive. Mainstream work organizations are not. Mentoring or buddy systems are
particularly helpful – assuming that the mentor understands Aboriginal
culture. This is particularly important since, when faced with discrimination, many Aboriginal Peoples will leave the situation.[7] This leads to a
spotty work history which makes it harder to get further employment.

Support also means learning to appreciate aspects of Aboriginal culture which differ from mainstream culture. When is respect and co-op-

### FIGURE 3-1

#### BASIC GEOGRAPHIC BACKGROUNDS OF ABORIGINAL PEOPLES

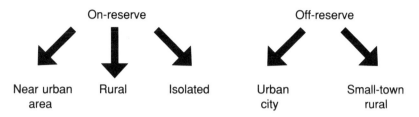

eration better than aggression and divisiveness? When is communication within the larger context better than just getting to the point? One employment barrier to be overcome is the assumption that cultural differences are so vast they cannot be bridged – this is not true.

**Stereotypes and racism:** Stereotypes affect the people who are the subject of the stereotypes. Stereotypes affect self-image and self-confidence. The stereotypes about Aboriginal Peoples held by the mainstream culture are predominantly negative, and these stereotypes have existed since the Europeans came to Canada. Negative stereotypes can be "in the air"; that is, one does not have to have any contact with the members of a particular group to know the common stereotypes. Other stereotypes come from contact with people and misinterpretation of their behaviour. For example, everyone in the mainstream culture "knows" that the appropriate way to behave in an interview is to look the interviewer in the eye and to give quick and direct answers to questions. Many Aboriginal applicants will not behave this way. For one thing, looking someone in the eye is a sign of disrespect in many Aboriginal cultures. Thinking carefully before one speaks is typical and getting to the point is not valued the same way as it is in the mainstream culture. The interpretation which is put on this "different" (not necessarily bad) behaviour in an interview is likely to reinforce negative stereotypes.

Stereotypes about Aboriginal Peoples, of course, are inconsistent with many realities. For example, between 1985 and 1989 there was a 66 per cent increase in university and post-secondary enrolments among First Nations peoples. Between 1981 and 1986 labour force participation among Aboriginal Peoples increased from 50 per cent to 60 per cent. The Aboriginal community is the only one in Canada which is getting younger.

**Harassment:** Harassment issues experienced by First Nations peoples are similar to that experienced by people of colour and are discussed in detail in Chapter 10.

### *How has the view of persons with disabilities evolved over time?*

The modern view of persons who have disabilities has evolved over time. Canada's history is one of nomadic tribes (Aboriginal Peoples) and westward movement (Europeans). Many of the Aboriginal tribes were nomads who followed the animals they hunted. European communities were established by trappers and traders. In both the Aboriginal and European settling of Canada, stamina and hard work were needed to succeed; weakness was a hindrance. Everyone in the community had to be able to do their share of what was necessary for survival. In some Aboriginal cultures the elderly, the weak or those who had a disability were expected to leave the community – a form of suicide. In European cultures persons with disabilities were the responsibility of their families. Later, institutionalization of persons with disabilities became common. Such institutionalization was felt to facilitate better care of persons with disabilities. It also served to segregate those with disabilities from the community. Such segregation reduced the interaction between able-bodied persons and persons with disabilities. This allowed able-bodied persons to escape the discomfort often experienced from such interaction.

People with disabilities have become more political over time and continue to demand greater integration into the community. Power was gained through the self-help movement when persons with disabilities joined together to help each other. This led to demands that persons with disabilities become involved in defining and redressing their own needs, rather than relying on social services professionals. Finally, many persons with disabilities have followed the example of the women's movement, anti-racism groups and Aboriginal rights groups and formed an advocacy movement. People with disabilities continue to demand full participation in society. One example is mainstreaming of children with disabilities into regular school classes (often supplemented with special classes). New technology has also facilitated integration by enabling people with certain disabilities to perform many functions which they previously were unable to do.

There are two potential pools of applicants with disabilities for an organization. First, those individuals who already have a disability and are seeking employment within the organization. Second, those who have acquired a disability while working for the organization. As difficult as it sometimes is for the second group to remain employed, the first group faces even more severe barriers.

### *What kind of employment barriers do persons with disabilities face?*

There are a number of attitudinal barriers which disadvantage persons with disabilities. These include:

- Generalization of inability;
- Feelings of discomfort and embarrassment;
- Over-protectiveness;
- Fear of the need to accommodate;
- Presumption that persons with disabilities make poor employees;
- Accessibility to buildings and work sites.

**Generalization of inability:** When an able-bodied person encounters a person with a disability he or she is likely to focus on the disability (and miss the person). In addition, able-bodied persons tend to generalize that someone who has a disability has other limitations. For instance, persons using wheelchairs often report that others talk to them more slowly and in simpler sentences, assuming that they do not have a normal level of intelligence. Numerous assumptions are made about what a particular disability means. Many sighted people feel that they would be lost without their vision. Therefore, they assume that someone who is blind cannot do anything which the sighted person cannot do with their eyes closed. They do not recognize that over time other senses (*e.g.*, hearing) and functions (*e.g.*, memory) can be used to compensate for loss of sight. Further, many people do not know that someone who is legally blind may still have some vision.

Focusing on the disability and assuming an understanding of what it means can prevent human resource professionals and supervisors from seeking the information they need to make a good employment decision. It is essential to ascertain if an applicant with a disability can do a particular job, given the necessary accommodation (more is said about this in Chapter 8).

**Feelings of discomfort and embarrassment:** Able-bodied people often do not like to be around persons with disabilities because they (1) do not know how to behave, (2) feel vulnerable, and/or (3) feel pity toward the person. People like to feel competent and dislike being in situations where they do not know how to cope. For example, what is the correct response when one tries to shake hands with someone who is missing their right hand? How does one react to a manic-depressive who is in the manic phase? What should one do if someone has an epileptic seizure? While these are not skills one is generally taught, they can be learned – often by talking with a person who has a specific disability. Studies show that increased positive interaction with persons with disabilities reduces fears and discomfort and leads to better acceptance. This is because, as one spends more time with someone who has a disability, the disability becomes only one of the things you know about the person rather than the only thing.

Most able-bodied people do not like to think about their vulnerability, or that many of us are temporarily able-bodied. Initially, interacting with a person with a known disability can make able-bodied persons feel vulnerable and fearful about themselves. Interacting with a person with a disability can result in an able-bodied person imagining what it would be like to have a disability and may lead to feelings of anxiety and dread. Some people may, erroneously, think or act as if disabilities are contagious.

Another common reaction is pity. Pity is inconsistent with feeling respect for a person. It often makes people over-protective (discussed below). Being pitied is an uncomfortable feeling since it communicates a lower status.

**Over-protectiveness:** Everyone takes risks throughout the day. Yet people often become overly-protective of someone with a disability, feeling that he or she should not be into a position where they might run the risk of being injured and/or increase the severity of their disability. Being "overly-protective" and denying persons with disabilities the dignity of risk is another common reaction that able-bodied people have when interacting with persons with a disability. The dignity of risk means that a person has a right to decide which risk he or she is willing to take and which ones to avoid. For instance, many employers argue against hiring a deaf person because if there was a fire that person would be unable to hear the alarm. Denying someone an employment opportunity based on the infinitesimal probability of fire is a poor argument. Further, the risk can be minimized by the ability to communicate a fire alarm in other forms (*e.g.*, a flashing light, a vibrating "beeper" or by human contact).

**Fear of the need to accommodate:** Employment equity requires that the essential duties of jobs may have to be changed to accommodate the needs of someone with a disability (this is discussed in detail in Chapter 8). This requirement can be a barrier in itself if human resources staff and managers see such accommodation as extra work requiring substantial sums of money. The presumption about cost is untrue in the majority of cases. Eighty per cent of accommodations cost less than $500. For example, four bricks under a desk to accommodate an employee using a wheelchair cost less than $5.00. It may be possible to work with the person who has the disability to obtain funding for equipment to enable them to perform their job duties (for example, a special keyboard designed for someone who has one arm). It may be better for an employee who has a disability to own the specialized equipment rather than the employer who would keep it if the employee left the organization.

It is true that accommodation takes some extra work. But many organizations are daunted by the task because they have no idea of what to do or how to go about it. An excellent source for this information is the person being accommodated. They, or an organization which works with persons with the particular disability, are likely to be familiar with what accommodations are needed and how to accomplish them. It is important to involve the person being accommodated. Some employers have found that they have done more than necessary or have done the wrong thing because they made incorrect assumptions about what kind of accommodation was needed. Another source for information on accommodation is the Job Accommodation Network (JAN). Their toll free number in Canada is 1-800-526-2262.

Another barrier comes from delays in getting equipment. Particularly in large organizations, bureaucratic paperwork delays getting purchase approvals through the system and delivered for use. A supervisor who believes that he or she is going to have a person on staff, unable to do their job because the necessary equipment cannot be obtained for four months, may balk at hiring a person with a disability even though they are the best qualified. Some organizations are setting aside money to be used for accommodations. This system has a faster approval process. Renting, rather than purchasing equipment, may speed up the process and is a good idea when there is some question over what the best technical aid would be.

**Presumption that persons with disabilities will make poor employees:** There is a presumption that persons with disabilities have higher rates of absenteeism, lower levels of productivity, require more training and added supervision, and will, generally, be harder to work with. Studies show these beliefs to be strong barriers with no relationship to reality.

**Accessibility to buildings and work sites:** Accessibility issues involve getting to work, getting into buildings or to work sites, getting around the work location to perform the job, using the cafeteria or bathroom, etc. Only some persons with a disability will face accessibility barriers (for instance, some people with mobility impairments or muscular-skeletal disabilities, some with visibility impairments, and some who have developmental disabilities).

### What has been the experience of racial minorities in Canada?

When we think of racial minorities in Canada we immediately think of immigrants. And it is true that if one goes back far enough in time each member of a racial minority in Canada can identify her or his immigrant roots. This is true of all Canadians (though those of Aboriginal ancestry have to go back thousands of years). What differs is how far back each has to go to find an immigrant ancestor. However, when one thinks "racial minority" one tends to reason:

Recent immigrant,
therefore
language problem.

While it is true that about 70 per cent of recent immigrants are people of colour this reasoning is flawed for three reasons:

1. Many people of colour are Canadian born.
2. Many immigrants of colour speak English or French.
3. Many immigrants of colour come as children and learn English or French before they enter the labour force.

Approximately 140,000 immigrants enter Canada in any one year – about one half of one per cent of the total population. Since the 1960s and 1970s, Canadian immigration changed to include an increasing number of immigrants from countries which are primarily populated with persons of colour, as shown in the map in Figure 3-2. These recent immigrants are joining other members of racial minorities in Canada who have been here since the 1700s (Blacks), 1800s (Chinese) and early 1900s (East Indians).

Immigrants to Canada have always come for the same reason – they felt that they and their children could have a better life here than in their current country. What has changed is that, at one time, moving from Northern Europe to Canada resulted in a higher standard of living; this is less true today. At one time moving from Southern Europe to Canada provided a better life; this is less true today as the standard of living has increased in European countries. Today, people are coming from third world countries to Canada because they can see that such a move is likely to increase their standard of living. Countries from which recent immigrants move are more highly populated with persons of colour.

Another reason for a higher proportion of immigrants who are persons of colour is that, in the past, Canadian immigration policies and laws were racist. Legislation and government policies designed to keep specific racial groups out of Canada have dotted our history. For example, in 1885 a tax was imposed on any Chinese person who wanted to immigrate. The Chinese were the only group which has had to pay in order to immigrate to Canada.

In 1908, the continuous passage requirement was imposed through an Order-in-Council. This required that immigrants to Canada must enter Canada from the country of their birth or citizenship by a continuous journey, that is, without stopping in another country.[8] While this rule was not specific to any country it did have a different impact on immigrants from Europe versus India, for instance. Continuous passage from Europe was easy; continuous passage from India was almost impossible.

**FIGURE 3-2**

**IMMIGRATION IS INCREASING FROM
RACIALLY DIVERSE GROUPS**

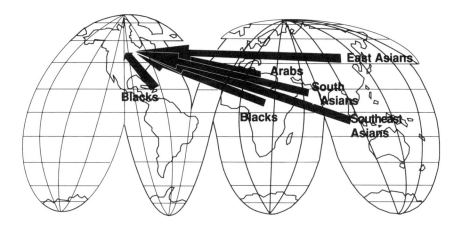

In 1923, Canadian immigration policy decreed that only citizens of Commonwealth countries with predominantly white populations would be considered British subjects and able to migrate to Canada.

In 1914, the head of the provincial administration of British Columbia, Sir Richard McBride, said "to admit Orientals in large numbers would mean in the end the extinction of the white people and we have always in mind the necessity of keeping this a white man's country".[9] This quote is similar to that made by William Lyon Mackenzie King, in 1947, when he was prime minister: "The Government will seek by legislation, regulation, and vigorous administration to ensure the *careful selection* [of immigrants]... [T]he people of Canada do not wish, as a result of mass immigration, to make a fundamental alteration in the character of our population" [emphasis added].[10] The continuous passage rule was one such regulation which effectively closed the door on immigration from India and Asia until the 1950s. Still, the *Immigration Acts*[11] of 1952 and 1957 barred persons from immigrating to Canada because of nationality, ethnic group, class, particular customs, habits, modes of life, or unsuitability to the climate. This resulted in preference being given to Whites. It was not until the *Immigration Act* of 1962 that Canadian immigration laws eliminated the racial component. However, immigration of people of colour was not particularly encouraged. In 1964, out of 32 Canadian immigration offices located in 22 countries, only four were in countries where the population is, predominantly, people of colour. Further, immigration officers had wide discretionary powers and could work against non-Whites. In 1967, regulations to the *Immigration Act* spelled out the objective criteria to be used in selecting immigrants. Anyone who achieved enough points, based on the criteria, and was in good health was admitted.

As with the other designated groups, one cannot talk about the experience of racial minorities as if this group is homogeneous. To highlight the heterogeneity within this designated group and to provide a background to the barriers faced by visible minorities, the remainder of this section will focus on the experiences of two different racial groups: Blacks and Chinese.

**Experience of Blacks in Canada:** Slavery existed in Canada. In 1687 the first known Black entered Canada as a slave. Most slaves worked as domestics. By 1783 there was a critical mass of non-slave Blacks, so one could not equate being black with being a slave. Slavery was outlawed in Ontario in 1793, the earliest date within the British Commonwealth. However, emancipation in Ontario was staggered by the age of the individual so that when Britain outlawed slavery in 1835, for itself and its colonies, there were still some slaves in Ontario.

As a tactic to subvert the economy of its rebelling colonies to the south of Canada, in 1775 the British promised freedom and land to any U.S. slaves who could get to Canada. They also promised land to non-slave loyalists who left the colonies. However, the British did not always fulfil their promises. For instance, only a third of these blacks were given land and many of those were given land inferior to that given to the white loyalists. Many of the Blacks who came to Canada at this time found themselves working for a quarter of the wages paid to whites. Blacks were not allowed to vote or sit on juries. There were no laws upholding these practices, but there were strong norms prohibiting these activities for Blacks.

The War of 1812 brought more black, former slaves to Canada. These new immigrants were welcomed initially because of the existing labour shortage. However, by 1815 the economy had taken a downturn and the Province of Nova Scotia tried to ban Black immigration. The period prior to, and during the Civil War in the United States, led to the underground railroad which brought many Blacks to Canada. About 75 per cent of those who came during this period returned to the United States for the opportunities offered to them during the Reconstructionist period which followed the Civil War.

Black communities that developed in Canada tended to be isolated from the white community, not by law, as in South Africa, but by social custom. However, segregated schools were allowed in Ontario by the Common School Act of 1850. Though schools were eventually integrated the discriminatory law remained until 1964.

In the 1890s, when immigration was being encouraged, the Canadian government, under Clifford Sifton as Minister of Immigration, sent special agents to the southern United States to discourage Blacks from coming to Canada. Black immigration did not begin again in significant numbers until the 1950s and 1960s, when the black population of Canada doubled; 90 per cent of these immigrants were from the Caribbean. Because of the new immigration laws in the 1960s, immigrants from the Caribbean (and elsewhere) tended to be people who were highly educated or those who would work as domestics.

**Experience of Chinese in Canada:** Chinese immigration began in the 1850s. It was greatly encouraged between 1880 and 1884 when the trans-Canada railroad was being built. However, Chinese working on the railroad were paid less than Whites for the same job. Because workers were needed but Chinese immigrants were not particularly welcome, immigration of men, not families, was encouraged. In 1885, after the railroad was completed, a head tax was imposed on Chinese persons who wished to immigrate to Canada. This head tax was raised from $50 in 1885 to $500 in 1904. Between 1923 and 1947 the *Chinese Immigration Act* prohibited Chinese immigration. Additionally, persons of Chinese ancestry were not allowed to enter certain professions such as law, teaching and pharmacy. Nor could individuals of Chinese extraction vote until 1947.

Past Chinese immigration policies provide an example of the retractable red-carpet approach which still characterizes Canada's immigration policy. Immigrants were encouraged to come when needed and then expected to leave when the task was finished or the economy took a downward turn. The difference in treatment between white immigrants and immigrants of colour was due to the fact that the latter did not "blend in". Both immigrants of colour and their descendants are noticeably different from the white majority in Canada. This was demonstrated to the Chinese community by an incident in 1979. The television program, W5, ran a segment called "The Campus Giveaway" which implied that qualified "Canadian" students were being denied places in Canadian universities because of the presence of foreign students. A scene during the show panned a classroom at the University of Toronto showing a large number of Asian students. The impression left by the program was that an Asian face could be equated with a foreign student. In reality most of the Asian students in the classroom were Canadian born or immigrants to Canada. The potential to disenfranchise people of colour is always present because they cannot "fit in" by changing their names or losing their accents. They will always be visible.

It is important to remember that "racial or visible minorities" is a catch-all label which may incorporate more heterogeneity than homogeneity. What is common about members of visible minority groups is that they are all seen as being different from white Canadians. This difference is related to having darker skin, being non-white. But racial minorities do not form a homogeneous group. A person of Japanese descent may hold the same stereotypes of East Indians as do Whites. The difference is that more Whites are in positions of power and, thus, can more greatly effect economic consequences for people of colour.

## What kind of employment barriers do racial minorities face?

Barriers faced by members of racial minorities include:

- Racism;
- Cultural differences and negative stereotypes;
- Assumption that all members of racial minority groups are recent immigrants;
- Racial harassment.

**Racism:** Many Canadians think of racism as a U.S. or South African problem, not as a Canadian issue. This has led Dan McIntyre, a prominent black leader, to label one barrier faced by racial minorities as the "there is no problem" problem. Canadian racism may differ from that exhibited in other countries, but it exists. What is racism? Racism is the assumption of the superiority of one racial group over another *and* the power to act on this assumption politically and economically. Racism assumes that members of different races have clearly discernable characteristics which are shared by all members of that race and are not shared with members of other races. The sense of superiority is tied to an assumption that everything good and important was created by members of the superior race and that other races have made no contribution. In Canada the group which sees itself as the racial group which has done everything good and important are Whites.

**Cultural differences and negative stereotypes:** There are differences among different ethnic groups – even those which belong to the same race (for example, among Caucasians there are those in the United Kingdom, Greece, Portugal and Sweden; among Blacks there are those in Africa, the Caribbean, and the United States). While we are sometimes tuned into ethnic differences, we are always tuned into racial differences. There is a presumption that members of different races are totally different. There are, typically, more differences between members of the same race than between members of different races. The important question is whether these differences are relevant to the work situation at hand. When someone presumes another person is different from them, they often expect to feel uncomfortable around that person. They feel they will not know how the other will behave; those who are different are unpredictable. In work situations predictability is desired. People want to know that others in a similar situation will respond in a similar manner. People feel they cannot assume this with others of a different race. This is related to the general assumption that there is only one way to accomplish something – and that is the way members of one's own race have always done it.

Members of the majority culture often do not recognize that they have a culture. Rather, they simply assume that their way of doing things is the standard and everyone else's way is deviant. The reality is that there are a number of ways of doing the same thing, only one of them is the white way.

The presumption of difference where race is involved tends to be tied to negative stereotypes. Stereotyping is a natural way to deal with too much information. People try to simplify the world by putting things into categories. The problem with stereotypes is the degree to which they are generalized and the assumption that they are true (and nothing else is) for every person who belongs to that group. Interestingly, it appears that negative feelings about different racial groups are formed first and then stereotypes are designed to support them. How else can one explain the negative stereotype that Asian students "study too much"?

Studies demonstrate that racism directly relates to a common negative stereotype about members of racial minority groups (as well as members of the other designated groups). In one study, Caribbean Blacks and South Asians were found to have lower incomes and higher levels of unemployment than others and only a small part of this could be attributed to differences in job qualifications.[12] Anglo-Saxon MBAs were hired more often, received higher salaries and advanced more rapidly than racial minority candidates, despite the fact that racial minority candidates submitted more job applications, attended more interviews and held similar qualifications.[13]

One particularly interesting study directly addressed the common belief that designated group members would be hired if only they were qualified.[14] There were two parts to this study. In the first part, four individuals in Toronto answered job advertisements in *The Globe and Mail* and *The Toronto Star*. Of these four individuals, one had a Jamaican accent, one an East Indian accent, one an Italian accent, and one a Canadian accent. All four called the same 201 advertisements. All four responded to the advertisements within a two-hour period and changed the order in which they responded. Each of them indicated that they had the qualifications required. The white, Canadian-sounding "applicant" was told 15 per cent of the time that the job was filled. The East Indian-sounding "applicant" was told 45 per cent of the time that the job was filled – three times the number of rejections received by the "white" applicant. Looking for work is a gruelling process – getting three times the rejections makes it even harder.

In the second part of the experiment four actors were used to apply to jobs advertised in the same two newspapers. The actors were a black man, a black woman, a white man and a white woman. The men were sent to apply for traditionally male jobs and the women applied for traditionally female jobs. One black and one white person applied for the same job. The researcher developed *equivalent* resumes for the two actors applying for the same job. The findings: for both the men and the women, the black applicant applying for the same job as the white applicant with equivalent qualifications was told three times more often that the job had been filled, treated rudely, not called in for a first interview, not called in for a second interview or not offered the job.

**Assumption that all members of racial minority groups are recent immigrants:** Being a member of a racial minority group is often confused with being an immigrant, as it is often assumed that non-Whites have recently come to Canada. Not all immigrants are visible minorities nor are all visible minorities immigrants (unless the word "immigrant" is being used to describe all Canadians). The assumption that visible minorities are synonymous with immigrants relates to the often false concern that racial minorities do not understand how things are done in Canada, do not have Canadian experience or that they do not understand or speak the predominant language. Obviously, these concerns are non-issues for members of visible minority groups who were born and/ or raised in Canada. Regardless, there is often no cause for these concerns. For instance, what is unique about Canadian experience in computer science, or the auto industry, or general labour? Yet, for all immigrants – Whites and people of colour – the requirement for Canadian experience where it is not needed is an employment barrier.

**Racial harassment:** Harassment on the basis of race is a clear employment barrier; it is discussed in detail in Chapter 10.

### What kind of employment barriers do women face?

Women, of course, include Aboriginal women, women of colour, disabled women and white women. Women who fall into more than one disadvantaged group are likely to experience multiple aspects of discrimination; double or even triple jeopardy. The issues discussed here are those traditionally associated uniquely with being a woman, and some may relate more to being a white woman without acknowledging the increased disadvantage of being both a woman and a member of one of the other target groups.

The following barriers will be discussed:

- The assumption that women do not need to work;
- The assumption that women do not want to do, or are unable to do, certain kinds of work;
- The presumption of greater loyalty to family than to work;
- The Invisible Woman Syndrome;
- Pay inequity; and
- Sexual harassment.

**The assumption that women do not need to work:** The assumption that women do not need to work can be a major barrier to consideration for certain jobs, to being taken seriously at work and to consideration for promotion.

A basic division of labour has, traditionally, been that between men and women. Beginning with the industrial revolution in the late 1700s until the 1970s there has been a basic separation between the appropriate roles for each gender: men as the providers who need to earn a living and women as economically dependent on men while tending the home (nurturers). If women were employed outside the home it was assumed they worked for extras (*i.e.,* pin money). This basic division of labour was particularly prevalent in North America during the 1950s.

Most of today's decision-makers were either the primary breadwinners or were children in such a family. The family of the 1950s, comprised of a breadwinner-father and a mother who stayed home to care for the children, is seen by some people as the proper and typical family structure. While this family structure is one of many acceptable family structures, it is no longer the norm. In the 1960s, 60 per cent of families had this traditional structure; today, only 16 per cent of families have a breadwinner-father, a stay-at-home mother and dependent children. More typical today are families with two wage-earners which comprise 36 per cent of Canadian families with dependents.

The reality is that women are working outside the home and they are doing so because they need the money. This is supported by the following facts:

- The number of two-parent families below the poverty line would increase by an estimated 78 per cent if only one person in the household was employed.
- Wives working full-time, year-round, contribute, on average, 40 per cent of family income. Those working part-time contribute, on average, 25 per cent of family income.
- Between 1971 and 1986 the number of women living in poverty increased by 110 per cent, compared to only a 24 per cent increase for men.
- Sixty-three per cent of women report that they work for economic reasons, as do 66 per cent of men.

**The assumption that women do not want to do, or are unable to do, certain kinds of work:** It is true that for every kind of work there are some women who do not want to do it – but the same thing can be said about men. An employment barrier faced by women is not that individual women have personal preferences about the kind of jobs they want, but the assumption that no women want to do "men's work". A primary reason women (and men) face systemic discrimination is due to societal perceptions that certain kinds of work are appropriate for each gender. Therefore, it is assumed that certain work should be done only by members of one gender or the other. This is called occupational segregation.

The occupations presumed appropriate for women are those which are an extension of the activities women have traditionally been responsible for in the home – nurturing, caring for the sick, teaching the young, preparing food. Consequently, women tend to be employed as nurses, elementary school teachers, child care workers, librarians, social workers, clerical and service workers. Even within an occupation, women tend to be found in particular subspecialties. As an example, female lawyers are more likely to be involved in family law than in corporate law.

Assumptions about appropriate work for women can be found among some women, as well as among those in positions to hire or influence women in their career choices. Occupational segregation results when women (and men) are restricted from moving into occupations for which they have the interest and ability but which are not seen as appropriate for their gender. An individual who persists in trying to get into non-traditional jobs will confront many barriers ranging from people telling them that they (the women) do not want to do this kind of work to harassment on the job.

There has now been enough experience with affirmative action and EE to know that for every kind of job there are some women interested. For example, women have shown an interest in mining, the military, religious ministry, medicine and management, to name a few occupations which have traditionally been highly male-dominated.

**The presumption of greater loyalty to family than to work:** As noted earlier, most women work because of economic necessity. Employed women have taken on the traditional male role of provider. However, they have maintained their role as nurturer. A large number of women balance the role of provider and nurturer, as do some men. Because of economic necessity mothers, particularly mothers of young children, are entering the labour force in record numbers. Figure 3-3 shows the change in participation in the labour force for women in different family situations. This graph shows the sharp increase in working mothers with children under three. Two-thirds of the mothers with children under three work full time.

FIGURE 3-3

INCREASE IN LABOUR FORCE PARTICIPATION
FOR WOMEN IN DIFFERENT FAMILY STRUCTURES

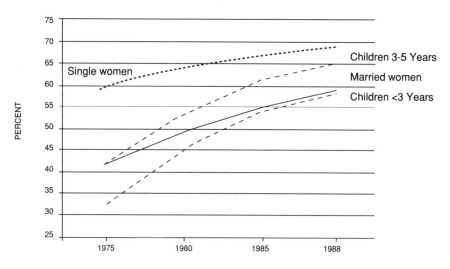

SOURCE: Statistics Canada (1990), "Women in Canada: A Statistical Report," 2nd ed., Cat. No. 89-503E, Tables 3 & 4, pp. 79, 80. Reproduced with the permission of the Minister of Industry, Science and Technology, 1993.

Family issues include parenting children, caring for elderly parents and other activities which support the family unit. Family issues have been perceived as women's issues because women have been the traditional caretakers of the family. Now that women are entering the labour force in record numbers the traditional separation of employment and family no longer works. Still, most organizations operate on the assumption that workers have a caretaker wife/mother at home and, therefore, organizations do not have to acknowledge the family needs of their employees. This creates a difficult balancing act for many women: one not required of most men.[15]

The reality is that, as of 1991, 58 per cent of women are in the labour force. Unlike the experience during the world wars, women are in the labour force to stay and organizations could not run without them. Even during the height of the recession in the early 1990s, when unemployment was running about 11 per cent, women comprised 40 per cent of those *employed*.[16] It cannot be argued that women should leave the labour force so that men can have jobs – the 817,000 unemployed men could not cover (even if they had the skills) the work performed by the 5,589,000 employed women.

Organizations have always been concerned about family issues – from the perspective of male providers. This is because it is recognized that people work to support their families (they do not have families to support their work). So, for example, benefits such as life insurance and dental care were provided by organizations so that their workers (who were primarily male at that time) would be better able to concentrate on their jobs rather than worrying about their families. What has changed is that there is no longer the same division of labour between men as employees who are providing for their families and women as family caretakers who stay home. Now both men and women are providers, and many women (and some men) continue to provide the caretaking that families need. At different life stages different family issues are likely to be relevant. For example, the needs of young children (pre-school) are different than school-age children, and adolescents. Further, help and care for elderly parents are also family issues, even for those who are single. Some potential means to balance work and family include flexible work arrangements, job-sharing, part-time work, maternity leave, child and eldercare as discussed in more detail in Chapter 7.

Because women have traditionally taken care of family matters and because it is assumed that they continue to do so, even when they are employed, there is a presumption that women are less committed to work than are men. It is more likely true that, for men and women at different life stages, work plays a different role in their life. But, for women, it is always assumed that their family will come first and, therefore, they will be less interested in promotions, less willing to travel and less able to work shifts. Let us examine the willingness to work shifts as a way of showing that stereotypes and reality often differ. Are women less willing to do shift work? It is often assumed so because one thinks of women's responsibilities to prepare dinner, help children with their homework and put them to bed and/or care for elderly parents or for a husband. However, nursing is one occupation which almost exclusively employs women and most nursing jobs require rotating shifts. Additionally, most nurses have family responsibilities. The stereotype does not fit the reality.

**The Invisible Woman Syndrome:** One does not have to talk with women very long about their experiences at work before someone will tell the following story. At a meeting the woman makes a suggestion which is right on target and provides a new way of solving the problem being discussed. No one acknowledges her suggestion. A few minutes later one of the men makes the same suggestion which everyone immediately thinks is a great idea and begins discussing. As a woman tells this story all the other women will nod their heads in agreement – this has happened to them too. Women often feel invisible, or noticed for the wrong thing (for instance, their looks).

**Pay inequity:** An EE concern is that women are not paid fairly for the work they do. In the 1950s and 1960s it was recognized that even when men and women performed substantially the same work they were not paid the same. That is, stewardesses were paid less than stewards on planes, as were maids compared to janitors, and often women teachers were paid less than men who taught. This problem was addressed by equal pay for equal *work* legislation which required that if women and men performed substantially the same kind of work they must be paid the same wage.

Because of occupational segregation, most women perform work which is different from that performed by most men. To address this the principle of equal pay for work of equal *value* (pay equity) was introduced in most provinces in Canada between the mid-1970s and the early 1990s for those working in the public sector. Pay equity requires that traditionally female jobs which are of equal value compared to traditionally male jobs, even though the type of work is completely different, must be paid the same when they are within the same organization. Some people confuse pay and EE. The differences between the two were discussed in Chapter 2.

**Sexual harassment:** Sexual harassment is a barrier that women commonly face whether they are working in traditionally women's jobs or not. Harassment is an exercise of power. While harassment also occurs on the basis of race and disability, sexual harassment is unique in that it is more likely to be denied as a problem. This occurs because it is confused with sexual attraction (as when someone jokingly says, "I wish someone would sexually harass me."), or it is denied as a problem because it is assumed that the women bring it upon themselves. Harassment, including sexual harassment, is discussed in detail in Chapter 10.

# NOTES

1. "Status" is a legal concept and it has evolved over time. Initially as Native peoples entered into treaty and reserve arrangements it was necessary to identify those who were entitled to treaty benefits from those who were not.
2. Now R.S.C. 1985, c. I-5.
3. Though the term "guys" is coming to mean a group comprised of members of both genders.
4. Rupert Ross, *Dancing with a Ghost: Exploring Indian Reality*, Toronto: Octopus Publishing, 1992, Chapter 3.
5. A story told by Dr. Clare Brant, a Mohawk, highlights this (from R. Ross, *Dancing with a Ghost: Exploring Indian Reality*, Toronto: Octopus Publishing Group, 1992, page 2). Dr. Brant's Mohawk band had invited a group of James Bay Cree to take part in a sporting tournament. The Mohawk have an agricultural tradition (which precedes the coming of the Europeans). A hospitality custom of the Mohawk is to set out considerably more food than their guests would consume (not unlike Jews and Italians). The Cree have a different custom. They are a hunter-gatherer people for whom scarcity is typical, so, as a means of showing respect for their hosts, their custom is to eat everything set out before them. Ross concludes: "The Cree considered the Mohawk something akin to gastro-intestinal sadists intent on poisoning them. The Mohawk, for their part, thought the Cree ill-mannered people intent on insulting Mohawk generosity."
6. There are provincial differences as shown in the following table.

### TABLE 3-5
### DISTRIBUTION OF ON- AND OFF-RESERVE POPULATION BY PROVINCE

| Region | Aboriginal Peoples | | | | Canadian Population |
|---|---|---|---|---|---|
| | On-reserve | | Off-reserve | | |
| Atlantic | 8,060 | 5.0% | 26,345 | 4.8% | 9.0% |
| Quebec | 21,600 | 13.5% | 59,325 | 10.8 | 25.8 |
| Ontario | 26,135 | 16.4% | 141,220 | 25.6 | 36.0 |
| Manitoba | 27,375 | 17.1% | 57,840 | 10.5 | 4.2 |
| Sask. | 27,025 | 16.9% | 50,620 | 9.2 | 4.0 |
| Alberta | 18,845 | 11.8% | 85,065 | 15.4 | 9.4 |
| B.C. | 30,045 | 18.8% | 96,260 | 17.5 | 11.4 |
| Territories | 580 | .4% | 34,925 | 6.3 | .3 |
| Canada | 159,665 | 100% | 551,600 | 100 | 100% |

SOURCE:   Adapted from Statistics Canada, "A Profile of the Aboriginal Population Residing in Selected Off Reserve Areas" prepared by the Aboriginal Data and Native Issues Unit of the Housing, Family and Social Statistics Division, February 1990.

7. "Focus on Aboriginal Women" Ontario Women's Directorate, Toronto, January 1993, page 5.
8. *Evolution of the Immigration Act* Ottawa: Immigration Branch, Department of Citizenship and Immigration, 1962.
9. *The Times*, London, England, May 23, 1914. © Time Newspapers Ltd., 1914.
10. Speech on Canadian Immigration Policy in the Canadian House of Commons, May 1, 1947. *Hansard*, pages 2644-2646.
11. Now R.S.C. 1985, c. I-2.
12. Jeffrey G. Reitz, "Ethnic Concentration in Labour Market and Their Implications for Ethnic Inequality", in R. Breton, *et al.*, *Ethnic Identity and Equality*, Toronto: University of Toronto Press, 1990, Chapter 5.
13. Elia Zureik, "The Experience of Visible Minorities in the Work World: The Case of MBA Graduates", Ontario Ministry of Labour, Human Rights Commission, 1983.
14. Frances Henry and Effie Ginzberg, "Who Gets the Work? A Test of Racial Discrimination in Employment," Toronto: The Urban Alliance on Race Relations and The Social Planning Council of Metropolitan Toronto, January 1985.
15. Though men face another barrier – one that denies their caretaking interest and abilities.
16. Census data shows:

**TABLE 3-6**
**MEN AND WOMEN, EMPLOYED/UNEMPLOYED, 1991**

|  | Men | Women | Total |
|---|---|---|---|
| Employed | 6,751,000 | 5,589,000 | 12,340,000 |
| Unemployed | 817,000 | 619,000 | 1,436,000 |
| Total | 7,568,000 | 6,208,000 | 13,776,000 |

SOURCE: Adapted from Statistics Canada, 1991 census data.

# REFERENCES

Patricia Aburdene and John Naisbitt, *Megatrends for Women*, New York: Villard Books, 1992.

Jane Allen, "Employment Equity: How We Can Use it to Fight Workplace Racism", Toronto: Cross-Cultural Communication Centre, 1988.

B. Singh Bolaria, *Racial Oppression in Canada*, 2nd ed., Toronto, Garamond Press, 1988.

S. Chandrasekhar. *From India to Canada: A Brief History of Immigration; Problems of Discrimination; Admission and Assimilation*, LaJolla, CA: A Population Review Book, 1986.

J.S. Frideres (ed.), *Native People in Canada*, Scarborough: Prentice-Hall, 1983.

Morley Gunderson and Leon Muszynski, *Women and Labour Market Poverty*, Ottawa: Canadian Advisory Council on the Status of Women, 1990.

Judy H. Katz, *White Awareness: Handbook for Anti-Racism Training*, Norman: University of Oklahoma Press, 1978.

Marilyn Loden, *Feminine Leadership or How to Succeed in Business Without Being One of the Boys*, Toronto: Random House, 1985.

McDonald Series, "Aboriginal Issues Today," Winnipeg: Cross Cultural Communications International, Inc., undated.

Penny Petrone, *First People, First Voices*, Toronto: University of Toronto Press, 1983.

D. Purich, *Our Land: Native Rights in Canada*, Toronto: Lorimer, 1986.

Subhas Ramcharan. *Racism: Non-whites in Canada*, Toronto: Butterworths, 1982.

Jeffrey G. Reitz, "Ethnic Concentration in Labour Markets and Their Implications for Ethnic Inequality," in R. Breton *et al.*, *Ethnic Identity and Equality*, Toronto: University of Toronto Press, 1990.

Rupert Ross, *Dancing with a Ghost: Exploring Indian Reality*, Toronto: Octopus Publishing Group, 1992.

Anne Wilson Schaef, *Women's Reality: An Emerging Female System in a White Male Society*, New York: Harper Paperbacks, 1985.

Deborah Tannen, *You Just Don't Understand: Women and Men in Conversation*, New York: Ballantine Books, 1990.

James W. St.G. Walker, *A History of Blacks in Canada*, Ministry of State, Multiculturalism, Published by Minister of Supply and Services Canada, 1980.

United States Commission on Civil Rights, *Accommodating the Spectrum of Individual Abilities*, Washington, D.C.: Clearinghouse publication 81, 1983.

# CHAPTER 4

# First Step: Preparation

Getting started on EE involves a number of steps. First, there must be a commitment to EE. The level of commitment can range from compliance (obey the legislation, but do no more) to strategic commitment (where EE is seen as an integral part of the organization's long-term human resource strategy). A second aspect of preparation is accountability. This may include the establishment of one or more positions devoted to EE. Some of the reporting relationships for EE positions within the organizational structure are discussed later. In addition, three processes are begun during the preparation stage but are on-going throughout the EE process. These are: communication, training, and consultation (with non-union employees and with unions). Since the issue of seniority is closely associated with unions, the seniority issues related to EE are discussed in this chapter.

## COMMITMENT AND ACCOUNTABILITY

*How is top management commitment obtained?*

Commitment to EE can come from a belief that EE is either the right thing to do, the necessary thing to do, or both. Legislation prompts many organizations to see the necessity of EE. However, many organizations which look beyond the legislative requirement find that there is a good business case for EE (see the section on the changing work-force demographics in Chapter 3). Sometimes the presence of legislation initially obscures the other reasons for EE. Education is typically needed to obtain top management support. To be blunt most employees, including senior managers, are likely to have the following initial feelings about EE:

> It is government intervention requiring reverse
> discrimination to hire unqualified people.

Further, there is a concern that engaging in EE too enthusiastically may be perceived as an admission of past discrimination.

Some important points to get across in early training, to grab attention and to begin changing the above perceptions of EE are:

- Employment equity requires change, but not blame.
- The demographics of the Canadian work-force are changing. Continuing to apply employment systems designed for a different kind of work-force will be ineffective in the future.
- There will be a labour shortage for many kinds of work by the late 1990s. There will be a skill shortage for many skilled, technical and managerial jobs. Employment equity initiatives can help address these shortages.
- Employment equity never means hiring unqualified people.

Getting these points across takes time (and repetition). For example, in recessionary times, it is difficult for most people to envision labour and skill shortages. These feelings are supported by predictions of continued unemployment levels at 11 per cent until 1997. However, the realities of the labour/skill shortages versus the surplus of labour need to be considered for each organization, rather than for the economy as a whole. For instance, any organization which needs experienced auto workers or steel workers will not face a labour shortage. But the high availability of workers who can do certain kinds of work can exist at the same time that there is a shortage for other kinds of skills. For example, organizations looking for computer specialists or health care professionals will still face a labour shortage even though there is a high proportion of unemployment among those who have worked in heavy manufacturing. And high unemployment may not help the dry cleaners needing unskilled labour whose wages will not appeal to those who are accustomed to making significantly more. Therefore, different industries and different organizations can find themselves simultaneously facing skill shortages and labour surplus for different jobs.

In some organizations support for EE has developed among senior managers who have a personal relationship with members of some of the designated groups. Senior managers who have daughters in college or entering the labour force are often more receptive to the need to remove systemic barriers for women. Senior managers who have had a personal relationship with a person who is disabled (a member of their family, a friend) are typically more aware of the abilities such a person can offer. If these personal situations make a senior manager more receptive to EE for some groups, links have to be made to the need for equality for all the designated groups.

While it is critical to get top management support for EE, the support and involvement of middle managers may be even more important. Where senior managers need to endorse the principles behind EE, middle managers and supervisors make it happen. Further, middle managers and supervisors often feel more threatened by the effects of EE on their careers. While many senior managers will retire before they find themselves competing with designated group members, those lower in the organizational hierarchy are likely to perceive stiffer competition because they will be competing for promotions with all other employees rather than only a subset (*i.e.*, non-designated group members). Involving middle managers and supervisors in setting EE goals is key to their commitment to making them happen. Ensuring that performance appraisals include how well supervisors and managers are achieving EE goals is also important. And, of course, training is critical. Change is required of senior managers, middle managers and supervisors in order to make EE successful. Therefore, these employees need skills training which will facilitate their competence in such things as managing a more diverse work-force, effectively handling a racial harassment complaint, knowing how to deal with a female employee who cries (rather than shouts) when angry. It is unfair to expect supervisors and managers to operate effectively in a changing workplace without providing them with the necessary skills.

Honesty is a factor in getting commitment from all levels of authority. Employment equity has many benefits for organizations. However, this does not change the reality that the old saw "no pain, no gain" is applicable.[1] Employment equity requires difficult changes for organizations. It can involve overcoming traditions long perceived as the only way to do things. It challenges personal values and beliefs. It involves making mistakes because it means trying things that an organization has never done before. Those in power are being asked to share power with others who are different.

### What does managerial commitment look like?

Talk is cheap. Commitment is judged by actions, not words. The kinds of visible support which demonstrate commitment include:[2]

- Financial commitment to support achievement of EE goals and targets.
- Hiring of designated group members into key positions.
- Placement of designated group members on the board of directors.
- Public statements supporting EE outside the company.
- Internal communication about the organization's progress in EE (not just "cheer leading" statements, but actual data).
- Training for employees at all levels about EE.
- Providing other resources needed to make EE work.
- Making positive connections between EE and other issues of concern to the organization, rather than keeping EE isolated as if it were irrelevant to the "real" operation of the organization.
- Not avoiding tough issues related to EE.

- Rewarding those in the organization who behave according to EE principles.

A key resource is the hiring of people to work in EE.

*As part of accountability, what kind of skills/duties should be part of the EE function?*

Working in EE can mean walking a tightrope. Those working in EE are attempting to achieve organizational change from the inside out. The *status quo* is often more comfortable than change. So EE practitioners must push their organizations to do things they would rather not do simply because it involves change. Where there is EE legislation there is also external pressure which helps make EE a priority. At the same time that EE staff are working to change the organization, they have to represent their organization's effort to external stakeholders who are impatient for change.

The activities EE staff must engage in include:

- Educating managers and employees about what EE is and is not, how it works and how it will affect them, why it is needed, and so on.
- Monitoring internal policies and practices. This goes beyond the formal systems review because many activities in organizations follow informal, unwritten policies. The EE staff must always be vigilant in barrier detection.
- Developing and implementing an EE plan: This involves the technical steps of EE such as a formal systems review, data collection and analysis, setting goals and timetables, implementing programs, and monitoring and evaluating.
- Providing advice on policy and fulfilling the role as a resource person. Employment equity practitioners will obviously be involved in EE policy. Since employment barriers are affected by all employment policies and can be affected by other policies, EE staff need to be available to help the organization see the EE implications in many of its activities. It is important, however, that the EE staff not be perceived as being "responsible for equity". This is a responsibility of all supervisors and managers and needs to be integrated into the workings of the organization.
- Speaking many "languages". To aid communication between groups which tend to perceive issues differently, EE staff need to be able to speak with each group and translate for other groups. For example, there is the language of the organization (whether it is "profit margin", "quality service", "curriculum" or "policing"), the lan-

guage of unions, the jargon of EE, plus politically correct language preferred by the various designated groups.

- Advocacy. This may be for the EE program, for particular changes, or for individuals who need support and understanding because they do not fit neatly into the mainstream way that things have been done.

- Monitoring the environment. There is an important link between EE and the environment with which the organization interacts. One task is to scan this environment to stay current on what is new. A second task is to make contact with various designated group communities. There may be unexpected and delicate situations to deal with, for instance, a salesperson from another organization may be accused of harassing one of your employees.

### How should EE be structured within the organization?

One of the "resources" which an organization provides its EE staff is its reporting relationship within the organization. This can facilitate or hamper success. Employment equity can be added to an existing job or one or more persons can be assigned specifically to the function. If EE is added as one more thing someone is expected to do there is a risk that EE will not get high priority. Unless the person has been relieved of some other duties when EE is added, the organization's commitment to EE is likely to be questioned.

In structuring the EE function within the organization two issues are (1) to whom should the EE function report, and (2) should it be a separate function or placed within the human resources area? Looking at the second issue first, EE and human resources activities are connected. The systems review examines employment policies and practices typically developed by the human resources function. Activities such as investigating allegations of harassment often fall into the human resources area. Changing recruiting and selection to ensure their ability to identify qualified designated group members requires interaction with the human resources department. Because of this, some argue that EE should be placed in the human resources area, while others argue, just as strongly, that EE and human resources should be separate. Incorporating EE with human resources places the responsibility for equity on those who have developed many of the practices. Because they are within human resources, it is expected that change will be easier. Those who argue on the other side point out that the EE function should be outside of human resources in order to operate as an effective critic and to avoid being co-opted by human resources. Either model can be right for different organizations. It depends on how open and knowledgeable human resources staff are about EE. Some, not understanding systemic discrimination, may feel that all EE initiatives are an accusation that they, the human resources staff, have been discriminatory. In other organizations, the human resources staff may simply be too bound to the polices and practices they have put into place to be able to assess them objectively for potential barriers. In some organizations, unfortunately, the human resources department has such a poor reputation that EE would be tainted by being included.

Another question of structure is to whom EE should report. This issue can impact on the ability to integrate EE into the organization. Having EE report to a position high in the hierarchy signals that EE is important. However, it is critical that such a reporting relationship signify true access to the top, rather than simply a diagram on the organizational chart. Alternatively, both EE and human resources can report to the same vice president, or director or Assistant Deputy Minister as a way to better coordinate the two functions, while keeping them separate.

A concern related to structuring the EE function is the conflict between making EE visible and ensuring its integration into the organization. Some organizations which have high-profile EE departments find that supervisors and managers adopt an attitude of "equity-is-the-employment-equity-department's-responsibility". To facilitate integration from the start, one organization put all its vice presidents on its EE steering committee[3] which was an effective way to integrate EE responsibility throughout the organization. Ultimately, as EE becomes integrated into organizations and is part of how "things are done around here" the issue of how to structure the EE function will disappear. Until then, visibility is a valuable resource which organizations need to provide to EE, at the same time they are working towards integration.

## COMMUNICATION AND TRAINING

Employment equity communication and training are on-going processes. Where a union represents the employees, joint communication and training is preferable. As noted (and discussed further in the section on backlash in Chapter 11) many people have preconceived, negative notions about EE. Others lack understanding or are confused. For example, virtually everyone believes that it is better, and fairer, not to notice people's race, gender and disability status when making hiring decisions. Yet, EE requires collecting information on these very characteristics. Employment equity involves refocusing: admitting that while Canadian society has as one of its principles to be colour-, and gender-, and disability-blind, the reality is that we are not. Part of the process of refocusing is to determine how well members of the designated groups are doing within work organizations, and how representative of the available labour force they are. The only way to assess the nature and extent of the problem of discrimination in employment is, *for a period of time*, to collect this information.

One reason communication and training is on-going is because EE principles challenge long-standing beliefs, stereotypes and assumptions. To facilitate the learning process, information needs to be available when people need it – not necessarily all at once. Such communication should be interactive so that employees have an opportunity to voice their concerns and get responses to their questions.

Some of the topics that should be covered in the various communication pieces and training sessions include:

- Systemic discrimination and how it differs from direct discrimination.
- Why EE is needed.
- How EE works.
- That EE never means hiring unqualified people.
- Why focusing on designated group status is part of the solution even though such characteristics should not matter in employment situations.
- Why EE is not reverse discrimination. It is removing barriers, not giving an advantage to otherwise equal groups.
- What EE means to each person in the organization.

Employees should be asked what they want to know about EE (this will obviously change as the organization goes through the process). The organization should share information with employees about what is happening in EE (*i.e.*, what goals have been set, how well the goals are being met). Employees should be given chances to be heard and to express their concerns and fears. For example, some white, able-bodied males assume that EE means they will never get another promotion while some white females fear they will always lose out to visible minority candidates in a job competition.[4] The data from the work-force analysis and annual changes should be shared. Most organizations move much slower at achieving a critical mass of designated group members than justifies the fears and concerns of employees. At least if people are going to be upset with EE efforts they should know what is really happening rather than making erroneous assumptions.

Include EE principles in all communications, not just those directly related to EE. For example, does the annual report show the diversity which exists in the organization (or that for which the organization is striving). Remember EE challenges long-held traditions. These traditions cannot be changed quickly or with a single communication. Repetition, answering your audience's concerns (regardless of what they are) are keys to good communication in this area. Variety is important too. In one organization the president sent out a yearly letter about EE – but it was

Employment Equity: Making It Work

the same letter every year! Make sure all communications use language which is inclusive and sensitive. The language of EE is developing and evolving. Sometimes it changes so fast it feels like it is impossible to stay on top of it. But do not get uptight if you are corrected for not being "politically correct". Find out why others prefer different language. Make the language issue the subject of a newsletter article. Some language usage was discussed in Chapter 3.

Some suggestions to consider in developing a communication strategy are:

- Develop a logo for the EE function so that communication is quickly identifiable.
- Utilize employer and union newsletters; publish articles and/or question and answer columns.
- Use EE posters.
- Make it known who employees can talk with about EE.
- Have bag-lunch sessions where anyone can ask or say anything, even if it is not "politically correct".
- Having asked employees for input on the work-force analysis, be sure to provide them with the over-all results.

The draft regulations for the Ontario *Employment Equity Act* outline a number of reports which must be made available to employees (and to the Employment Equity Commission upon request). Two reports are required — one at the beginning of the three-year EE plan and one at the end. All the numerical data provided in the first report must be repeated in the second report so that employees can see the progress that has been made. The numerical data required differs for employers of different sizes as shown in Table 4-1.

Other information to be provided in the report includes:

- Goals set out in the plan. (Not required of small employers.)
- Number of opportunities for hiring/promotion into each occupational group during the plan and the number that were filled by members of each designated group. (Not required of small employers.)
- List of qualitative measures that have been put into place by the end of the term of the EE plan.

This report must be prepared within six months after the end of the term of the EE plan.

TABLE 4–1

INFORMATION TO BE PROVIDED TO EMPLOYEES UNDER ONTARIO *EMPLOYMENT EQUITY ACT*

| Data to be reported at the beginning and the end of 3-year EE plan | Small employers: private sector employers with fewer than 100 employees and broader public sector employers with fewer than 50 employees | Employer Size | |
|---|---|---|---|
| | | Private sector employers with between 100 and 500 employees; and broader public sector employers with between 50 and 500 employees | Large employers (more than 500 employees) |
| Number of total employees and number of designated group employees | Yes (numbers within the entire work-force) | Yes | Yes |
| by occupational groups | No | Yes | Yes |
| by geographical area | No | Yes | Yes |
| by permanent full-time, permanent part-time, term, and seasonal employees | No | Yes | Yes |
| by salary quartile* | No | No | Yes |
| Total number of employees who filled out and returned a work-force survey question-naire | No | Yes | Yes |

* Actual salary amounts do not have to be included, just the total number of employees and of the designated group members in the first, second, third, and fourth salary quartile for each occupation.

# CONSULTATION

Consultation should include members of the designated groups. These may be current employees or community groups. The Ontario Employment Equity Commission will furnish information on how to address barriers likely to be faced by each designated group. The Ontario *Employment Equity Act*[5] requires consultation with non-union employees and with unions. Consultation with non-union employees must cover:

1. The work-force survey,
2. The employment systems review, and
3. The development, implementation, review and revision of the EE plan (or part of the plan) which covers the employees.

To assist in the consultation process with non-union employees, Ontario employers will be required to provide employees with a description of the consultation process, the results of the work-force audit, a summary of the outcomes of the systems review, and proposals for the elimination of barriers and the qualitative goals set. Employees are only entitled to the information relevant to their workplace.

Co-operation between unions and management will facilitate EE goals. The Ontario Act requires consultation with unions to fulfil a series of joint responsibilities (e.g., workplace survey, systems review, development of EE plan). It is the bargaining agent's responsibility to consult with its members who are members of designated groups. Employment equity demands a different relationship between the two workplace parties than that used for collective bargaining and the settlement of grievances. These traditional union-management activities are adversarial in nature; equity should not be. To achieve co-operation it is vital to remember that EE is addressing systemic discrimination and, thus, there is no issue of blame involved (see Chapter 1). Neither party is to be blamed for participation in past negotiations which may have led to employment systems which are now perceived to be barriers for the designated groups. That was then and this is now.

It is impossible to say a great deal about union-management relations in general, since the reality depends on the particular situation. Many labour unions have been active in areas of EE for a number of years, as have some public and private employers. The labour movement has also been instrumental in lobbying for EE legislation in various provinces. However, all union locals do not take a positive stand on EE. Within a specific organization, one needs to consider the past labour relations history between the two parties. What is the relationship, if any, between the various unions representing those working for a single employer? Who have traditionally been members of the union – Whites, men, the able-bodied? What does EE have to offer current members? It is probable that, within any particular organization, management will like some aspects of EE and dislike others; each union will probably like other aspects and dislike some that management approves. Getting the parties to buy-in and set priorities will be difficult. In the Ontario *Employment Equity Act* where joint union-management co-operation is required there will be a mechanism for either workplace party to bring impasses to the Employment Equity Commission. However, in many situations intervention by a third party is not preferred by either party.

Hiring is typically done at management's discretion, except where there are hiring halls. So the initial recruitment and selection issues associated with EE are management's responsibility. However, retention, not just hiring, is crucial to EE. Here, both union and management play an important role. For that reason management should always include co-operative unions in all aspects of EE. This includes joint training, joint communications and, of course, joint decision making. Any union member working on EE, or attending workshops (in or out of the organization) should be paid for this time. Many unions have good educational and training material on EE and related issues. For example, the Canadian Auto Workers have produced an anti-harassment film. Particularly when training union members, having someone from the labour movement as a trainer or co-trainer is an excellent idea.

### Seniority

A major issue which arises when EE is discussed is seniority. Seniority is typically used for some things even in non-union environments, but it is virtually always a part of a collective bargaining agreement. The purpose of seniority is to protect current union members. Once designated group members become members of a union, seniority will work to protect them. However, the current situation is that many designated group members are on the outside looking in. To understand seniority within the EE context it is important to review the uses of seniority. Seniority is a commonly used criterion for allocating desirable rewards such as transfers, promotions, later lay-off and earlier recall.[6] In transfer situations seniority may become a barrier because many occupations (and, thus, the unions representing them) are associated with gender, such as clerical versus technical jobs. There have also been some occupations associated with members of racial minorities, such as porters working for railroads and maid services in hotels. Where the career ladder is shorter in occupations associated with female or minority jobs, then seniority earned for time worked within a department (versus within the organization as a whole) is a barrier. It prevents members of designated groups near or at the top of their occupational ladder from being able to move into higher paying jobs represented by another union because they would have to start at the entry-level.

When seniority is used for promotion purposes it is not typically the only criterion.[7] It is often incorporated into a "sufficient ability clause" where if the most senior person is qualified he or she gets the job. Alternatively, seniority and performance can be incorporated into a "competitive clause" where if there are two or more relatively equal candidates the most senior gets the job. In either case, if seniority is credited only within a department it can greatly block those trying to move into jobs they have not traditionally performed.

The use of seniority for lay-off and recall, while potentially an employment equity barrier, is generally recognized as being justifiable. This use of seniority results in last-hired-first-fired; designated group members will disproportionately be among the last hired. However, the Ontario legislation explicitly states that using seniority for lay-off and recall is not an employment barrier. This is consistent with the notion that remedies of systemic discrimination do not involve blame. It would be difficult to justify that those who have held their jobs longer should be laid off sooner and called back after newer employees.

There are some ways to mitigate the impact of seniority as the criterion for lay-off within seniority systems. Some of the ways which have been tried, either in Canada or the United States, are:

- Use organizational-wide seniority rather than department or union seniority.
- Employees cannot use their non-bargaining seniority to get jobs within the bargaining unit, but once in they are credited with all their organization-wide seniority.
- Retroactive seniority. In jobs where there is under-representation, when designated group members pass probation they are credited with having seniority which is equal to the average seniority of those on the job (or in the union).
- Have separate seniority lists for designated group members and non-designated group members. For example, in case of lay-off, the person with the least seniority from the designated group list is laid off first, then the person from the non-designated group list, followed by the person with the next lowest seniority from the designated group list, and so on.
- Encourage more senior people to retire or job share, decreasing the number of lay-offs of more recently hired employees.

Note that none of these solutions reject the use of seniority systems; rather they adapt seniority systems. Some of the alternatives change the seniority system for all employees (*e.g.*, using organization-wide seniority rather than department seniority). Others only address the seniority of designated group members (*e.g.*, retroactive seniority) and are only used for positions where there is an underrepresentation of a particular designated group.

Some unions have gone further than what is suggested above. For example, the Steelworkers entered into an arbitrated first settlement with Placer Dome Inc. which incorporates a Native Employees' Employment Equity Plan. One clause in the contract reads:

> In all cases of vacancy, promotion, transfer, lay-off and recall from lay-off, Native employees shall be entitled to preference if they have the ability and physical fitness to perform the work, notwithstanding their seniority.

Retroactive seniority has been agreed to by the Grain Services Union and has been put on the table with the Saskatchewan Wheat Pool. With retroactive seniority, upon completion of probation, members of designated groups which are underrepresented in the position, are granted seniority equal to the average seniority of those within the job. The Communications Workers of Canada and Bell Canada allow a certain number of "employment equity moves" of women from the female-dominated operators' bargaining unit to the higher-paid, male-dominated technicians' unit. The women retain their full seniority. Further, a limited number of openings have been set aside to be filled exclusively by designated group members. To help women become qualified to move into non-traditional jobs, a Qualifications Development Program was established to place women temporarily in technicians' jobs in order to gain the skills necessary to qualify for the jobs permanently. Once a woman is qualified, she can then be considered for placement in one of the positions set aside for EE moves or compete openly with any other qualified candidate.

The Carpenters Union, Local 27, in Toronto, has removed barriers by ensuring that entry to apprenticeship is no longer based on "old-boy" or family networks. Initially, a separate apprenticeship program was run for designated group members. Now the local has an integrated program where 50 per cent of the places are filled with members of the target groups. English as a second language and math tutoring is also provided. In recognition of other barriers, seminars on eliminating racial and sexual harassment are being developed.

## NOTES

1. This section is based on an article by Paul Scott, "Is the Senior Level Really the Place to Go for Commitment to Employment Equity?", *Equal Times*, vol. 2(6), August, 1989.
2. Francine S. Hall and Maryann H. Albrecht, *The Management of Affirmative Action*, Santa Monica, CA: Goodyear Publishing Company, Inc., 1979, pages 159-160.
3. The human resources department took on the responsibility of scheduling the meetings and facilitating the committee but the vice president of human resources was no more accountable than all the other vice presidents.
4. Employment equity can lead to unrealistic expectation for some designated group members as well.
5. Bill 79, introduced for 2nd reading July 12, 1993.
6. Seniority can be used as the basis for making many other decisions where there is potential conflict, such as who gets first choice at scheduling their vacation, who gets to work overtime (where there is a desire to), or using inverse seniority to decide who works overtime when there is no desire to.
7. Kathryn MacLeod, "The Seniority Principle: Is It Discriminatory?" Queen's University School of Industrial Relations Research, Essay Series No. 11, 1987, pages 11-12.

# REFERENCES

Carol Agocs, Catherine Burr, and Felicity Somerset, *Employment Equity: Co-operative Strategies for Organizational Change*, Scarborough: Prentice-Hall, 1992.

Francine S. Hall and Maryann H. Albrecht, *The Management of Affirmative Action*, Santa Monica, CA: Goodyear Publishing Company, Inc., 1979.

*Without Bias: A Guidebook for Nondiscriminatory Communication*, 2nd ed., New York: Wiley, 1992.

CHAPTER 5

# Data Collection and Analysis

One of the ultimate goals of EE is to have representation of designated group members throughout the organization. In order to know when this goal has been accomplished it is necessary to know (1) the designated group status of the organization's work-force, and (2) the availability of designated group members in the labour force. This chapter discusses the data collection and analysis for the EE process.

## INTRODUCTION TO DATA COLLECTION

*Why collect information on designated group status of current employees?*

Data on the designated group status of one's current employees is collected for three purposes:

1. *To identify where EE initiatives are needed.* This data will help guide the organization's decisions as to what EE activities are needed. For instance, consider two organizations, a print shop and an insurance company. The print shop finds that only 10 per cent of its employees are women and they are all employed in clerical positions. Employment equity activities need to focus on recruitment and placement of women into non-traditional, technical jobs. The insurance company finds that 70 per cent of its employees are female, but only 15 per cent of its managers are female. The insurance company needs to focus on getting more women into management positions, through promotions and outreach.
2. *To set goals and timetables.* Employment equity goals and timetables are based, in part, on the work-force analysis. This information is combined with information about the organization (its strategic direction, growth areas, short- and long-term human resource needs), information about employment systems and other information to develop realistic, obtainable goals.
3. *To assess the organization's accomplishment towards a representative workplace.* The ultimate goal of EE is for the work-force of the organization to mirror the available work-force. That is, if 5 per cent of the available work-force, in the recruiting area, is comprised of visible minorities then 5 per cent of the employees should be members of

racial minority groups. In order to know if the organization's work-force is representative, one needs to know the designated group characteristics of the work-force, and of the available working age population.

## DATA COLLECTION

*What data reporting form should I use?*

Each governmental agency which requires data be collected has slightly different requirements. The data collection forms and requirements are provided in the appendices. Those for the federal program are found in Appendix B and for the Quebec program in Appendix C. Based on the draft regulations the kind of data required in Ontario is shown in Appendix D. Most EE activities are not legislation specific. That is, most organizations will find that EE requires involvement in accommodation, anti-harassment training, work and family policy, regardless of the legislative mandate. Data collection, however, is one important activity which is legislation-bound. Because each jurisdiction has specific data collection requirements, it is advisable for workplace parties to familiarize themselves with the legislative requirements for data collection. Though the legislation is pending in Ontario, this does not prevent an organization from beginning EE. While the work-force analysis is critical to the EE process, it is not essential in order to begin. In most organizations the underrepresentation of the four designated groups is obvious. As a generalization, most Canadian organizations employ few, if any, Aboriginal Peoples. Employees with disabilities also tend to be few in number and seldom in management positions. Racial minority employees are found in organizations in major urban areas – but, typically, not in positions above the level of supervisor. Women are employed in traditional female clerical, service and helping professions but not in technical, trade or top level jobs. Even without a formal work-force analysis most organizations can identify some EE initiatives that are needed.

This chapter does not focus on the data collection requirements and analysis required in any particular jurisdiction. Rather, the illustrations and examples are designed to equip the reader with the skills to complete whichever data collection form is required. For organizations addressing EE on a voluntary basis, review the various forms and select the one that is best, or adapt one of the forms. Many possible ways to analyze the data are discussed – more than are likely to be used by a single organization.

*What information needs to be reported?*

While there are some differences as to how terms are defined, all the jurisdictions require the same basic pieces of information:

- *Designated group status* of the work-force indicating the composition by gender, racial group (including whether someone is of First Nations ancestry) and disability status. Specifically, data is typically reported on female and male Natives, female and male racial minorities and males and females with disabilities, in addition to the totals for males and females within the organization.
- *Occupational groupings.* Data related to organizational level is typically reported in two ways. First, showing the designated group characteristics within occupational categories, such as senior management, middle management, supervisor, manual, clerical, etc. (The occupational categories may differ across different jurisdictions.) Figure 5-1 is an illustration of a form for reporting on the occupational distribution of employees. The organization's job titles are put into the occupational groupings.
- *Salary groupings.* A second way of showing organizational level is to report the data by salary levels as illustrated in Figure 5-2. This information is reported in terms of salary bands (*e.g.*, $20,000 to $39,999; $40,000 to $59,999). The Ontario legislation is requiring salary quartiles, but does not require that the actual salary amounts be reported (see Appendix D).
- *Flow Data.* Transaction data or flow data shows the pattern of movement through the organization in terms of hires, transfers, promotions, demotions and terminations. Flow data is needed to keep the organization's work-force analysis up to date once it has been collected. It also can provide valuable information on employment barriers.
- *Employment status.* Some jurisdictions (*i.e.*, federal, Ontario) require that the above information be reported separately for employees working permanent full-time, permanent part-time, term, or seasonal. This is because designated group members often are underrepresented in permanent full-time jobs.

*What questions should be asked to collect information on designated group status?*

Examples of two questionnaires which can be used to collect designated group status information from employees are shown in Boxes 5-1 and 5-2. The work-force audit questionnaire should be limited to collecting designated status information. Information on designated group status is

FIGURE 5–1

ILLUSTRATION OF DATA REPORTING FORM BY OCCUPATIONAL GROUPING

| Occupational group | Women | Men | Visible minorities | | Aboriginal Peoples | | Persons with disabilities | |
|---|---|---|---|---|---|---|---|---|
| | | | Women | Men | Women | Men | Women | Men |
| Management | | | | | | | | |
| Supervisors | | | | | | | | |
| Professionals | | | | | | | | |
| Blue collar | | | | | | | | |
| Clerical workers | | | | | | | | |
| TOTAL | | | | | | | | |

FIGURE 5–2

ILLUSTRATION OF DATA REPORTING FORM BY SALARY LEVELS

| Salary levels | Women | Men | Visible minorities | | Aboriginal Peoples | | Persons with disabilities | |
|---|---|---|---|---|---|---|---|---|
| | | | Women | Men | Women | Men | Women | Men |
| $80,000 per year or more | | | | | | | | |
| $60,000 to $79,999 | | | | | | | | |
| $40,000 to $59,999 | | | | | | | | |
| $20,000 to $39,999 | | | | | | | | |
| Less than $20,000 | | | | | | | | |
| TOTAL | | | | | | | | |

---

## Box 5-1

### EMPLOYMENT EQUITY QUESTIONNAIRE
(Short Version)

Employee name or identification number _____

1. For the purposes of EE, a person is an Aboriginal person if he or she is a member of the Indian, Inuit or Métis peoples of Canada.
   Based on this description, do you consider yourself to be an Aboriginal Person?

   Yes___ No___

2. For the purposes of EE, a person is a member of a racial minority if, because of his or her race or colour, the person is in a visible minority in Ontario (e.g., Black, Asian, East Indian). The fact that a person is an Aboriginal Person does not make him or her a member of a racial minority.
   Based on this description, do you consider yourself to be a member of a racial minority?

   Yes___ No___

3. For the purposes of EE, a person is a person with a disability if the person has a persistent physical, mental, psychiatric, sensory or learning impairment and,

   i. the person considers himself or herself to be disadvantaged in employment by reason of that impairment, or
   ii. the person believes that an employer or potential employer is likely to consider him or her to be disadvantaged in employment by reason of that impairment.

   Based on this description, do you consider yourself to be a person with a disability?

   Yes___ No___

4. For the purposes of EE, all women, including Aboriginal women, women with disabilities and women who are members of racial minorities are included as members of the designated group "women".
   Are you a woman?

   Yes___ No___

---

# Box 5-2

## EMPLOYMENT EQUITY QUESTIONNAIRE
(Long Version)

Employee name or identification number _____

**Sex**
1.  Please indicate if you are:

___ Female
___ Male

**Racial ancestry**
Questions 2 and 3 are about your racial ancestry. If you are of mixed ancestry you can either check two or three categories or the one with which you identify most or the one which you think others identify you with.

Racial ancestry is *not* about citizenship or nationality. For example, people from Jamaica can be Black, Asian (Chinese) or White. Black, Asian or White are racial characteristics.

2.  Do you consider yourself a North American Indian, Métis, or Inuit/ Eskimo

___ Yes    Unless you are of mixed ancestry you can skip question 3 and go to question 4.
___ No     Go to question 3.

3.  Check the line or lines which best describe(s) your racial ancestry or origin, not your citizenship or nationality.

___ Black
___ East Asian, Oriental, Chinese, Fijian, Japanese, Korean, Polynesian, Other Pacific Islanders.
___ South Asian, Bangladeshi, Bengali, East Indian, Gujarati, Pakistani, Punjabi, Singhalese, Sri Lankan, Tamil.
___ South East Asian, Burmese (Myanmar), Filipino, Cambodian, Laotian, Thai, Vietnamese, Indonesian, Malay.
___ West Asian and Arab, Egyptian, Iranian, Lebanese, Syrian, Turk.
___ Other racial minority (persons who, because of their race or colour, are a minority in Canada, such as South American Aboriginal Peoples, etc.)
___ White (i.e., English, Greek, Italian, Portuguese)

Please go to question 4 on the next page.

---

Box 5-2 (Cont'd)    PAGE 2

### EMPLOYMENT EQUITY QUESTIONNAIRE
(Long Version)

**Persons with disabilities**
Persons with disabilities are persons who, for the purposes of employment, consider themselves or believe that an employer would likely consider them disadvantaged by reason of any persistent physical, mental, psychiatric, learning or sensory impairment.

4. Do you have a disability?

___ Yes    Please answer question below.
___ No     You have completed the questionnaire. Thank you.

It would help us to address the needs of different disabilities if you would check the line or lines which describe(s) any condition that you feel applies to you as a persistent disability.

Visual impairment (if glasses or contact lenses correct vision, do not include yourself in this category)

___ Partially sighted
___ Blind

Hearing impairment

___ Hard of hearing
___ Deaf

Others

___ Co-ordination or dexterity impairment
___ Learning impairment (e.g., dyslexia)
___ Mental impairment
___ Mobility impairment
___ Non-visible physical impairment (e.g., epilepsy, haemophilia, heart condition)
___ Psychiatric impairment
___ Speech impairment

You have completed the questionnaire. Thank you.

sensitive and employees may feel uncomfortable providing it. A communication program (discussed later) is needed to ensure that employees understand why they are being asked for this information. One important assurance to give employees is that this data is being used *only* for EE purposes. Therefore, it is best if the questionnaire deal only with designated group status and nothing else, reinforcing the singular use of the data.

The first of the two sample questionnaires provided, is a short form (Box 5-1). It asks the four questions required in Ontario legislation (as found in the draft regulations). The longer version (Box 5-2), asks for more details. For example, if the employee completing the form is a member of a racial minority, information is collected as to which racial group they belong. Or if a person is disabled, information on the kind of disability is collected. The short form provides all the information which is currently required by all the jurisdictions requiring formal data collection. It is likely that over time more programs will require the kind of information collected by the longer form. At some point in time, it may be useful to have the more extensive information to help in setting goals and timetables. At the present time the more detailed information is not required;[1] and an organization has to decide if more detailed information would be helpful. If you are designing such a questionnaire be sure to avoid two common mistakes:

- Include "White" under racial ancestry.
- Use terminology which is meaningful to the people who will be completing the questionnaire. While certain words are becoming more acceptable (such as "Asian" rather than "Oriental", "Inuit" rather than "Eskimo") it is best to use all the words employees are likely to use to ensure that they do not make mistakes because they are unfamiliar with the newer terminology.

### *Is it essential to include the employee's name or identification number on the questionnaire?*

Yes, in order to keep the data base up to date. If information is collected with employees' names it is possible to link the designated group status information with the other information needed to report (*e.g.*, occupational grouping and salary), with employment status (*e.g.*, part-time, temporary) and to up-date the information for employees (*e.g.*, promotions, terminations). If identification is not included

- a full data-collection process will have to be repeated every year, and

- employees will have to include information about their salary and job title on the questionnaire, rather than their name.

The draft regulations for the Ontario legislation require names be on the survey form. Employees have the right to decide to complete the form or not but they must return it.

## How is designated group status data kept up to date?

Once data has been collected on designated group status – assuming a good participation rate and accurate data – such a massive data collection process will not have to be done again,[2] as long as there is some employee identification (names or identification number) on the questionnaire. The only additional data to be collected will be on new hires and transaction data every year (*i.e.*, transfers, demotions). Designated group data on new hires should be collected at the same time that other personal information (*e.g.*, payroll deductions) is collected. It should be done after the person has been hired (collecting designated group status on applicants is a separate process). New employees must understand why this information is being completed and what it will be used for. This can be adapted from the communication material provided to current employees (discussed later). The same questionnaire which was used in the original survey can be used to collect this information from new employees.

Up-dating includes revising information for current employees. Both designated group status information and occupation and salary information can change. A change in designated group status is most likely to occur because an able-bodied person becomes disabled or someone with a disability may no longer believe that they have a persistent physical, mental, psychiatric, learning or sensory impairment. Further, unless there was 100 per cent participation on the original survey, employees may later wish to supply this information. So there is a need to establish a procedure to enable employees to change the information on their designated group status.

Information on employment changes (*e.g.*, transfers) need to be put into the system to ensure up to date data. For example, salary increases, promotions, demotions, terminations all need to be recorded so that when an EE report is run it is a true picture of the work-force at a point in time. Further, an employee's employment status (*e.g.*, part-time) can change. It is expected that, over time, target group members will move into jobs which they have not traditionally held. This means that the organization is succeeding at EE, thus, it is essential that these accomplishments be picked up in the data.

## How can data on designated group status be collected?

The question here is whether employees or someone else provides the information. Some jurisdictions specify how the designated group status information must be collected, others do not. For instance, under the federal[3] and Ontario[4] *Employment Equity Acts* employees must provide the information on themselves; this is not required under the Federal Contractors' Program. There are three typical ways of collecting information. These are:

- *Self-identification*: Each employee is asked to specify her/his characteristics in terms of each of the four designated groups.
- *Third party identification*: Someone other than the employee is asked to specify each employee's characteristics in terms of each of the four designated groups. The person doing the specifying is usually the supervisor or someone in human resources.
- *Third party identification with verification*: Someone other than the employee specifies the designated group characteristics and this is then given to the employee for her/his verification.

### Which data collection method should one use, if there is a choice?

There are advantages and disadvantages to each of the three data collection methods. Table 5-1 compares the three methods on four criteria: Accuracy, participation, confidentiality of personal information and cost of collecting the data. The assessment in Table 5-1 assumes that there has been thorough communication to all employees and training to supervisors about data collection for EE purposes (these topics are discussed later).

Use self-identification when

- there is a high level of trust within the organization,
- there is union-management support,
- employees have been fully informed about the purpose and use of designated group status data,
- you have the time to collect the information.

Use supervisory identification with verification when

- time, accuracy and participation are important considerations,
- supervisors have been trained.

Use third party identification when

- low trust or suspicion is likely to result in sabotage (incorrect information being reported),
- data is needed quickly,
- there is no time to train supervisors or employees as to why data needs to be collected,
- one of the other two techniques will be used in the future.

TABLE 5-1

COMPARISON OF THREE METHODS FOR COLLECTING DATA

|  | Self-identification | Supervisory identification with verification | Third party identification |
|---|---|---|---|
| Accuracy | Potential highest<br><br>May be sabotage (incorrect inform-ation given) | High because typically employees will correct inaccur-ate information<br><br>Employees may feel their privacy has been invaded | Lowest<br><br>Enforcement agencies might question accuracy of data<br><br>Employees may feel their privacy has been invaded |
| Participation | Requires most work to get participation | High. May not get verification from all employees but will have third party identification | High |
| Confident-iality of personal information | High | Low | Low |
| Cost | Highest for both collection and communication<br><br>Longest time to collect | Middle but closer to self-identification in cost of communi-cation and collection and length of time to collect | Lowest |

While accuracy potentially is highest with self-identification it may not be if some employees express their dissatisfaction with EE by marking their questionnaires incorrectly. With all three methods of data collection it may be impossible to get information on invisible disabilities (*e.g.,* diabetes) unless there is a high level of trust with self-identification or it is known to the third party identifier.

Regardless of the method used employees and supervisors do not like the data collection process. Communication is the key.

# COMMUNICATION ISSUES

*Why is communication so important?*

Asking employees to identify themselves in terms of their race and whether or not they have a disability is sensitive. It is part of the Canadian value system that such personal characteristics should not matter in employment (and they should not). Further, many believe it is illegal to ask such questions. This is *not* true. It is legal to ask for this information *when it will be used for EE purposes*. For example, section 15(2) of the *Canadian Charter of Rights and Freedoms*[5] allows special programs to redress systemic discrimination. Data collection is part of this process because it provides statistical evidence as to whether systemic discrimination is likely to be operating. That is, if an organization's work-force does not mirror the available labour force then it is assumed that there are employment barriers.

The communication strategy is somewhat different depending on whether one is using self-identification, third party identification, or third party identification with verification. With self-identification it is best to focus on a census day. A day on which all the data is to be collected. This approach is superior to sending out the questionnaires and asking employees to return them, say, within a week. The participation rate is likely to be lower with the latter approach because employees will forget or lose their questionnaires. A census day provides a focus for the survey. It also allows other techniques to be used to increase the participation rate. For example, all employees within a work unit can get together at the same time (*e.g.*, 11:00 a.m.) so that each person can complete her or his questionnaire. This allows questions about the survey to be asked and answered so that everyone hears the same information. It also prevents employees from putting off the task or forgetting about it. Employees should seal their questionnaires in envelopes with identification numbers on them. This allows verification of who has completed the form without seeing the data.

When third party identification is done without verification (the least favoured option) there is less pressure to have a specific time noted for identification. It may be more practical to work with one division or department at a time.

Some examples of communication material are provided in Edward Harvey's 1988 book which is noted in the references for this chapter.

*What is essential for a communication strategy?*

As noted in Chapter 4, communication about EE should be on-going. Communication about the collection of designated group status should not be the first EE communication employees receive. Still, it is important that there be clear communication to all employees when self-identification is being used. The points to stress in communication are:

- Collecting such information is legal. In support of this, it is a good idea to send the questionnaire to the relevant provincial or federal human rights agency for review. This will serve two purposes. First, it will ensure that your questionnaire is not inadvertently wrong in some way. Second, you will be able to reassure employees that you have approval for the questionnaire from human rights.
- Why the information is being collected. Saying that it is legally required is not sufficient. Employees need to understand something about EE and systemic discrimination which makes workforce analysis necessary.
- How the data will be used. Ensure that employees know that it is the aggregate data, rather than the data on any particular individual which is important. It is important that employees understand that this data will be used to establish goals and timetables and to assess how well the organization is doing at meeting its goal of representation. It is also important to inform employees that the information will not be used in making transfer, promotion, demotion or termination decisions.
- Assure confidentiality. It is important employees know that this information will not be made part of their personnel file. Nor will it be reported in such a manner that they could be identified. Usually, if there are less than three employees in a "cell" on the reporting form the data is not reported. For example, if there is only one Aboriginal professional, the salary data for this person is not reported.
- Provide results to employees. Share with employees the basic make-up of the organization. Some organizations have gained employees' or senior management's interest by asking them to describe the organization in terms of their estimates of designated group membership within the organization. This can than be compared against the actual data once it is collected.

It is vital that supervisors fully understand the need for data collection. This holds true regardless of the means of collection used. Particularly with self-identification, supervisors' attitudes, ability to answer questions to employees' satisfaction and their handling of the process can have a strong impact on the return rate and the accuracy of the information.

### Do we have to collect designated group data on applicants?

For jobs where there is an underrepresentation of designated group members and a lack of applicants may be part of the problem, yes. It is necessary to determine where barriers are. For instance, if racial minority candidates are not making it through the selection process, then this, and not the number applying is the problem.

Where it is necessary to collect applicant information, it should be kept separate from the application form, and candidates names should not be kept with the designated group status information (this differs from what is done with employees). So with each application a separate form (and self-addressed envelope which goes to a different location than the application) can be attached. This form should ask for the title of the job applied for and whether the candidate is female or male, a member of a racial minority or white (if non-white, whether of Aboriginal ancestry or not), and whether disabled or able-bodied. The form should also inform applicants as to why this information is being collected and how it will be used.

## ANALYZING THE DATA

This section discusses a number of potential analyses which can be made using the data collected from the work-force analysis questionnaire. The kind and number of analyses will depend on the information needed to set goals and timetables. Further, the number of analyses will depend on the ability of decision-makers to absorb the information (there is such a thing as information overload). The basic calculations require percentages, which are discussed next.

### Using percentages

Percentages are used in analyzing the data. While many people are familiar with percentages and feel comfortable with them, others have not had to calculate them or work with them directly. Material in Boxes 5-3, 5-4 and 5-5 provides some basics on understanding, calculating and reporting percentages.

## Box 5-3

### UNDERSTANDING PERCENTAGES

A per cent tells us what portion of a "whole" we are focusing on. For example, if the data shows that 40% of the organization's employees are women, we know that 60% are male. Per cents always add to 100; that is, 100% represents the whole.

One way to illustrate percentages is to use a pie chart as shown in Figure 5-3. The entire pie equals 100%; each piece of the pie is some portion or part of the pie. The pie in Figure 5-3 shows the proportion of the Canadian work-force comprised of each designated group and of white, able-bodied men.

### FIGURE 5-3

### COMPOSITION OF CANADIAN LABOUR FORCE

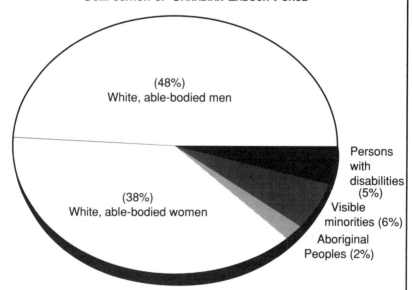

SOURCE: Adapted from 1986 Census and Health & Activities Limitation Survey.

Table 5-2 provides the numbers which were used to create the pie chart in Figure 5-3 (calculating percentages is discussed in the next section). Both Table 5-2 and Figure 5-3 provide similar information; column 1 in Table 5-2 provides the "raw numbers" or "raw data" used to calculate the percentages which are shown in column 2 of the Table and in the pie chart. The percentages show the proportion each designated group forms of the whole labour force.

## Box 5-3 (Cont'd)

### Table 5-2

#### Number and Percentage of People
#### in Various Groups in Canadian Work-force

|  | Availability in the Canadian Labour Force* | |
|---|---|---|
|  | **Number** | **Percentage** |
| White able-bodied women | 5,245,000 | 38% |
| White able-bodied men | 6,693,000 | 48% |
| Visible minority women | 406,000 | 3% |
| Visible minority men | 467,000 | 3% |
| Women who are disabled | 314,000 | 2% |
| Men who are disabled | 439,000 | 3% |
| Aboriginal women | 133,000 | 1% |
| Aboriginal men | 161,000 | 1% |
| TOTAL | 13,858,000 | 100%** |

SOURCE:  Adapted from combined data from Employment Equity Availability Data Report, Tables 8 and 12 (provided by Employment Immigration Canada) which is based on data from 1986 Census and 1986 Health and Activities Limitation Survey (the latter provides data for persons with disabilities).

*   Labour force is comprised of all those 15 to 64 years of age who are employed or are looking for work (are unemployed).

**   Adds to 99% due to rounding.

## Box 5-3 (Cont'd)

Table 5-3 shows one of the important ways percentages can be used – to make comparisons. The first 2 columns of numbers show the numbers of people in the various designated groups with Ordinary Organization Ltd. and within the Canadian labour force. While these numbers were needed to calculate the percentages it is impossible to compare them in any meaningful way because the Canadian labour force is so much larger than the work-force of Ordinary Organization Ltd. (200 employees compared to 13 million people). Percentages overcome this problem by allowing comparisons between the proportions of the same thing (designated group members) in organizations of very different sizes; as can be seen in the last 2 columns of Table 5-3 which show percentages based on the raw data. This is because with percentages the total is always 100%. Two hundred employees is 100% of the employees at Ordinary Organization Ltd. and 13,858,000 people is 100% of the Canadian labour force. With per cents the total is always 100%. So with percentages we do not know anything about the *absolute size* of the total. Percentages tell us something about the *relative size*.

### TABLE 5-3

#### COMPARISON OF DESIGNATED GROUPS IN ORGANIZATION TO AVAILABILITY WITHIN CANADIAN WORK-FORCE

|  | Raw data | | Percentages | |
|---|---|---|---|---|
|  | Ordinary Organization Ltd. | Available in Canadian work-force | Ordinary Organization Ltd. | Available in Canadian work-force |
| White able-bodied women | 122 | 5,245,000 | 61% | 38% |
| White able-bodied men | 46 | 6,693,000 | 23% | 48% |
| Racial minorities (men & women) | 26 | 873,000 | 13% | 6% |
| Persons w/a disability (men & women) | 4 | 753,000 | 2% | 5% |
| Aboriginal men & women | 2 | 294,000 | 1% | 2% |
| TOTAL | 200 | 13,858,000 | 100% | 100%* |

* Adds to 99% due to rounding.

## Box 5-3 (Cont'd)

Figure 5-4 shows the proportion of designated group members in 2 departments of Ordinary Organization Ltd. (here the data is shown in the form of a bar chart).

### Figure 5-4

### Comparison of Gender Composition in Two Departments of Ordinary Organization Ltd.

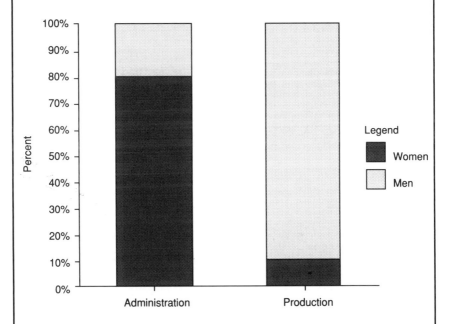

From Figure 5-4 it is clear that the Administration Department has a higher *proportion* of women than does the Production Department. But Figure 5-4 tells us nothing about the absolute size of these 2 departments. The Production Department has 100 employees, 10 of whom are women (10%). The Administration Department has only 10 employees, 8 of whom are women (80%). So, there are more women (in terms of absolute numbers) in the Production Department (10 women) than in the Administration Department (8 women). But the proportion of the department which is female is higher in Administration 80% (= 8 ÷ 10) than Production 10% (10 ÷ 100). So percentages allow comparison of relative relationships between departments, between organizations, and between an organization and availability in the external work-force. The fact that such departments, organizations or the external labour force are of different sizes is irrelevant since each has a total of 100%.

## Box 5-4

### CALCULATING PERCENTAGES

A per cent is the number representing the portion (*e.g.*, women) divided by the total (or whole) (*e.g.*, all employees). For example, there are 8 women working in the Administration Department of Ordinary Organization Ltd. The Administration Department has a total of 10 employees. The percentage of women in the Administration Department is

$$\frac{8}{10} = .8$$

If you divide 8 by 10 with a calculator, the screen shows: .8 (or .80 or .800). This is **not** expressed as a percentage, but can easily be transformed into a percentage. To do this you can either:

- Move the decimal point (.) 2 places to the *right* and add the "%" sign, so .8 becomes 80%; .80 becomes 80%; .800 becomes 80.0% which is the same as 80%.

OR

- Multiply .8 by 100 and add the "%" sign. (.8 X 100 = 80; add "%" for 80%; .80 X 100 = 80; and .800 X 100 = 80)

The important thing to remember in calculating a percentage is to divide the total into the portion as shown below:

Portion of total
Total

The number on top, when analyzing work-force analysis data, is always smaller than the one on the bottom since it is a portion of the total. The total can be defined differently – it could be all the employees in the organization, all the employees in an occupational category, all the visible minority employees in the organization, etc.

To calculate a percentage you usually need to know the portion and the total – but not always. Sometimes you use the knowledge that percentages always total to 100%. For example, if you know there are 15 *women* in a department of 90 people, you can determine the percentage of *men* working in the department.

(1) Determine the percentage of women in the department: 15/90 = .16 or 16%
(2) All the people who are not women are men so if 16% of the department is women then
100% − 16% = 84% must be men.

(Another way to solve this problem would be to say that if 15 of the employees in a department of 90 are women then 75 (= 90 − 15) are men. So the percentage of men is 75/90 = .84 or 84%.)

## BOX 5-4 (CONT'D)

If you know that
      32 % of your employees are women
      6 % are visible minority men
      0 % are Aboriginal Peoples
      4 % are men with a disability

you can determine the proportion who are white, able-bodied males by:

(1)  Adding the percentages of the designated group members together:
                  32%
                   6%
                   0%
                   4%
                 42% of the employees are members
                     of the four designated groups

(2)  Subtract the percentage of employees who are NOT white, able-bodied males from 100%
        100% - 42% = 58% of the employees are white,
                    able-bodied males.

Assume an organization has 150 people. Using this, plus the percentages given above, you can determine how many men with disabilities are employed in this organization. The proportion of men with disabilities is 4%.

When multiplying by a percentage, convert it to a number with a decimal point. This can be done by either

(a)  Changing the % sign to a decimal point (.) and moving the decimal point 2 places to the *left*. So 4% becomes 4., and the decimal point is then moved 2 places to the left and it becomes .04. A zero (0) needs to be put in front of the 4 in order to move the decimal point (.) *2* places. [It is a mistake to convert 4% to .4, since .4 equals 40%.]

or

(b)  Dropping the % sign and dividing 4 by 100
           (4/100 = .04)

So the number of male employees with a disability is determined by:
      Multiplying the total by the percentage number
                150 x .04 = 6
      150 total employees X .04 (proportion who are men with
        disabilities) = 6 male employees who have a disability

The trickiest thing about working with percentages is to know how to read the "%" sign when there is a decimal point in the percentage number

## Box 5-4 (Cont'd)

---

## Box 5-4 (Cont'd)

(7.5%, for example). If you calculate a per cent and your calculator shows .46 this is the same as 46% (you move the decimal point 2 places to the right and add the "%" sign). If when you calculate a percentage the calculator shows .058 this is 5.8%. Alternatively, if the number reads .005, the percentage is .5% which is half of 1%. Forty-six per cent (46%) is almost half (50%), 5.8% is not quite 6% and .5% is less than 1%. So it is important to know which number you are looking at. You use the number without the "%" sign and with the decimal point in front (.46, .058 and .005) when you need to use the number in a calculation (*e.g.*, to determine the number of persons with disabilities in the total organization). When you report the data you should use the percentage sign so that it is clear to the reader that the number is a percentage.

---

## Box 5-5

### Reporting Percentages

When reporting a percentage it is important to make clear what total the percentage is a portion of. For instance, in 1991, the following 2 facts were true:

- 45% of the labour force are women.
- 58% of women are in the labour force.

It is important to read each fact carefully in order to understand its meaning. In the first, "45% of the labour force are women", the "whole" are all the people (both men and women) in the labour force. The labour force is comprised of all those 15 to 64 years of age who are either employed or looking for work. To arrive at this percentage one needs to know the total number of people in the labour force (13,757,000) and the portion who are women (6,188,000). This is used to calculate the percentage:

$$\frac{6,188,000}{13,757,000} = .45 \times 100 = 45\%$$

Graphically, this is shown in Figure 5-5.

The second fact given above is that "58% of women are in the labour force". This fact is based on the "whole" being all the women who are of working age (15 to 64) in the Canadian population. The 58% is the proportion of the total of all women who are in the labour force (the other 42% [= 100% − 58%] are students, housewives, retired, in institutions (*e.g.*, prison) or idly rich). The figures used to develop this percentage are:

- 6,188,000 women in the labour force
- 10,629,000 women between the ages of 15 and 64 in Canada

## Box 5-5 (Cont'd)

### Figure 5-5

#### Percentage of Men and Women in the Labour Force

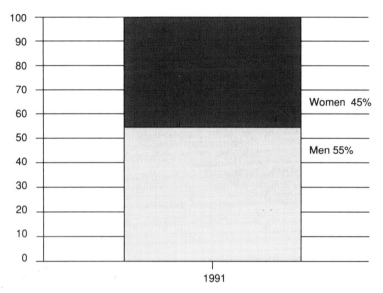

SOURCE: Adapted from Statistics Canada, 1991 data, Cat. No. 71-220. Reproduced with the permission of the Minister of Industry, Science and Technology, 1993.

So the percentage is calculated:

$$\frac{6,188,000}{10,629,000} = .58 \times 100 = 58\%$$

Graphically, this is shown in Figure 5-6.

Notice that both these 2 percentages are based on the same portion (6,188,000 women in the labour force); what is different is the "whole". The first is the proportion of the labour force which is comprised of women (45%) – comparing women (part) to the labour force (whole). The portion comprised of women (45%) and the proportion comprised of men (55%) will equal 100%. The second percentage is the proportion of women in the labour force – comparing women in the labour force to all women of working age. The portion of women in the labour force (58%) and the proportion of women not in the labour force (42%) will add to 100%.

When reporting percentages it is critical that the reader always know what "whole" is being referred to. So, the easiest way is to contract the information as shown in Figure 5-7.

124

Box 5-5 (Cont'd)

FIGURE 5-6

PERCENTAGE OF WOMEN IN THE CANADIAN LABOUR FORCE
1991

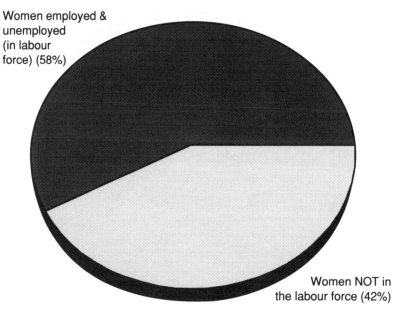

Women employed &
unemployed
(in labour
force) (58%)

Women NOT in
the labour force (42%)

SOURCE:  Adapted from Statistics Canada, 1991 data.

FIGURE 5-7

REPORTING OF PERCENTAGES

"45%      of      the      labour      force      are      women"

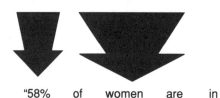

Percentage                    Whole                    Part represented
                                                        by percentage

"58%    of    women    are    in    the    labour    force"

## What information is needed to analyze the EE data?

Table 5-4 shows the data needed to do work-force analysis, and the source of the data used. Most information is needed on individual employees (see rows 1, 2 and 3). However, it is important to remember that the analyses are based on aggregated data. That is, the individual data is added together. Note from Table 5-4 that some of the employee data is collected from the designated group status questionnaire (row 1), some is found in current personnel files (row 2) and some is collected whenever there is an employment transaction (*e.g.*, promotion) (row 3). The final kind of data used is external availability data which is provided by the federal or provincial government.

The kind of data required in row 1 (designated group status) has been discussed, and the data required in row 3 (flow data) and row 4 (availability data) will be discussed later. At this time it is useful to review the data required in row 2 – (data from current human resource files). The first piece of information noted in row 2 is employment status, whether employees work full-time or part-time, on a permanent or casual basis. This information is used in one of the analyses discussed later to assess if designated group members are likely to have more tenuous employment status. The second item in row 2 is a job code. This is needed in order to report the data in terms of occupational categories. If your organization must report to only one jurisdiction then the occupational categories rather than job codes can be stored in the data base. However, if the organization has to report to two or more jurisdictions then it is necessary to keep job code data since the occupational categories required in reports can differ from jurisdiction to jurisdiction. By storing the data with a job code it is then possible to aggregate the data into the required occupational categories.

Salary is the third piece of information noted in row 2 of Table 5-4. Annual salaries have typically been reported. Geographic location, the fourth item noted in row 2, needs to be included for organizations which operate in more than one city. The availability data provided by the relevant government will be broken down into different geographic areas. For instance, the data provided by the federal government has national data, provincial data and data for the standard metropolitan areas (SMAs) of the largest cities in the country. The availability of First Nations people and racial minorities are likely to differ greatly by geographic area. For example, the proportion of racial minorities is much greater in Vancouver than in Halifax. The availability of women and persons with disabilities is similar across different geographic areas. (Availability data is provided in Appendix A.)

It is a good idea to include the date of employment in the data base so that seniority can be calculated and updated. Seniority may be useful in

TABLE 5-4

DATA REQUIRED FOR EMPLOYMENT EQUITY ANALYSIS

| Row # | Data | Source |
|---|---|---|
| 1 | **Designated group status data** aggregated for all employees:<br>• Name or identification number<br>• Designated group status<br>  — Gender (female or male)<br>  — Racial minority or white<br>  — Aboriginal ancestry or not<br>  — Disabled or able-bodied. | Collected once and up-dated as necessary.<br><br>Collected via designated group status questionnaire (for self-report). |
| 2 | **Employment information** associated with each employee:<br>• Employment status (full-time, part-time, etc.)<br>• Job code and corresponding occupational category<br>• Salary, salary band or salary quartiles<br>• Geographic location<br>• Date of employment or seniority. | Information in current human resource records. Linked with designated group status information. Updated as necessary. |
| 3 | **Flow or transaction data** on new hires, transfers, promotions, demotions, terminations and retirements; and changes in employment information or designated group status. | Whenever such a transaction occurs, the data must be recorded for employment equity purposes. Periodically (quarterly or annually) must be added to employment equity data base. |
| 4 | **External availability data** for each of the designated groups. | From government agency requiring employment equity reporting. |

understanding the data. For example, it may be found that, among supervisors, those who are members of a racial minority group are paid significantly less than are employees who are white. Analysis can be done to determine if this is due to race or to lower seniority among racial minorities who have more recently been promoted into supervisory positions. Differences due to race are problematic; showing that supervisors with the same amount of seniority, regardless of race, are paid the same, shows that racial discrimination does not exist in salaries.

External availability data (row 4) is used as a comparison standard for some of the EE analyses. It allows the question – does our organization mirror the available labour force? – to be answered. The potential problem with the external availability data is its lack of precision for those located in some areas. For example, the 1986 census shows the following data for racial minorities:

6.3%  Canada
9.0%  Ontario
16.3%  Metro Toronto

What is the appropriate availability figure for the City of Hamilton which is a 45-minute drive from Toronto? It is probably more than 9 per cent but certainly less than 16 per cent, even though some people live in Toronto and work in Hamilton.

This discussion has provided an outline of the information which is needed for the analyses of the work-force audit data (flow data is discussed later). The next sections discuss the potential analyses which can be done.

### How do we analyze the data?

Data analysis for EE requires calculating percentages and comparing them with other percentages (standards). It is important to ensure that data analysis does not become an end in itself, but is always focused on answering questions which will help the organization identify and address its EE needs. The data analysis is a starting point. Areas of concern indicate where one should begin looking to identify barriers. The analyses are done for each designated group separately. Three primary questions which data analysis can answer are:

1. What proportion of the work-force is comprised of designated group members? (Representation)
2. What proportion of each designated group are employed in each occupational category (and salary range)? (Distribution)
3. What proportion of incumbents in each occupational category (and salary range) are members of each designated group? (Occupational representation)

To help address these questions it is necessary to compare the data (percentages) against standards. These standards can be either internal or external. One internal comparison is to compare a percentage for a designated group against its "reciprocal". A reciprocal is the complementary or opposite: the reciprocal of racial minorities is Whites, of Aboriginal Peoples is those not of First Nations ancestry, of persons with disabilities is those who are able-bodied, of women is men. The external standard is the availability data which provides information on the presence of designated group members in the community from which the organization recruits. Representation, occupational representation and positions of authority can be examined in terms of availability.

*Representation*

Representation measures the proportion of each designated group found in the total organizational work-force. One of the ultimate goals of EE is representation of designated group members throughout the organization (at various occupational levels). In order to have this it is necessary that the organization have an overall representation which mirrors that found in the area from which the organization recruits.[6] If an organization's work-force does not match the external available work-force then the potential barriers to look for are those which keep members of designated groups out of the organization. For instance, barriers could be that (1) information about job openings are not available to them; (2) designated group members believing that they are unwelcome (because there is no one else like them working in the organization); (3) that unnecessary job qualifications are keeping qualified designated group members out; (4) invalid selection procedures are screening them out; or (5) they are getting hired but do not stay.

Data for a fictitious organization in Regina, Saskatchewan is shown in Table 5-5.

There are no Aboriginal employees, 5 per cent of the employees have disabilities, 1 per cent are members of racial minority groups and 48 per cent are women (45 per cent and are white, able-bodied women). These percentages describe the organization. Is there a problem? In order to begin to answer this question one needs to compare the representation percentage with availability data. This comparison is shown in Table 5-6.

The availability data shows that this organization's representation of women matches that for Regina. However, the barriers which are keeping First Nations peoples and racial minorities out of the organization need to be identified. There are no Aboriginal Peoples and only a small number of racial minorities (1 per cent) though there are 3 per cent to 4 per cent of each group in the labour force. The organization needs to build on its success of hiring persons with disabilities and increase its representation somewhat from 5 per cent to closer to 8 per cent. While

## TABLE 5-5

### REPRESENTATION FIGURES FOR ORGANIZATION

| Designated groups | Representation |
|---|---|
| Aboriginal Peoples | 0% |
| Persons with disabilities | 5% |
| Racial minorities | 1% |
| Women (48%): white, able-bodied women | 45% |
| TOTAL DESIGNATED GROUPS WITHIN ORGANIZATION | 51% |

## TABLE 5-6

### COMPARISON OF REPRESENTATION DATA WITH AVAILABILITY DATA

| Designated groups | Representation | Availability** | |
|---|---|---|---|
| | | Saskatchewan | Regina |
| Aboriginal Peoples | 0% | 4% | 3% |
| Persons with disabilities | 5% | 8% | N/A |
| Racial minorities | 1% | 3% | 4% |
| White, able-bodied women (45%); Women | 48% | 43% | 47% |
| TOTAL | 51%* | 58% | N/A |

\* Total based on 45% white, able-bodied women; not 48% which is all women in the organization.
\*\* Based on 1986 Census for Saskatchewan and Regina
N/A = Not available

the percentage difference between the organizational and availability data for Native peoples, racial minorities and for persons with disabilities are all the same (3 per cent) the situations may be quite different. There are no Aboriginal Peoples working in the organization (0 per cent) and very few racial minorities (1 per cent) while there are some (5 per cent) employees with disabilities. It is typically more difficult to hire the "first" from any designated group than to add to an existing critical mass.

Formula for calculating representation:
   Part:       Membership in each designated group
   Whole:      Organization's work-force

REPRESENTATION = Total number in a designated group
                           Total number of employees

### Distribution

"Distribution" analyzes how each designated group is distributed across the occupational levels (and salary levels). It answers the question – Where are the persons with disabilities employed in our organization? – and so on for each designated group. The concern is that members of designated groups will be concentrated into specific occupations which are either low paying, limiting in terms of career movement and/or do not utilize the talents of the members of the designated groups. The objective is to have designated group members distributed across occupational groupings similarly to those who do not belong to the designated group. The occupational distribution data for the Regina organization noted above is given in Table 5-7.

### TABLE 5-7

### DISTRIBUTION OF DESIGNATED GROUP MEMBERS
### ACROSS OCCUPATIONAL LEVELS

| Occupational categories | Aboriginal Peoples | Persons with disabilities | Racial minorities | Women |
|---|---|---|---|---|
| Management | 0% | 2% | 0% | 0% |
| Professional | 0% | 40% | 0% | 10% |
| Technical | 0% | 30% | 100% | 0% |
| Clerical | 0% | 28% | 0% | 90% |
| TOTAL | 0% | 100% | 100% | 100% |

Since the distribution analysis shows the placement of each designated group across different occupational levels it is possible to get a sense as to whether there is an overrepresentation (concentration) or under-representation of the various designated groups within the various occupations. For example, women are concentrated into clerical jobs (90 per cent of the women work in clerical jobs) and racial minorities are concentrated into technical jobs (100 per cent of racial minorities are in such jobs). Such concentration raises issues about barriers which block entry into other occupations within the organization. For instance, in many organizations it is almost impossible for individuals working in clerical jobs to move into any other kind of work. There is not only a glass ceiling preventing employees from moving up but also glass walls preventing them from moving into technical, maintenance and other such jobs. This barrier is often caused by the assumption that women, the predominant holders of clerical jobs, do not want, or cannot do, jobs traditionally done by men. Stereotypes often work to keep racial minorities in technical jobs rather than their moving up or moving laterally.

Table 5-7 shows that persons with disabilities are not concentrated into any one occupational grouping but are found throughout the organization. To assess this further in terms of potential underrepresentation, it is necessary to compare the distribution percentages for persons with disabilities with their reciprocal group, able-bodied employees. This is shown in Table 5-8.

## TABLE 5-8

### COMPARISON OF DISTRIBUTION OF EMPLOYEES WITH DISABILITIES WITH ABLE-BODIED EMPLOYEES ACROSS OCCUPATIONS

| Occupational categories | Persons with disabilities | Reciprocal group: Persons who are able-bodied |
|---|---|---|
| Management | 2% | 8% |
| Professional | 40% | 38% |
| Technical | 30% | 28% |
| Clerical | 28% | 26% |
| TOTAL | 100% | 100% |

The proportion of persons with disabilities in each of the occupations is similar to the proportion of able-bodied people found in these occupations, with the exception of management. Only 2 per cent of employees with disabilities hold management jobs, compared to 8 per cent of employees who are able-bodied. So, persons with disabilities are underrepresented in management jobs (as are Aboriginal Peoples, racial minorities and women, all of whom have no members holding management jobs, as shown in Table 5-7). Barriers associated with movement into management jobs need to be identified and changed.

Formula for calculating distribution:
    Part:      Number of designated group members in each occupation.
    Whole:   Total number of designated group members.
              (Note that in Table 5-7, the percentages of designated group members adds to 100 per cent.)

$$\text{DISTRIBUTION} = \frac{\text{Designated group in each occupation}}{\text{Total number in each designated group}}$$

## Occupational representation

Distribution and occupational representation both use occupational data. The difference is that occupational representation is the proportion in each occupation (whole) held by the various designated group members (part); while distribution is the proportion of each designated group (whole) in the various occupations (part). Occupational representation data is used to assess if the proportion of designated group members across occupations match the reciprocal and the availability data. Table 5-9 shows the occupational representation. (Note that it is the rows (occupation) which add to 100 per cent while in Table 5-7 it is the columns (designated group status) which add to 100 per cent.) The occupational representation analysis shows that virtually all (99.7 per cent) management jobs are held by white, able-bodied men. This group also holds the vast majority (92 per cent) of technical jobs, 66 per cent of the professional jobs, but only 2 per cent of the clerical jobs. Are designated groups well represented in the various occupational groups or not? The answer to this question requires a comparison. Two comparisons are possible - one internal and one external. These are shown in Table 5-9.

The internal comparison shows underrepresentation in management for all groups. While white, able-bodied men comprise 49 per cent of the organization's work-force they hold 99.7 per cent of the management jobs. Persons with disabilities hold .3 per cent of the management jobs though they comprise 5 per cent of the organization's work-force. There

## TABLE 5-9

### OCCUPATIONAL REPRESENTATION

| Occupational categories | Aboriginal Peoples | Persons with disabilities | Racial minorities | White, able-bodied women | White, able-bodied men | TOTAL |
|---|---|---|---|---|---|---|
| Management | 0% | .3% | 0% | 0% | 99.7% | 100% |
| Professional | 0% | 10% | 0% | 24% | 66% | 100% |
| Technical | 0% | 5% | 3% | 0% | 92% | 100% |
| Clerical | 0% | 3% | 0% | 95% | 2% | 100% |
| INTERNAL COMPARISON | | | | | | |
| Representation | 0% | 5% | 1% | 45%* | 49% | 100% |
| EXTERNAL COMPARISON** | | | | | | |
| Management | 1% | 3% | 5% | 28% | 63% | 100% |
| Professional | 1% | 2% | 4% | 50% | 43% | 100% |
| Technical | 6% | 3% | 6% | 20% | 65% | 100% |
| Clerical | 1% | 2% | 3% | 80% | 14% | 100% |

\* White, able-bodied women only.
\*\* Figures in these tables are estimates rather than actual availability data.

are some persons with disabilities in the pipeline within the organization (10 per cent of professional jobs are held by persons with disabilities). Employment equity initiatives need to be found either to prepare professional employees who are interested in management jobs or to remove barriers which have prevented professionals with disabilities from moving into management.

There are no Aboriginal Peoples, racial minorities or white, able-bodied women in positions of authority – but their circumstances differ. For Aboriginal Peoples the concern is getting some people of First Nations ancestry into the organization. For racial minorities and white, able-bodied women the issue is moving them up into management positions. The white, able-bodied women have more representation in the pipeline closest to the management ranks (24 per cent of professional jobs are held by this group). Members of racial minorities are all in technical jobs. Has anyone ever moved from technical positions to management? If not, is this an appropriate career path? Depending on the answer to this question, EE efforts should be put into changing the career path and preparing technical staff for management jobs or recruiting outside the organization for managers from racial minorities or both. Recruiting from outside the organization into management jobs is an option for all the designated groups since the availability data (shown in Table 5-9) indicates that there is a higher proportion of each designated group available in the external labour force than is found in the organization.

There is a severe problem of overrepresentation of women in clerical positions. While white, able-bodied women comprise 45 per cent of the employees they represent fully 95 per cent of clerical employees. This is an even greater concentration than found in the external work-force where 80 per cent of clerical jobs are held by white, able-bodied women. Where the overall representation data showed that this organization had an adequate representation of women, the occupational representation shows that barriers need to be addressed to get women into non-clerical jobs. Employment equity initiatives may involve either hiring women into non-clerical jobs directly or encouraging movement of current clerical employees into other kinds of work, or both. The comparison with the availability data (external comparison) also shows that women are underrepresented in technical jobs – there are none in this organization compared to 20 per cent of the technical jobs being done by white, able-bodied women in the labour force. The proportion of professional jobs performed by women is also low compared to availability data (24 per cent compared to 50 per cent). On the other hand, this organization has a higher proportion of professional jobs being performed by staff who have a disability than is true in the external work-force (10 per cent compared to 2 per cent). Racial minorities and Aboriginal Peoples are underrepresented in all the occupational groupings since there are none in the organization.

Formula to calculate occupational representation:
>Part:     Designated group members within occupation
>Whole:    All employees within occupation

>                          Total designated group members
>OCCUPATIONAL     = within occupational group
>REPRESENTATION   Total employees in occupational group

## What exactly is availability data?

Availability data refers to those who are available to work in the occupation but are not currently working. There is both internal and external availability data. Internal availability refers to those within the organization who are qualified or readily qualifiable to work in occupations which are non-traditional for them, for example, female clerical employees who want to work in manual jobs. Barriers such as perceptions that "women do not want to get dirty," unnecessary qualifications, and not informing clerical staff of openings in manual jobs can block those within the organization from moving freely between occupations.

External availability data refers to those outside the organization. This data is typically obtained from census data. It is provided by the government which is requiring EE. The data provides the percentages to compare with an organization's representation, distribution and occupational representation data. The availability data can be based on the population in general, the working age population, or those in the labour force. Typically, the proportion of designated group members in the population is greater than the working age population, which is larger than the proportion in the labour force. The working age population are those 15 years of age and older. The labour force includes those 15 and older who are employed and those available and looking for work (the unemployed). Those not in the labour force include students, those caring for home and family, those who are retired, those in institutions (*e.g.*, prisons) and the idly rich.

Approximately two-thirds (68 per cent) of the population is between the ages of 15 and 64. Approximately 75 per cent of the working age population (or about half the total population) is in the labour force.[7] But the population and working force availability figures are not always that far apart for some of the designated groups. For example, in Ontario, 2 per cent of the population and 1.5 per cent of the labour force are comprised of First Nations peoples; 8.5 per cent is the proportion of racial minorities in the population and in the labour force. For women and persons with disabilities the figures diverge more: women comprise 51 per cent of Ontario's population and 44 per cent of its labour force, while persons with disabilities comprise 14 per cent of the population and 11 per cent of the labour force.

Either the working age population or the labour force data is best for EE purposes. The availability data based on the labour force is conservative because past discrimination may have led to a larger proportion of designated group members (compared to non-designated group members) leaving the labour force. That is, designated group members who have left the labour force, *would* be available to work if they felt there were jobs. The working age population provides the upper limit of the potential number of people available. However, some individuals within this age group do not want to work, at least for a period of time, such as students, those caring for their families, and those who take early retirement. While it can be debated which availability figures are best, for most organizations beginning EE it is irrelevant since most organizations are far from having a representative work-force regardless of which standard they are compared with. The Ontario draft regulations indicate that the working age population will be used.

*Measures of flow data*

There are two kinds of data – stock and flow. Stock data provides a snapshot at one point in time. This is the kind of data which has been discussed so far. Flow data provides information on the movement of people through the organization due to hires, transfers, demotions, and promotions. Flow data is also called transaction data because it is based on various human resource transactions. Comparing stock data at two points in time (*e.g.*, January 1, 1994 and January 1, 1995) does not provide the same information as that provided by flow data. For example, look at Table 5-10 which provides an example of stock data at two points in time for racial minorities within an organization.

If one looks at this stock data one could conclude that the organization has, overall, increased its number of members of racial minorities, but that it has done better hiring professionals than entry-level positions or supervisors and with no change in skilled or managerial jobs. However, the flow data, shown in Table 5-11 provides a more comprehensive picture. For instance, while there is a decrease of racial minorities in entry-level jobs this does not represent a problem. This decrease is due to a large number of promotions (24 employees promoted). Even though there was a large number hired from the outside (20) into entry-level positions, more were promoted out of entry-level jobs. On the other hand, the lack of change in the number of racial minorities in skilled jobs may mask a problem. While hires (3) and promotions (7) look good, the number of quits (8) is very high. Who are the people leaving – the ones who have been in the job for a period of time or those new to the job? Why are they leaving?

The flow data does not reveal any problems with either supervisory

**TABLE 5-10**

**EXAMPLE OF STOCK DATA AT TWO POINTS IN TIME**
**FOR RACIAL MINORITY EMPLOYEES**

| Occupations | NUMBER OF EMPLOYEES | | |
|---|---|---|---|
| | At beginning of period | At end of period | Difference |
| Entry-level | 50 | 45 | -5 |
| Skilled | 10 | 10 | 0 |
| Professional | 40 | 60 | +20 |
| Supervisory | 5 | 2 | -3 |
| Management | 1 | 1 | 0 |
| TOTAL | 106 | 118 | +12 |

staff or management. Rather, the stock data indicates that given the number of racial minorities in professional jobs, goals need to be set and initiatives begun so that over time members of racial minority groups will be ready to move into supervisory and management jobs.

*Conclusion about analyses*

The important thing to remember about data collection and analysis is that these measures are tools. They are a means to an end, not the end. The purpose of the data collection and analysis process should always be kept in mind:

- To identify barriers so EE initiatives can be used to remove them.
- To set goals and timetables.
- To assess the organization's accomplishments towards its goals of a representative work-force and employment systems which work for all employees.

*Establishment of EE data base*

When designated group members status is collected with the employee's

TABLE 5-11

EXAMPLE OF FLOW DATA FOR RACIAL MINORITY EMPLOYEES

| Occupations | Beginning | Hired from outside (+) | Promoted in (+) | Promoted out (-) | Quits (-) | Terminations (-) | Retirement or death (-) | End |
|---|---|---|---|---|---|---|---|---|
| Entry-level | 50 | 20 | 0 | 24 | 1 | 0 | 0 | 45 |
| Skilled | 10 | 3 | 7 | 2 | 8 | 0 | 0 | 10 |
| Professional | 40 | 11 | 17 | 1 | 2 | 0 | 5 | 60 |
| Supervisory | 5 | 1 | 2 | 0 | 4 | 1 | 1 | 2 |
| Management | 1 | 0 | 1 | 0 | 0 | 0 | 1 | 1 |
| TOTAL | 106 | 35 | 27 | 27 | 15 | 1 | 7 | 118 |

name or identification number, it is necessary to establish a data base which

- ensures confidentiality, and
- allows the information to be combined with transactions such as promotions, transfers, demotions and terminations.

The latter is necessary so that the information as shown in Table 5-11 can be generated each year. This will enable an analysis of progress, or what is referred to as flow data. The importance of flow data was demonstrated above.

### Isn't data collection like human resource planning?

There is certainly a relationship. Human resource planning is concerned with ensuring that an organization has the right number of people with the right skills at the right places at the right time, doing what results in both the organization and the individual receiving maximum long-term benefits. So it is broader and more comprehensive than the data collection needed for work-force analysis. Some organizations which want and need more sophisticated human resource systems, become involved in human resource planning rather than just focusing on EE data collection. Obviously, an organization's human resource planning system must be able to provide the necessary data for EE analyses.

## NOTES

1. Except by the City of Toronto contractors' program which is being phased out because the Ontario government is bringing in legislation.
2. Except in Ontario where draft regulations state:
   (1) Data must be kept up to date, and
   (2) A new survey must be done 9 years after the original.
3. R.S.C. 1985, c. 23 (2nd Supp.).
4. Bill 79, introduced for 2nd reading July 12, 1993.
5. *Constitution Act, 1982*, Pt. I of Schedule B, en. by the *Canada Act, 1982* (U.K.), 1982, c. 11.
6. Having representation of each designated group within the organization is a necessary but not sufficient condition for achieving the ultimate goal, however. It is possible to have an organizational workforce which mirrors the community but for designated group members to be concentrated into certain occupations rather than found throughout the organization. Occupational representation, the third analysis discussed, looks at this issue.
7. The figures for 1986 are:

| | |
|---|---|
| Canadian population | 25,300,000 |
| Working age population | 17,219,000 |
| Labour force | 12,746,000 |

# REFERENCES

Edward Harvey, *Information systems for Employment Equity: An Employer Guide*, CCH Canadian Ltd., 1988.

Edward Harvey, Eric J. Severn and John H. Blakely, *Computing for Equity: Computer Applications for Employment Equity*, CCH Canadian Ltd., 1990.

# CHAPTER 6

# Employment Systems Review

*What is an employment systems review?*

When one thinks of direct discrimination the primary barriers confronting disadvantaged groups is presumed to be the attitudes and behaviours of prejudiced people. However, EE is needed because of the operation of systemic discrimination. That is, barriers become embedded, unintentionally, in employment systems. The purpose of the employment systems review is to identify and remove the barriers from the systems while allowing the systems to continue to operate effectively without a discriminatory effect. Because systemic discrimination is subtle and unintentional, and because the employment systems are designed for a non-discriminatory purpose, it is often difficult to perceive systemic discrimination unless one is looking for it. The employment systems review is the mechanism used to look for systemic discrimination. The ultimate outcome of the systems review is that employment systems will work equally well for all kinds of employees – white, able-bodied men, Aboriginal Peoples, racial minorities, persons with disabilities and women. Another way to state this goal is that all employment systems will be free of barriers and will not have an adverse impact on any group.

Two examples of systemic discrimination, in educational assistance programs and through word-of-mouth recruiting, were given in Chapter 1. Other examples include:

- Job postings being available only to those in particular departments or within a particular functional area, rather than organization-wide postings which would help employees who are currently underemployed or interested in moving into an area of work which is non-traditional for them.
- Decisions as to who should attend training and development activities sometimes work against designated group members who are less likely to be perceived as wanting to move up and/or as less suited for higher level jobs.
- Using employment agencies which do not cultivate access to representative labour force.
- Work environments which have materials (*e.g.*, pin-ups) which are likely to be offensive to some employees.
- Supervisors and managers who do not understand their responsibility for accommodating employees, or who do not want to accommodate employees because "it is a bother".

- Rotating middle managers through different geographic locations could be a barrier for some designated group members. There may be particular issues for racial minority employees whose community is found in major urban areas, not in small towns where they will be a highly visible minority. Some accommodations for persons with disabilities may have to be duplicated. This may cost little in time or money, but where buildings in outlying areas require retro-fitting it could be expensive. Moving employees – both female and male – with employed spouses can be problematic.

### What is the purpose of employment systems review?

Identification and elimination of all existing discriminatory practices, both formal and informal. The systems review provides input for qualitative goals and the designing of special measures. Such a review often leads to the realization of the need for EE and/or a valuing of diversity policy.

### Which policies should be reviewed?

All employment systems and various communication systems. That is, what images are being communicated about the organization through annual reports, sales promotions, company videos and other communication vehicles. It is important to portray the diversity which exists, or is desired, within the organization. Communication related to human resources (*e.g.*, recruitment) is expected to be (and should be) sensitive to EE principles. But when other communications are similarly sensitive they are very powerful. The goal is to have communication which is inclusive (showing racial minority as well as white employees) but which avoids stereotypes.

Another area to review is the work environment – both physical and psychological. In what way is the environment welcoming or threatening to those who are different than the mainstream employees? What kind of climate is there for reciprocal banter or for put-down jokes against certain groups (but not others)? How are people who require accommodation treated – with respect and understanding or with resentment? What happens between employees which includes everyone and what happens which is exclusive?

The employment systems to be reviewed include:

- Accommodation
- Recruitment and selection
- Orientation and integration
- Training and development
- Compensation and benefits
- Performance management and appraisal
- Succession planning and career development

- Promotions and transfers
- Mobility between occupations
- Discipline
- Health and safety
- Terms and conditions of employment (including employment status, hours of work, and working conditions, etc.)
- Termination, lay-off and recall
- Retirement
- Workplace accessibility

Both formal and informal employment systems require review. Begin with the formal, written policies. But since these policies are seldom followed exactly as written, the informal practices are critical. What actually happens within the organization is more important in terms of identifying barriers. Informal systems are more difficult to review for a number of reasons:

1. They are not written down, so there is no place one can go to ensure one has considered all the policies.
2. It is often hard to get a handle on all informal policies because (a) they are often seen as the "only way things can be done" rather than a policy or practice which can be reviewed, and (b) one must go through a full annual cycle in order to become aware of many of them (*e.g.*, how summer jobs are given out).
3. While there may be a single set of written policies for the organization, it is typical that, except in very small organizations, the informal applications of policies will differ throughout the organization. Different departments or work units are likely to behave differently; even within the same unit a particular supervisor may put her or his unique stamp on the way the system works. Further, employment systems for jobs at different levels are typically treated differently.
4. Some informal policies may not be a barrier at present but may become a barrier in the future. Employment equity success changes the situation and may result in some practices becoming barriers. For instance, until there are women in technical jobs, barriers presented by some safety equipment may not be realized.

Because of the inability to identify more subtle barriers until the more obvious ones have been dealt with, because of the inability to deal with all systems at once, and because of the periodic nature of some activities, systems review is not something done only once. Rather, systems review is an on-going process. Even the review of formal policies is likely to be required more than once (over a number of years). Review of informal policies is likely to go on longer.

It is impossible to review all formal and informal systems at the same time. Priorities can be set using the following guidelines:

- *Entry-level positions*: Even if the organization is not hiring now, it is useful to identify the "ports" of entry into the organization. There are generally more than one key entry jobs within organizations based on job function (clerical versus shop floor) and organizational level (entry-level unskilled versus entry-level professional). Ports of entry jobs where future hiring is likely and where there is an under-representation of one or more of the designated groups are a good place to begin reviewing employment systems related to recruitment and hiring.
- *Mobility channels*: What are the typical paths of progression or movement through the organization. Identifying the mobility channels which are likely to be affecting one or more designated groups in the future is a good place to begin the systems review related to promotions.
- *Revolving doors*: Are members of one or more of the designated groups leaving the organization in disproportionate numbers? If so, the terms and conditions of employment, the work environment, the support of co-workers or supervisors and other systems affecting retention need to be examined.
- *Identification of barriers by organizational members*: Input from human resource staff, supervisors and employees can help identify barriers. Input may be sought formally or individuals may mention (often casually) a barrier they perceive to be operating. Formal input can be obtained through an attitude survey or through focus groups with various designated and non-designated group members.

The purpose of a systems review is change. Change takes time. Change typically takes longer than one expects. For that reason a systems review of the organization's recruiting sources should be done long before it is expected that any recruitment will be done. It is common for a systems review to reveal that the systems not only contain barriers but also are inadequately fulfilling their intended purposes. Rather than redesigning the system to remove barriers, it needs to be totally reworked to ensure that the system works for the organization. This reworking of systems is one of the important and useful side benefits of the EE systems review. But it can add considerable time to the process.

### What are the criteria for reviewing employment systems?

When assessing employment systems the basic issue is:

> Does this policy or practice promote or hinder equality?

To answer this certain criteria can be used to ascertain if the policies and procedures are consistent with EE. These criteria are:[1]

- *Legality*: Does the policy or practice conform to relevant work-force equity legislation, including human rights, labour standards, pay equity, the *Charter of Rights and Freedoms*?
- *Consistency*: Is the policy or practice applied in the same way for everyone – except where the specific needs of designated group members are met through accommodation?
- *Job-related*: Is the policy or practice (*e.g.*, job qualifications, tests, work schedule, manner of performing the job) directly linked to the effective performance of the essential job requirements?
- *Validity*: Is the policy or practice (*e.g.*, employment test, employee survey) objective and predictive – does it measure what it sets out to measure?
- *Adverse impact*: Does the policy or practice have a greater negative impact on designated group members (which is not job-related)?
- *Business necessity*: Is the policy or practice essential to the safe and efficient operation of the organization – have all realistic alternatives to the practice causing adverse impact been explored – will the removal or modification of the policy or practice impose hardship on the organization?
- *Non-discriminatory language*: Is the policy or procedure documented in non-sexist language that is inclusive rather than limiting, and in language that does not promote racial, ethnic or other stereotypes?

The job-related and business necessity criteria require some additional comment. Because systems have been operating in a certain manner there may be a presumption that they are job-related and/or done this way because of business necessity. Even if the system was originally designed to be consistent with these criteria it cannot be assumed that it has remained so. Tradition is a powerful force and employment systems often continue regardless of changes which should result in redesigning the systems. Job-relatedness and business necessity must be examined, they cannot be assumed.

### Who should be involved in the systems review?

The potential people to involve in reviewing employment systems, in addition to human resources staff, include:[2]

- Senior staff with overall responsibility for the systems.
- Supervisors responsible for implementing the systems.
- People affected by the system, both members of designated groups and those who are not.

- Community input (particularly for public sector organizations).

When considering who to involve, remember that people who have designed, benefited from, or progressed through the system should not be the only critics of that system. In particular, the role of human resources in the review should be related to their ability to be open to suggestion about their systems and their willingness to make changes. Ironically, human resource staff are often disadvantaged in the review process because of their understanding of how the systems are supposed to work. What is needed is a critical assessment of how the systems are actually working. Input from outside the organization (*e.g.*, consultants, community representatives) or from within (*e.g.*, new employees) can provide a different perspective and a questioning of how things have traditionally been done. Exchanging information with EE people in other organizations allows each organization to gain from the other's discovery of systemic discrimination. Data from work-force analysis can be informative. Flow data can be helpful in identifying where in the selection process designated group members are "falling out" of the system (*e.g.*, they do not know about job openings, their applications are not considered, individuals do not pass the selection criteria, or are offered jobs but do not accept them).

The role of unions in systems review (*e.g.*, contract provisions) is critical. Most terms and conditions of employment and employment systems are jointly negotiated between management and unions. These systems need to be jointly reviewed. The selection of employees into the port-of-entry job(s) within each union is typically a management prerogative, except in the case of hiring halls where it is done by the union. Whoever has responsibility for hiring has the responsibility for reviewing the recruiting and selection systems – though input from the other party could prove helpful.

### How is an employment systems review done?

It is impossible to do a system review treating the four designated groups as a single unit. Rather, it is critical to remember that each group faces different barriers (see Chapter 3). As noted in the previous section, it is important to have the systems reviewed from different perspectives to increase the likelihood that systemic discrimination will be detected. To review the formal policies an organization could assign a committee or task force. If there are a large number of policies more than one committee can be assigned – each committee can review a subset of the policies. The role of the task force could be either:

1. Identification of barriers;

2. Identification of barriers and development of potential solutions to remove the barriers. If these two steps are performed by the same task force they could be done at different times.

A committee of six to eight people with diverse membership is appropriate. In organizations with a human resource function, a member of that department should be on the task force or serve as a resource. In small organizations (up to about 50 people) a review of the formal systems can probably be completed in two to three months. In medium sized organizations (50 to 400 people) three to eight months is usually required while in large organizations six months to a year will be needed. The length of time depends on the members of the task force(s) being able to schedule meetings.

Some organizations have utilized the services of outside EE consultants to bring a new perspective. However, there is no substitute for the involvement of in-house managers and employees in the process. They possess the knowledge of how the systems actually operate, and their involvement is critical in making the changes required and in providing on-going feedback.

Repeating what has been said so far about the review of formal policies:

- Set priorities if all policies will not be reviewed at once;
- Establish one or more committees to review policies.

A series of questions is needed for the committee to use in reviewing the various policies. An excellent set of questions for systems review is provided in *Employment Equity Systems Review Guide*[3] which is published by the Employment Equity section of Employment and Immigration Canada. There are sections on recruitment, selection, training and development, upward mobility, job evaluation, compensation, benefits, conditions of employment, lay-off, recall, disciplinary action and termination. The section on training and development is reprinted in Box 6-1.

Review of informal policies and practices:

- Make informal policies and practices explicit;
- Sensitize human resource staff, supervisors, and managers and other employees about systemic discrimination;
- Encourage people to share concerns about systemic discrimination with those responsible for EE;
- Periodically use focus groups, employee attitude surveys and/or seek input from designated group networks as to systemic barriers.

## Box 6-1

### Focus on Training and Development

**Purpose of training and development:**

To improve an employee's performance in his/her current job and to enable the employee to acquire the necessary skills and knowledge for future opportunities.

An organization's training and development program may range from on-the-job training to educational leave with all tuition fees paid. While many organizations offer training and development opportunities, all employees may not have access to such opportunities.

For example:

- designated group members may not be able to avail themselves of training opportunities if information concerning available training, including eligibility criteria, is not disseminated company-wide;

- designated group members may be subtly encouraged to stay in lower level jobs because they are only provided with training to perform their current jobs better, rather than with developmental training to enhance their advancement opportunities;

- consideration of variables such as salary levels and occupational status, particularly if training and development are restricted to employees at the more senior levels, could have an adverse impact on designated group members who tend to be under-represented in the upper ranks of many organizations;
- training centres that are not equipped with ramps and accessible washroom facilities preclude the participation of some disabled employees.

The review of your organization's training and development system should assist you in assessing the extent to which employees have access to training opportunities. For employers who are committed to employment equity and to meeting the challenge of managing a diversified workforce, effective training and development initiatives are critically important in ensuring that present and future corporate skills needs are met.

## Box 6-1 (Cont'd)

**Reviewing your training and development system**

Determine:

- the purpose, policies and practices governing your organization's training and development system;

- whether the policies are applied consistently throughout the organization;

- the types of training and development opportunities which your organization offers;

- how employees are selected for training and development opportunities; for example, by:

  | | |
  |---|---|
  | Supervisor | ____ |
  | Employee request | ____ |
  | Seniority | ____ |
  | Performance appraisal results | ____ |
  | Career counselling results | ____ |

- whether training is available to all employees regardless of salary level or occupational group;

- the participation rate of designated group members in the training programs that are offered, through the compilation and analysis of data;

- whether the practices and related systemic issues which have been described in the following sample exercise module are evident in your training and development system.

Implement:

- the suggested remedies and alternatives you deem appropriate or develop alternatives that best meet your organization's needs.

## Box 6-1 (Cont'd)

| Systemic Issues | Suggested Remedies/ Alternatives |
|---|---|
| **Information, dissemination and selection criteria** | |
| If your organization lacks an up-to-date and comprehensive equity-based training and development policy: | • develop and publicize a policy;<br><br>• ensure company-wide distribution, and include training and deve-lopment in orientation materials;<br><br>• ensure that wording and graphics of training ads/brochures include designated groups; consider using lan- |
| If authorization for employees to attend training and obtain developmental opportunities is solely at the discretion of managers: | • encourage managers to recognize the developmental value and organizational benefit of training that is not necessarily related to employees' current jobs. |
| If eligibility for training and development is based on seniority, job level, earnings, next-in-line status, permanent and full-time status or is linked to current job: | • consider eliminating all such requirements as they perpetuate systemic discrimination; sensitize managers to view designated groups as resources to be developed; make managers accountable for maintaining a non-discriminatory eligibility system;<br><br>• survey employees to determine who seeks and who actually gets training; track this information by designated group status. |

## Box 6-1 (Cont'd)

| Career counselling services | |
|---|---|
| If career counselling is not available, or is available but is not publicized or is restricted to employees at middle and senior management levels: | • assist all employees to identify skills, career goals and in-house advancement opportunities;<br><br>• consider a career counselling program to provide advice and assistance to employees at all levels of the organization. |
| If career counselling does not include specific remedial and special support measures for designated group employees: | • provide counsellors with up-to-date career path guidance and organizational development information; include designated group members among counselling and training staff; provide counsellors with skills needed to deal with designated group issues. |
| If application, enrolment, or training program completion rates are low among designated group employees: | • ensure that information on training programs and how to apply for them is disseminated to all employees;<br><br>• invite input from designated group employees to identify and resolve any problems identified, i.e., interview trainee dropouts on a voluntary basis, to determine reasons for termination;<br><br>• review training materials for racial and gender biases and eliminate any found;<br><br>• ensure that trainers reflect equity principles and that they encourage participants to do so as well. |

## Box 6-1 (Cont'd)

| Specialized training | |
|---|---|
| If supervisors are not trained to develop and maintain a climate of equity and understanding and to manage a multicultural/multiracial workforce: | • provide awareness sessions for managers on such topics as managing in an employment equity environment, communications and race relations; interview techniques for decision-makers, and human rights in the workplace. |
| If designated group employees need remedial training: | • provide training programs on such topics as interview skills for candidates, career planning, management/ leadership skills, workplace English (or French) as a second language, as appropriate;<br><br>• reimburse and reward employees who complete such training programs at university or community college. |

### Training and development system checklist
If you are unable to answer yes to the following questions, you are encouraged to develop appropriate solutions to remedy the situation.

| | | Yes | No |
|---|---|---|---|
| 1. | Does your organization have a training and development policy based on employment equity principles? | | |
| 2. | Are **all** employees aware of the organization's training and development opportunities? | | |
| 3. | Do **all** employees have access to training and development opportunities? | | |
| 4. | Have you ensured that there are no restrictions to training opportunities based on occupational levels and earnings? | | |
| 5. | Are training centres accessible to disabled persons? | | |
| 6. | Do employees have access to in-house or company-paid career counselling? | | |

## How are systems corrected?

Each organization is unique and, therefore, their employment systems must reflect this uniqueness. Even organizations which find similar barriers will remove them differently. It is impossible to delineate all the possible ways this can be done. It is important to keep in mind that there is usually more than one way to change a system in keeping with EE principles. Creativity, an understanding of the organization's mission and of EE principles are all important in identifying the best solution.

For example, corporate culture that schedules many dinner meetings may find that this adversely impacts on the parents of young children. Since women more than men still have primary responsibility for child care, this could be systemically discriminatory against women. Assuming that attendance at such meetings is critical, a couple of options to remove this barrier are:

- Decreasing dinner meetings to a reasonable number. ("Reasonable" would depend on what other evening obligations are expected of these employees.)
- Re-scheduling the meetings as lunch meetings.
- Providing and/or paying for child care during dinner meetings.

## What is the outcome of systems review?

The outcome of the review of the formal employment systems will be changes to the written policies *and* an integration of these into the actual practices of the organization. All the changes will not happen at one time. Some policies are easier to change than others. Some policies will be more critical to making EE progress. Linking the work-force analysis with results of the systems review will be a useful way of helping to set the priorities. Vigilance as to how systems actually operate will be required for a long time to ensure the removal of all systemic barriers. Maintaining vigilance so that things do not slip back to the old way of doing things is also required. The results of the systems review – both formal and informal – are an input into the development of goals and EE measures (discussed in the next chapter).

It is important to communicate the results of the systems review to employees.

To keep systems free of barriers, the review should be kept up to date. That is, policies and practices should be reviewed periodically. This is necessary because the understanding of how systemic discrimination operates is evolving.

# NOTES

1. Adapted from material provided by Employment and Immigration Canada, *Employment Equity: A Guide for Employers*, 1989, p. 24 and Ontario Human Resources Secretariat, Workforce Planning and Employment Equity Branch, "Employment Systems Review: Technical Assistance Package" (Draft), 1991, pp. 2-3.
2. From a talk given by Susan Lewis, then Manager, Employment Equity, Metropolitan Toronto Police Force, June 2, 1992 TEEPA workshop.
3. Employment and Immigration Canada, *Employment Equity Systems Review Guide*, 1991, Cat. No. MP 43-232/1991, pp. 19-22. Reproduced with the permission of Employment and Immigration Canada and Supply & Services Canada, 1993.

# CHAPTER 7

# Implementation

## MODEL OF EMPLOYMENT EQUITY PROCESS

This chapter focuses on implementation issues – the setting of goals and the implementation of initiatives to achieve them. Before getting into the process of setting goals and timetables and implementing specific programs it is useful to take a moment to summarize the EE process. To help in this, the model of the EE process, shown in Figure 7-1, is used.

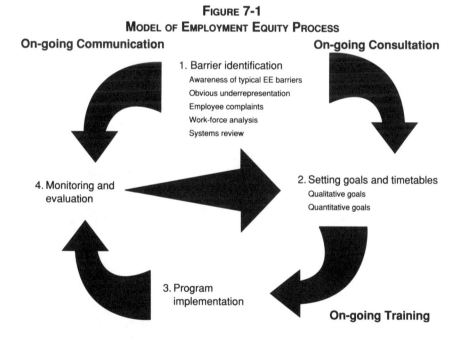

FIGURE 7-1
MODEL OF EMPLOYMENT EQUITY PROCESS

On-going Communication                    On-going Consultation

1. Barrier identification
   Awareness of typical EE barriers
   Obvious underrepresentation
   Employee complaints
   Work-force analysis
   Systems review

4. Monitoring and evaluation

2. Setting goals and timetables
   Qualitative goals
   Quantitative goals

3. Program implementation

On-going Training

This model assumes that commitment and accountability have already taken place. On-going communication, on-going training and on-going consultation are needed throughout the EE process, not just at the start. This model covers barrier identification including data collection and systems analysis, goal setting and implementation, and monitoring and evaluation.

Figures 7-2 to 7-5 show each step in the model separately. As Figure 7-2 shows the process begins with barrier identification. Barriers can be identified in the following ways:

- Awareness of typical EE barriers (for example, this chapter and chapters 8 to 10 highlight EE issues found in many organizations.
- Barriers can be raised by employees.
- Obvious underrepresentation as shown by work-force analysis, can indicate that barriers are operating. (Under-representation is often obvious because there are no women technicians, no Aboriginal employees at all, few racial minorities above the level of supervisor or few persons with disabilities in the organization. A formal work-force analysis is often not required to begin EE.)
- System analysis highlights barriers.

The barriers to be overcome are input for the goal-setting process (discussed in detail in this chapter).

There are two kinds of EE goals which need to be set. Numerical (or quantitative) goals typically based on work-force analysis (formal or obvious) and qualitative goals based on the awareness of typical EE barriers, employee complaints and systems review. An example of qualitative good is development of a anti-harassment policy and training of all staff.

### FIGURE 7-2
### EMPLOYMENT EQUITY PROCESS, BEGINNING WITH DATA COLLECTION AS INPUT TO SETTING OF GOALS AND TIMETABLES

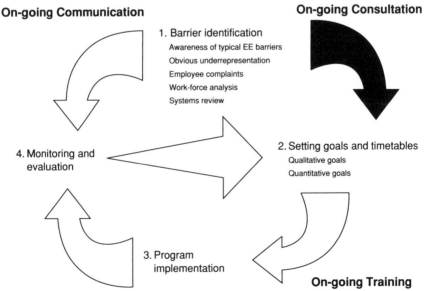

The achievement of both kinds of goals require EE initiatives designed to change how things are currently being done within the organization. Once these initiatives have been articulated they must be implemented, as shown in Figure 7-3.

Employment equity initiatives must be monitored and evaluated to ensure that they are fulfilling the goals, as shown in Figure 7-4. The monitoring and evaluation of programs is discussed in Chapter 11.

The steps shown so far have assumed that an organization is going through the EE process for the first time – collecting data for the first time, setting the first set of goals, implementing the first programs. However, the EE process is a long-term process continuing until EE is achieved so information from some steps in this model provides feedback to other steps. This is illustrated in Figure 7-5. Evaluation of the initial programs, transaction data, plus awareness of barriers in employment policies and practices not noticed in the initial systems review all become input for the second set of qualitative and quantitative goals which are set. These revised and new goals are implemented (as shown in Figure 7-3), then evaluated along with new data (as seen in Figure 7-5) leading to the goals for the next round. This continues until EE is achieved.

The focus of this chapter is on goal setting and program initiatives (steps 2 and 3 in the EE process model).

## FIGURE 7-3
### NUMERICAL AND QUALITATIVE GOALS ARE INPUT IN PROGRAM IMPLEMENTATION

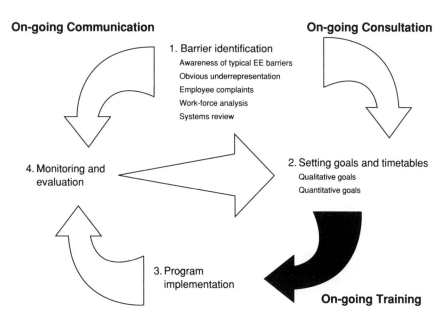

On-going Communication  On-going Consultation

1. Barrier identification
   Awareness of typical EE barriers
   Obvious underrepresentation
   Employee complaints
   Work-force analysis
   Systems review

4. Monitoring and evaluation

2. Setting goals and timetables
   Qualitative goals
   Quantitative goals

3. Program implementation

On-going Training

160

**FIGURE 7-4**
**MONITORING AND EVALUATION OF INITATIVES**

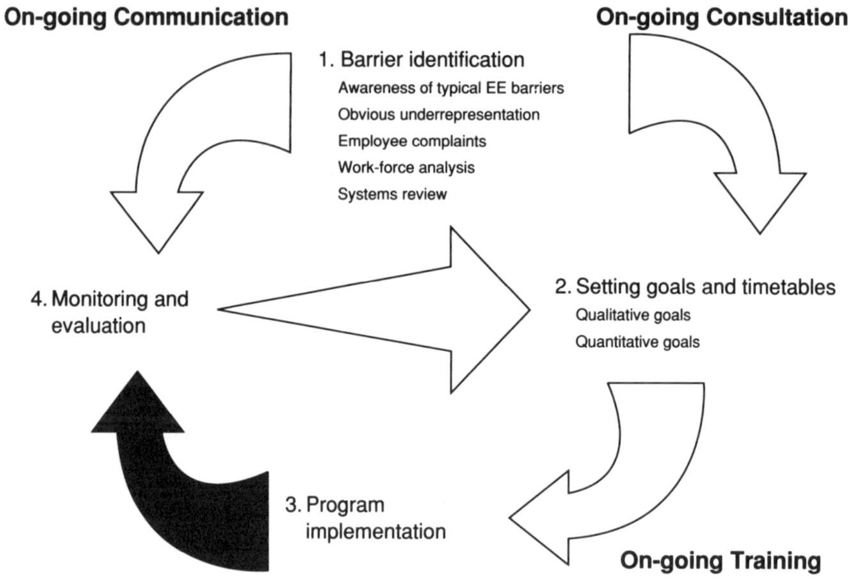

**FIGURE 7-5**
**ON-GOING PROCESS OF ASSESSMENT, GOAL SETTING AND IMPLEMENTATION**

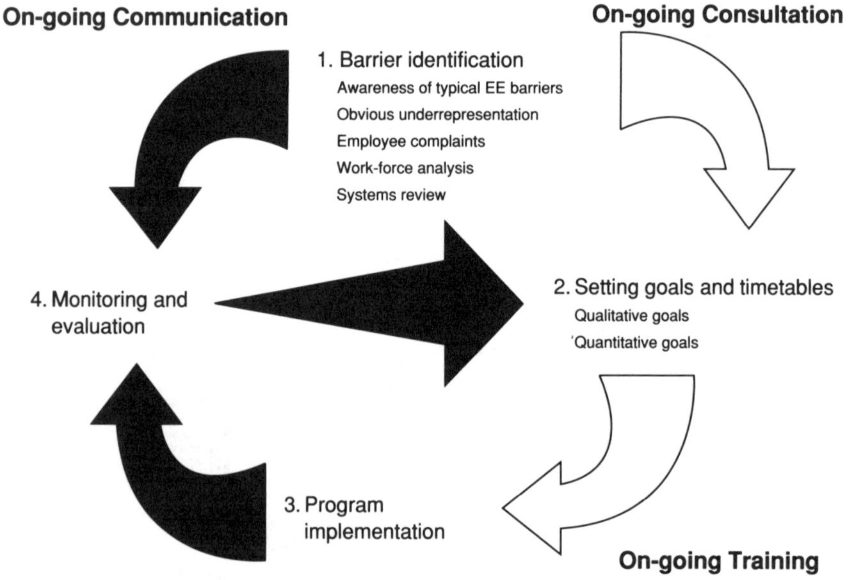

# SETTING GOALS AND TIMETABLES CONSISTENT WITH THE ORGANIZATION'S NEEDS

Before getting into the heart of goal setting, some terms need to be defined.

## *Terminology.*

The word "goals" can be used in a number of ways. For example, the ultimate goal of EE is a representative work-force and employment systems which work equally well for everyone. Goals can also refer to the specific steps needed to achieve this ultimate goal. While some talk about the former as the "goal" and the latter as an "interim goal" or "objective" in the remainder of this chapter the following terms will be used:

**Target:** The ultimate desired outcome. Representation of First Nation peoples, persons with disabilities, racial minorities and women at all levels in the organization in proportion to their representation in the relevant labour market, and employment systems which work well for all. For instance, an organization in Toronto will have a different target for its representation of employees who are racial minorities than will an organization in Thompson, Manitoba.

**Objectives:** Specific action-oriented procedures to achieve the target. These would be set annually. For example, to help fulfil the target of representation of persons with disabilities, the objective of developing functional physical demands analysis for all entry-level jobs could be set.

**Timetable:** The period of time set for the achievement of the targets and for specific objectives. For example, given the current representation of persons with disabilities in the organization's work-force and in the available labour force it might be decided that it will take four years to achieve representation. The length of time for completion of physical demands analysis for key entry-level jobs could be six months.

**Program implementation:** Carrying out the actual programs or initiatives set out in the annual objectives to bring about the target. To fulfil an objective of a harassment-free work environment could involve a program incorporating:

- Development of anti-harassment policy;
- Anti-harassment training;
- Identification and training of those who would investigate allegations of harassment;

• Employee attitude survey of the work environment.

The timetable could be set to implement the first three parts of the program in the first year while the attitude surveys would be conducted in the second year.

Goals, as used earlier in this chapter, and typically used in EE (*e.g.*, setting goals and timetables) sometimes refers to targets, to objectives, or to both.

Targets are fairly stable. For example, targets related to numerical objectives will only change when new availability data is released. Availability data is usually based on the census which is conducted every five years. Objectives change year to year. Objectives are set, monitored and revised each year (or more often) in order to ensure that they are helping achieve the target. Objectives must be revised because they are actualized or because of the realization that another avenue must be taken to move closer to the target. Once the target is achieved then no additional objectives or implementation efforts are needed (except to maintain the target). Hopefully the organization is working "naturally" to maintain representation and EE principles have become embedded in the organizational culture.

### How does an organization set objectives and timetables?

Setting objectives and timetables for EE is the same as setting objectives for any other business activity. Three pieces of information are needed:

1. The organization's current situation.
2. The target of where the organization wants to be.
3. Organizational circumstances in the short-run and the long-run.

These are shown in the model in Figure 7-6.

Objectives provide a map of how to get from the present situation to the target, taking into consideration organizational circumstances.

The organization's present situation is assessed using formal or informal means of identifying barriers. Informal means include knowledge of staffing patterns for jobs. For example, a visual scan of a senior managers' meeting within most organizations indicates the lack of representational designated group members. Often there are no racial minorities in the sales force, no women on the shop floor and no one of Aboriginal ancestry anywhere in the company indicating barriers. Such an informal assessment can be reinforced by a formal work-force analysis. However, in most organizations a work-force analysis is not essential to identify that the organization's work-force lacks representation. Of course, the work-force analysis enables the comparison of the actual organizational

FIGURE 7-6

BASIC GOAL-SETTING MODEL

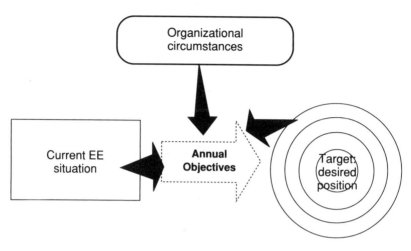

work-force statistics with the availability data. Such a comparison is essential to indicate when the organization has achieved representation. However, as noted in Chapter 5 on Data Collection, those who will be covered by Ontario legislation may want to wait until the regulations are available before beginning their work-force analysis because the regulations are likely to have specific requirements related to reporting. However, as noted, a formal work-force analysis is not required for most organizations to begin implementation of some EE initiatives.

Barriers can also be identified by educating human resource and supervisory personnel about EE and systemic discrimination. This will provide sensitization for the identification of barriers. They can then bring barriers they become aware of to the proper person. An organization can also survey its employees about potential barriers. A formal systems review is yet another way to identify barriers.

Figure 7-7 shows how to identify the current situation. This information provides both a sense of the organization's current representation of designated group members and some of the barriers in employment policies and practices.

A second piece of information needed before objectives and timetables can be developed is an assessment of the organizational circumstances and factors, in addition to EE, which are pressuring for change. Figure 7-8 shows four factors which should be taken into consideration in terms of their short- and long-term impact on the objectives and targets being set.

**FIGURE 7-7**

**COMPONENTS OF GOAL-SETTING MODEL**
**DETERMINANTS OF CURRENT SITUATION**

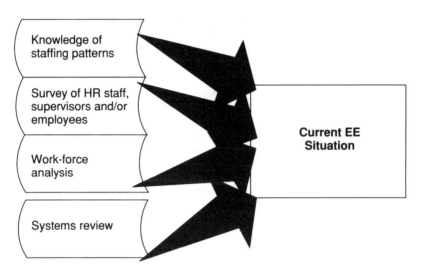

**FIGURE 7-8**

**COMPONENTS OF GOAL-SETTING MODEL**
**DETERMINANTS OF ORGANIZATIONAL CIRCUMSTANCES**

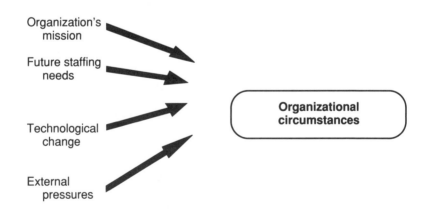

The organization's mission should be made explicit and clear. Is it likely to change? What is the expected change in staffing needs in terms of the numbers of employees and the skill mix? What is the likely growth in the various sub-units? Even in organizations which are declining or remaining stable overall some units may grow. What kind of technological change is likely in the short- and long-run and how will this impact on the mix of skills which will be needed within the work-force? Will employees be required to keep up with new developments in existing technology? Will a totally new technology be introduced? If so, how much cross-over will there be from the skills current employees possess? Remember, technological changes may involve equipment or machinery, but may also involve a new style of management (self-managed teams) or a new process. Finally, what anticipated external pressures are likely to have an impact on the kinds and levels of skills required of employees in the long term? The answers to these questions will have an impact on the appropriate objectives and to some extent could affect the EE targets.

In addition to being influenced by organizational circumstances, the target, and thus the objectives, will be affected by the external availability data *and* the likely growth or decline in demand for employees in each job as shown in Figure 7-9. Anticipated growth or decline is used, recognizing that it is rare for this figure to be known with certainty. The

**FIGURE 7-9**

**COMPONENTS OF GOAL-SETTING MODEL**
**FACTORS AFFECTING TARGET**

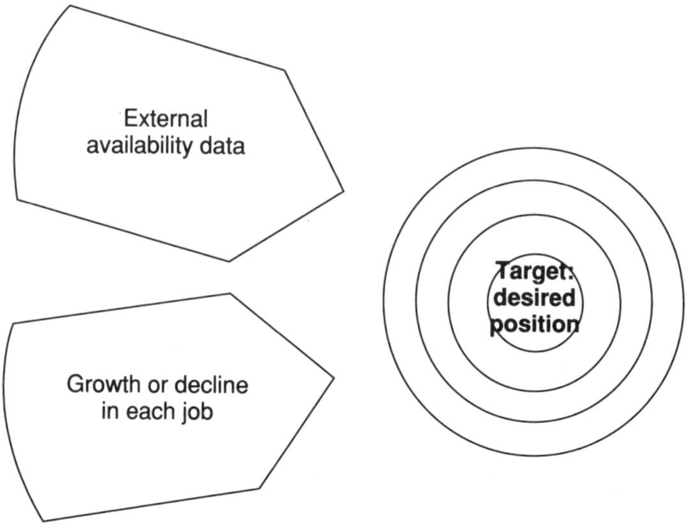

External availability data

Growth or decline in each job

Target desired position

external availability data provides information as to the representation of the designated group members in the labour force. In the draft regulations for the Ontario legislation a number of sources of availability data are to be taken into consideration in the setting of numerical goals. They include those available within the organization:

- Number of designated group members in the employer's work-force who are qualified or who the employer could train to be qualified.

And those available outside the organization:

- Working age population in the geographical area;
- Persons in the geographical area who are in the occupational group;
- Persons in the geographical area who have the necessary skills.
- Persons graduating from Ontario educational and training programs with the necessary skills.
- Other reliable data (*e.g.*, industry data).

(Except for the last, this data will be available from the Ontario Employment Equity Commission.) While each of the data sources must be considered, it is recognized that different data will have different relevance to various organizations. In the EE plan it must be explained how the availability data was used to arrive at the numerical goals. The complete goal-setting model is shown in Figure 7-10.

The target indicates where the organization ultimately wants to be. Objectives are typically set on an annual basis. A number of objectives will be set each year. These will be monitored during the year and at the end of the year. New annual objectives will be set based on how effective the organization was in moving towards reaching its target. The Ontario regulation stipulates a three-year EE plan but annual goals should still be set.

An example of how this model works for the fictitious company, Sales Unlimited, will help illustrate the working of the model. Assume this organization currently employs no First Nations people (current work-force picture). There is a reserve close by, so 5 per cent of the local labour market for entry positions at Sales Unlimited is comprised of First Nations people (external availability data). There will be no change in the kinds of skills nor in the number of employees Sales Unlimited will need in the short-run, though in the long-run it is expected to require greater computer skills in entry-level jobs (future staffing needs). About 15 entry-level positions are likely to become vacant over the next year in various areas of the company.

Based on this information some objectives need to be set which will move Sales Unlimited from its present situation of no First Nations em-

FIGURE 7-10

COMPLETE GOAL-SETTING MODEL

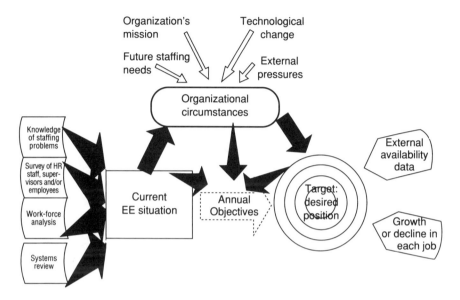

ployees to its desired target work-force which will include approximately 5 per cent First Nations peoples throughout the organization.

The Ontario draft regulations specify the way to express numerical goals. The goal is to be expressed as the proportion of the opportunities for entry (through hiring, transfer or promotion) into the occupational group which will be filled by designated group members. The goal set is to constitute reasonable progress toward achieving representation. So, in this example, to move from zero to 5 per cent representation of Aboriginal Peoples, Sales Unlimited could set a goal of hiring Native persons into a third to a half of the 15 new entry-level hires (five to eight people). While annual goals should be set, the EE plan in Ontario runs for three years. So exactly where to set this goal would depend on the expected hiring in the next two years, representation of the other designated groups and the qualitative measures being put into place.

How to achieve this goal will depend on an analysis of why there are no First Nations peoples currently working for the organization (determined in part from systems review). Geographic location cannot be the reason since the reserve has been located near Sales Unlimited since the company was founded. Some additional information is needed to determine how best to get from the current situation to the target. For example, the discrepancy between the present situation and the target could be due to:

- People on the reserve not knowing about openings at Sales Unlimited.
- People from the reserve applying for jobs, but their applications are not being considered.
- Applications being considered, but individuals not passing the selection criteria.
- First Nations peoples being offered jobs, but not accepting them.
- Persons of First Nations ancestry being hired, but not staying.

Assume that the data collection and analysis shows that few First Nations peoples apply. There is now enough information to set some objective for next year in order to change this situation. Some of the initiatives which might be implemented are:

- Make contact with the reserve community.
- Publish job openings in the reserve newspaper/newsletter or post notices in public buildings.
- Target Native high school students for internship programs.
- Identify sources for communicating with First Nations peoples who are living off the reserve (*e.g.*, Indian Friendship Centres).
- Hold an open house at the company for the First Nations community to introduce them to the kinds of work available and the physical surroundings of Sales Unlimited.
- Educate human resources personnel and line managers, who make hiring decisions, about First Nations culture and some of the likely differences between First Nations and mainstream cultures which may be exhibited by applicants during the selection process.

Not all of these initiatives would be implemented during a single 12-month period. But two to four of them could be incorporated as part of the means of achieving the annual EE objectives (along with objectives for the other three designated groups). Others might be implemented the next year, or the following, and so on. Other initiatives will become obvious depending on the success and failure of the first ones.

### What characteristics should objectives have?

Objectives should be attainable, realistic and measurable. Objectives should be expected to have a significant impact on achieving the targets.

Objectives (and goals) are not quotas. A quota is always numerical and fixed. For example, it is a quota if every fourth person hired must be a person with a disability. If three able-bodied people are hired then, with a quota, no additional hires can be made until a person who has a disability is found to do the job. Quotas often become ceilings: no more than a fourth of the new hires would be persons with a disability. Alternatively, an objective might be: 50 per cent of new hires will be people of colour. If anywhere between 45 per cent to 55 per cent of the positions were filled with people of colour then the organization is meeting its objective (and subsequent target) as desired.

Unlike quotas, objectives can also be non-numerical in nature such as:

- Ensure the fire alarm system is designed to work for deaf employees and customers.
- Review and revise the orientation program so that it demonstrates organizational commitment to valuing of diversity.
- Conduct an attitude survey to assess employees' needs in the area of balancing work and family concerns.

Non-numerical objectives provide the support necessary to ultimately achieve the fair representation of designated group members which is the target of EE.

## How does the organization begin setting objectives?

First, because the barriers faced by each designated group differs and because their representation and distribution within the organization is likely to differ, it is necessary to consider objectives separately for each designated group. Some basic questions which are likely to be useful to most organizations include:

- What can be done to increase the supply of persons from a designated group into occupations where they are currently underrepresented?
- What are entry-level jobs within the organization? Remember there is almost never a single entry-level job within an organization. Rather, there are different ports of entry for unskilled, skilled, professional and managerial jobs and for blue and white collar jobs. What are the mobility channels through the organization from each entry-level job? Do these mobility channels serve the organization well or are they followed simply because of tradition?
- Where does the organization experience high turnover (which kinds of jobs, which departments, which locations) – why?
- What has been learned about barriers within the organization?

## What if an organization does not achieve its objectives?

Anyone who has ever set objectives knows that some are achieved, some are missed for good reasons, some are missed for lack of commitment and some become irrelevant. Thus, when EE objectives have not been achieved it is important to determine:

- Why were the goals not achieved?
- Was it for lack of trying (*e.g.*, insufficient resources, no accountability)?
- Was it because of a misdiagnosis of the problem and how it should be addressed?
- Was the goal partially achieved? What contributed to the partial success and to the partial failure?
- What was learned from the failure to achieve the goal?

The Ontario *Employment Equity Act*[1] states that the criteria to be used in assessing an organization's EE endeavour is "reasonable effort".

The objectives will need to be assessed annually, at a minimum, and often quarterly, and revised as needed. Do not wait until the end of the year to revise an objective which is not helping reach the targets. Revisions will be needed because of the achievement of some of the objectives, or the realization that an objective was not achieved because of a reason such as the following:

- Extenuating circumstances (*e.g.*, the organization had planned to hire 20 engineers and only five were needed).
- Failure to recognize and eliminate a barrier which blocked goal achievement.
- Lack of sufficient effort or resources applied to achievement of the goal.
- Unintended consequences (*e.g.*, all designated group members turned down the job offers).

Remember, mistakes will be made in moving from an organization's current circumstance to fulfilment of EE targets. What is important is that lessons are learned from the mistakes and that they are not repeated.

## IDENTIFYING POSSIBLE EMPLOYMENT EQUITY INITIATIVES

To summarize the previous section: objectives are based on unique organizational considerations, the present situation and the ultimate EE targets. Because every organization is different, its targets will be different, and the objectives it sets to achieve the targets will be unique. Therefore, it is impossible to identify exactly what all organizations will have to do to achieve EE. However, it can be said with some certainty that every organization is likely to have to become involved in some way in the following areas: accommodation and diversity (Chapter 8), outreach recruiting (Chapter 9), anti-harassment policy and training (Chapter 10) and balancing work and family (discussed later in this chapter). But the specific initiatives to meet the needs of each organization will vary. Box 7-1 outlines a number of potential EE initiatives – and this list is far from exhaustive. Creativity is important. Being open-minded is important. For example, one organization which had recently begun hiring designated group members saw that their efforts were likely to erode if they approached up-and-coming lay-offs in the traditional manner. They considered job-sharing among their most senior employees who wanted to ease into retirement. This initiative would:

- Maintain more of their newly-hired designated group members; and
- Maintain seniority; and
- Address some of the problems caused by the traditional, "cold-turkey", style of retirement.

In order to be creative in identifying EE initiatives it is important to avoid thinking in terms of being forced into EE by government intervention. This may lead to defensive reactions. Rather, first identify existing problems within the organization and then think of EE solutions to these problems. For instance, asking a group of managers what the organization can do to hire more women is likely to lead to resistance. Beginning with the problem of an insufficient supply of mechanics, and presenting the training of women to fill these jobs as part of the solution changes the focus of the issue.

### What initiatives are likely to be legally required?

Because EE initiatives must fit the unique needs of particular organizations it is unlikely that specific initiatives (*e.g.*, internships) will be legislated. It is possible, however, to talk about four different kinds of EE initiatives which are likely to be required:

1. Barrier elimination
2. Accommodation
3. Supportive measures
4. Positive measures

## Box 7-1

### SAMPLE OF SOME
### EMPLOYMENT EQUITY INITIATIVES

**General**
- Commitment to employment equity.
- Employment equity policy.
- Review of human resource policies and practices – both formal and informal.
- Data collection and analysis on composition of work-force.
- Negotiating employment equity into labour contracts.
- Communication strategy (jointly for unionized employees).
- Providing mechanism for managers, staff, union representatives, etc., to provide input on potential barriers.

**Recruitment**
*External*
- Contacts and development of on-going relationship with visible minority, disabled and Aboriginal communities.
- Advertising in other than English and mainstream papers (*i.e.*, ethnic papers) and locations.
- Outreach or providing non-traditional role models to speak to high schools, college and university students, career fairs, etc.
- Obtain data on representation in labour markets (rather than vague impressions).
- Stating a commitment to employment equity in advertising.

*Internal*
- Posting system which informs everyone of opportunities.
- Up-to-date skills inventories.
- Career counselling for all staff.
- Avoidance of informal practices (*e.g.*, "old boys" network) for filling of permanent jobs or casual, part-time or secondment which leads to permanent jobs.
- Designing bridging positions; using short-term leaves or summer opportunities for current employees to try non-traditional jobs.

**Hiring and promotion**
- Review of job descriptions to determine qualifications truly needed to do the job.
- Physical demands analysis for all jobs.
- Validate selection devices.
- Management training programs for women, visible minorities, Aboriginal Peoples and persons with disabilities.
- Train supervisors on bias-free interview techniques and ensure they are practised.

---

**Box 7-1 (cont'd)**

- Communication enhancement programs (*e.g.*, literacy, English as a second language, accent modification).

**Training and orientation**
- Review of how decisions are made as to who to send to training programs.
- Integrating employment equity into on-going supervisory and other training programs.
- Training employees on why employment equity is needed.
- Anti-racism training.

**Providing experience**
- Internship programs
- Bridging program
- Secondment

**Work climate and environment**
- Orientation for non-traditional employees.
- Policy for racial and sexual harassment-free environment.
- Training for managers and staff on racial and sexual harassment.
- Ensure dress codes are able to accommodate dress requirements of ethnic and religious practices.

**Interaction between work and other aspects of life**
- Facilitate persons with disabilities getting to your location and accessibility within and around work site.
- Work scheduling to facilitate caring for family members:
    Working at home
    Flexible work schedules
    Job-sharing
    Part-time work
    Parental leave

**Lay-offs and recall**
- Design seniority so that designated groups are not unduly affected by lay-offs.

---

## What are barrier elimination measures?

Barrier elimination is not unique to EE. It is required under human rights obligations such as in Ontario legislation which refers to systemic discrimination. Unlike human rights legislation, however, EE requires immediate action rather than waiting for a complaint. Barrier elimination is the purpose of the employment systems review. The systems are reviewed to identify potential barriers so that they can be removed. Employment equity also includes the positive obligation to search for barriers, to be ever vigilant and to respond quickly when barriers are identified.

Certain barriers are found in most organizations. Because of this there are initiatives which virtually all organizations will have to implement: outreach recruiting, examination of job requirements to ensure they are job-related and not excessive, development of an anti-harassment policy and accompanying training, and strategies to enable employees to balance work and family. Some barriers will be unique to particular organizations.

## *What are job accommodation measures?*

Job accommodation requires balancing the needs of the job with the abilities and needs of the people who perform them. Accommodation recognizes that there is typically more than one right way to accomplish a task. The duty to accommodate has been recognized by the Supreme Court of Canada as an obligation of all employers and of unions (*Central Alberta Dairy Pool v. Alberta (Human Rights Commission)*[2] and *Renaud v. Central Okanagan School District*[3] cases). Because of the importance of accommodation to EE and because all organizations must accommodate this, Chapter 8 covers accommodation in some detail.

Flexibility is the key to accommodation. Accommodation replaces the emphasis on consistency as the only way to be fair. The need for flexibility flows from the increasing diversity found in the labour force (in terms of gender, ethnicity, religion, disability status, sexual orientation, and other factors).

## *What are supportive measures?*

Supportive measures remove barriers which have a greater impact on designated group members, but removal of such barriers also improves the workplace for all employees. Examples include:

- Policies and practices which facilitate balancing of work and family.
- Flexible work scheduling.
- Mentoring and career development programs.

If supportive measures improve the workplace for all employees, why are they not done routinely? One reason is that the need is not always recognized because of the stereotypes about the traditional worker – white, able-bodied men. For example, when one thinks of employing women, issues of parenting are likely to arise. The reality is that more men are finding themselves having to manage work and family. Yet, the stereotype of men as providers does not lead one to recognize these needs. One must first recognize the work and family issue women face and then realize that it is increasingly an issue for men too.

Two of the supportive measures – balancing work and family and flexible work scheduling are discussed later in this chapter.

*What are positive measures?*

Positive measures are proactive remedies designed to overcome the effects of past discrimination in an affirmative manner. The purpose of positive measures is to speed up the rate of change. Positive measures (unlike the other three) are temporary measures which stop as soon as equitable representation is achieved. The rational behind positive measures is that the hiring and promotion of designated group members needs to be achieved as quickly as possible and one of the best ways to increase the hiring of designated group members is to hire designated group members. That is, once there is a critical mass of designated group members within an organization, it is easier to hire additional people from the designated group. This is because of the communication of job opportunities among designated group members and the creation of an organizational environment which is supportive of all employees – designated group and mainstream.

Some examples of positive measures are:

- Targeted outreach where designated group members are encouraged to apply through advertisements and job information is disseminated primarily to sources which are known to designated group members. This differs from outreach recruiting (discussed in Chapter 9) in that targeted outreach includes the message that preference will be given to designated group members while outreach recruiting does not.
- Fast tracking designated group members within organizations.

## BALANCING WORK AND FAMILY

An organization's effort to help their employees balance work and family is an example of eliminating barriers, an accommodation measure and a supportive measure. One major challenge every organization will face is the way work has been structured. The work environment of today is still based on the assumption that fathers work outside the home while stay-at-home mothers take care of all family needs. In the past employees were a more homogeneous group. But today, only 16 per cent of Canadian families have a breadwinning husband and a stay-at-home wife. The "family responsibilities" which now concern employees differ from those of the past. In the past the workplace needed to be responsive to family needs from the perspective of fathers who needed to provide financially for their families. For instance, many benefits (*e.g.*, life insurance) were introduced to enable men to focus on their work, knowing that their families would be cared for if anything happened to them.

Today there is a high proportion of mothers in the labour force. In 1988, 58 per cent of mothers with children under three years of age were in the work-force. Mothers of children under three are the fastest growing group of women entering the labour force as shown in Chapter 3, Figure 3-3. In addition, increased longevity means that many workers today have to deal with family responsibilities associated with both children and aging parents simultaneously. With both mothers and fathers in the labour force, organizations have to support employees' needs to balance work and family.

Family responsibilities have traditionally belonged to women and to a great extent, this is unchanged. But it is wrong to equate family issues and women. First, all women are not mothers and, second, many fathers are increasingly becoming involved in caring for their children. In almost 75 per cent of families with children under three both parents work full-time, and 40 per cent of working parents had irregular work schedules (*e.g.*, late shift, working evenings routinely).[4] A U.S. study about executives (*i.e.*, men) of the 1,000 largest companies found that almost half (49 per cent) are finding that the number of ambitious executives willing to work long hours on a fast career track has decreased over the past five years. The overwhelming reason (59 per cent) is the desire for more time with family.[5] Additionally, both men and women are being called upon to help their parents and other aging relatives. Many people of prime working age find themselves sandwiched between the demands of both children and aging parents. Both female and male workers are willing to make trade-offs to achieve balance. A U.S. study found 78 per cent of American adults said they would take flexible hours even if it meant slower career advancement.[6] In Canada, The Conference Board published a study in 1989 which showed that 10 per cent of their informants had left a job because of work and family conflict, 14 per cent were considering leaving their current job for this reason, and 66 per cent reported some difficulty balancing family and work. The survey included both men and women.

One reason organizations will have to become involved in helping employees balance work and family is because there will be few, if any, employees who will not, at some point in their work life, need such services. Time is a non-expandable resource. Time facilitates people's ability to manage all the aspects of their life. In fact, "Leisure time – not money – is becoming the status symbol of the 1990s",[7] therefore, work-family policies and practices will focus on flexibility. The need for time will mean flexibility as to when one is required to be at work; sometimes it will mean working part-time or it may mean help in researching and selecting support services which can no longer be provided by the family (*e.g.*, elder "day care" programs). It is unlikely that any employee will desire all the various initiatives to balance work and family. It is very likely that most employees will need some flexibility during part of their working life.

**Examples of work-family policies:**

*Flexible hours:* With flexible hours employees work a full day, but the hours they work differ. Usually the organization sets core hours (*e.g.*, from 10:00 to 3:00) during which time everyone is expected to be working. Employees have flexibility as to the schedule they choose to start and finish work. For example, employees could start between 7:00 a.m. and 10:00 a.m. with corresponding quitting times being seven and half hours later, between 3:00 p.m. and 6:00 p.m. Flexitime allows employees to balance their own rhythms (*i.e.*, morning people), family needs, and commuting schedules with full-time work. It enables organizations to have greater coverage; something that is particularly useful when doing business across numerous time zones.

*Compressed work week:* Another option for those working full-time is to provide flexibility by allowing workers to work longer hours per day but fewer days per week. For example, four ten-hour days rather than five eight-hour days. The ability to manage family responsibilities on the day off and to avoid long commuting times are the advantages to the employee. The organization is able to have more staff resources on busier days when employees work longer hours.

*Part-time work:* Is it really possible that the vast majority of jobs are best scheduled Monday to Friday from nine to five? Not really. Most jobs have cycles, be they daily, weekly, monthly, quarterly or annually. Such cycles mean that there is more work during some periods than others. Think of accounting jobs, city bus drivers, bank tellers. Permanent part-time jobs enable the organization to staff for its busy periods and provide part-time opportunities to balance work and family. This is looking at part-time work from the organization's perspective.

It is also necessary to look at part-time work from the perspective of an employee who desires to work part-time for a certain period. One mother of a young child found that taking every other Wednesday off (working 90 per cent time) made all the difference. Others find that part-time work is a good way to ease back into employment after maternity leave. It may be a healthy way to ease out of work and into full retirement. It also can be used to go back to school. Part-time work can be part of a day, a week or a year. There are people who work part-time throughout their working lives. But much more common are employees who want to work part-time for a part of their working lives. As we approach a skill shortage, retaining skilled and talented employees will become an important organizational strategy. Allowing people to work part-time for a number of years will be part of that strategy.

Part-time work can involve doing the whole job for part of the time or doing part of the job. Examples of the former are supermarket cashiers or transit drivers; they are doing the whole job and should be paid the same compensation (salary and benefits) per hour as others working full-time. The latter, those who are doing part of the job, should be paid a fair compensation pro-rated to the amount of the job they do. Training and promotion opportunities should be made available to part-time workers of either kind who are interested.

*Job sharing:* A special kind of part-time work is job sharing where two people are responsible for one job. While requiring additional co-ordination efforts, job-sharing provides the organization with greater flexibility. For instance, when one person is on holiday, the other is there and may even be able to increase her or his hours if necessary. If one person quits there is still someone performing the job.

*Maternity and parental options:* Flexibility, on a regular basis, is needed when there are young children in the home. Policies are needed beyond those legally required. Some examples are: allowing mothers to return to work when they are ready, rather than at the end of a legally prescribed maternity leave; allowing mothers to return part-time, to job-share and/or to do some work at home; ensuring that fathers who take parental leave are treated with respect rather than like disloyal and uncommitted employees. Another way to promote flexibility is to allow employees to say "not now" to promotions, and not interpreting this as "never".

*Child care:* Organizations need to find out what their employees' child care needs are and how the organization can best help them. This might be on-site day care, but it could also be a referral service which helps employees find the child care situation they desire. (A similar referral service for elder care is becoming increasingly important.) Some other options: support for community child care facilities; sponsorship of training for in-home care providers; emergency babysitting; ensuring coverage for those working on shifts and emergency on-call work;[8] and subsidies to parents for child care services.

*"Home work":* The age of computers, modems, faxes and cellular phones is the age when white collar work can often be performed equally well at the office or in the home. Loss of control is the concern of many managers when they contemplate their employees working at home. This is often because organizations are better at measuring (controlling) how much time people work, rather than what they accomplish. Home work requires that productivity, rather than time, be measured. The concept of home work has existed for a long time in some traditional women's areas, such as the garment industry, and often raises issues of exploitation, creation of unsafe work environment within the home and other prob-

lems. Obviously, home work arrangements for any employee must overcome these negatives. In addition, it must not become a barrier which prevents employees from advancing in their organizations, if they wish to.

Working at home may be the preferred work location for some employees; for others it can be interspersed with days at the employer's worksite; it can be used to extend parental leave; or it can be used in case of an emergency.

*Personal leave:* Everyone has emergencies, ranging from a parent who falls and breaks a hip to the need to see a house one is considering buying between 3:00 and 4:00 on a Wednesday afternoon, to the need to be at home when the plumber comes. Emergencies are not a vacation, nor are they traditionally allowed under most sick leave plans. Allowing personal leave time or the flexibility to make up the time is useful.

*Allowing sick leave to be used for family medical matters:* When a child or a relative has a doctor's appointment many employees are forced to lie and say they are sick to take the time off. To maintain the lie the employee has to take the whole day off rather than the few hours needed for the doctor's appointment. Allowing employees to use their sick leave to care for medical needs of family members recognizes the reality of balancing work and family.

*Unpaid leaves and sabbaticals:* The opportunity to take an unpaid leave – with a guarantee of a job to return to – can be just the thing for those who need to deal with an intense family emergency (*e.g.,* a dying parent in another city) or to avoid burnout. Some organizations are doing creative things with sabbaticals: providing employees with full pay while they do volunteer work for a not-for-profit organization; or arranging for employees to receive 80 per cent of their pay for four years and then allowing them to take the fifth year off with the 80 per cent salary (20 per cent x four years) they have banked over the previous four years. This can also be done for shorter periods of time.

*Flexible benefits:* Benefit costs are high. Yet organizations are throwing some of the money away. This is because organizations typically provide benefits which their employees do not need, do not want, do not use and yet are a cost to the employer. Most benefit programs were designed with the breadwinner-husband, stay-at-home-wife model in mind. Today, over 60 per cent of Canadian families have two incomes, thus, many benefit dollars are being wasted when each partner is provided with the same insurance and other benefits. Further, family structures and needs differ. Flexible benefits give organizations a better return for their benefit dollar and give employees more of what they need for the money the employer is paying. Some flexibility can be provided by offering employees the option of picking from three or four basic benefit programs (and the ability to change as their family needs change). Others provide a few core benefits and allow each employee to spend their benefit dollars at a benefit "cafeteria", customizing the best benefit package they can and increasing employees' awareness of their benefits at the same time.

There are many mechanisms which can help employees balance work and family. Organizations will be forced to employ many of these in response to the labour/skill shortage. For example, take the case of the Intermedic Company, located in Texas next to a large Dow Chemical plant. The small company was unable to compete with Dow for high-calibre people. That is, until it put in a child care centre. Suddenly, Intermedic had a recruiting edge.[9]

# NOTES

1. Bill 79, introduced for 2nd reading July 12, 1993. To become effective in 1994.
2. [1990] 2 S.C.R. 489, 72 D.L.R. (4th) 417.
3. (1992), 71 B.C.L.R. (2d) 145, [1992] 6 W.W.R. 193, 141 N.R. 185 (S.C.C.).
4. Donna Lero, Hillel Goelman, Alan Pence, Lois Brockman and Sandra Nuttall, "Parental Work Patterns and Child Care Needs"; Canadian Nation Child Care Study Centre, July 1992.
5. Study conducted by Robert Half International and reported in *Human Resources Professional*, February 1992, p. 19.
6. Survey by Robert Half International reported in "USA Snapshot" in *USA Today*, November 20, 1990.
7. Patricia Aburdene and John Naisbitt, *Megatrends for Women*, New York: Villard Books, 1992, p. 222.
8. Only 55 per cent of parents with children under 13 have a standard, nine-to-five work week. In almost 75 per cent of Canadian families with children under three, both parents work full-time. Donna Lero, Hillel Goelman, Alan Pence, Lois Brockman and Sandra Nuttall, "Parental Work Patterns and Child Care Needs" from Canadian Nation Child Care Study Centre, July 1992.
9. Felice N. Schwartz, *Breaking with Tradition: Women and Work, The New Facts of Life*, New York: Warner Books, Inc., 1992, p. 208.

# REFERENCES

*The Emerging Role of the Work-Family Manager*, New York: Conference Board, 1992.

*Introduction: Changing Family Structure and an Aging Population*, United Steel Workers of America, Policy Paper, 1989, Canadian Policy Conference.

*Issues for an Aging America: Employees and Elder Care*, Bridgeport, CT, 06601, University of Bridgeport, Center for the Study of Aging, 1987.

*Work and Family: The Crucial Balance*, Toronto: Ontario Women's Directorate, (undated).

*Work and Family Responsibilities: Achieving a Balance*, New York: Ford Foundation, 1989.

Patricia Aburdene and John Naisbitt, *Megatrends for Women*, New York: Villard Books, 1992.

Betty Beach, *Integrating Work and Family Life: The Home-Working Family*, Albany, N.Y: State University of New York Press, 1989.

Lou Ellen Crawford, *Dependent Care and The Employee Benefit Package*, New York: Quorum Books, 1990.

Ann Duffy, *Few Choices: Women, Work and Family*, Toronto: Garamond Press, 1989.

Ann Duffy, *Part-time Paradox: Connecting Gender, Work and Family*, Toronto: McClelland and Stewart, 1992.

Marianne A. Ferber and Brigid O'Farrell (eds.), *Work and Family: Policies for a Changing Work Force*, Washington D.C.: National Academy Press, 1992.

Janice L. Gibeau, Jeane W. Anastas and Pamela J. Larson, "Breadwinners and Caretakers and Adult Day Health Services as an Employee Benefit", National Association of Area Agencies on Aging (600 Maryland Ave. SW, Ste. 208), Washington, D.C., 1986 and 1987.

Donna Lero, Hillel Goelman, Alan Pence, Lois Brockman and Sandra Nuttall, "Parental Work Patterns and Child Care Needs" Canadian Nation Child Study Centre, July 1992.

Phillip Mahfood, *Home Work: How to Hire, Manage and Monitor Employees Who Work at Home*, Chicago: Probus Publishing Company, 1992.

Barney Olmsted and Suzanne Smith, *The Job Sharing Handbook*, Berkeley: Ten Speed Press, 1983.

William F. Roth, *Work and Reward: Redefining Our Work-Life Reality*, New York: Prager, 1989.

Andrew E. Scharlach, Beverley F. Lowe, and Edward L. Schneider, *Elder Care and the Work Force: Blueprint for Action*, Toronto: Lexington Books, 1991.

Felice N. Schwartz, *Breaking with Tradition: Women and Work, The New Facts of Life*, New York: Warner Books, Inc., 1992.

Sheldon Zedeck (ed.), *Work, Families and Organizations*, San Francisco: Jossey-Bass, 1992.

# CHAPTER 8

# Duty to Accommodate

## INTRODUCTION

Achieving EE for the four designated groups involves both the duty to accommodate and the valuing of diversity. One could say that the duty to accommodate will facilitate EE and that EE requires the valuing of diversity. It is also true that the duty to accommodate and the valuing of diversity can be separated from EE and are issues of merit on their own. The duty to accommodate is part of human rights requirements in Canada. As noted in the discussion of demographic trends in Chapter 1, the Canadian labour force is becoming more diverse. Organizations which value this diversity can harness a synergy and creativity which is unavailable to organizations which require everyone to fit into the same mould.

## ACCOMMODATION

### What is the duty to accommodate?

Accommodation recognizes that different people do the same things in different ways, each being effective. The duty to accommodate requires employers to balance the needs of the job with the needs of their employees, as related to their membership in groups protected by human rights legislation. There are, of course, obligations on employees who need to be accommodated, these are discussed later. An organization has a duty to accommodate unless it would cause undue hardship. What constitutes undue hardship is discussed later in this chapter. The duty to accommodate short of undue hardship recognizes the diversity among employees. It recognizes that equality does not mean identical treatment, but can require differential treatment because of differing circumstances.

### Is the duty to accommodate part of EE?

Accommodation is required to make EE work and it is totally consistent with EE principles. But even without EE, the duty to accommodate is part of human rights laws in Canada. This was decided in *Central Alberta Dairy Pool v. Alberta (Human Rights Commission)* by the Supreme Court of Canada in 1990.[1] Because the duty to accommodate is part of human rights, employers must accommodate members of all the groups protected by the human rights legislation which governs their organization. Thus, the duty to accommodate involves more than just the four designated groups under EE.

The *Alberta Dairy Pool* case involved Mr. Christie, who worked for the Central Alberta Dairy Pool. Mr. Christie had become a member of the World Wide Church of God. According to the tenets of this religion, members were not to work on Easter Monday. Mr. Christie gave his employer sufficient notice that he wanted to take Easter Monday off for religious reasons. His employer refused on the grounds that Mondays are particularly busy days at the Dairy Pool, because milk brought in over the weekend has to be canned on Monday. Mr. Christie filed a complaint of religious discrimination which went all the way to the Supreme Court of Canada. The Court was very clear that employers have a duty to accommodate where adverse impact exists. Adverse impact results from a rule, practice or job qualification which is neutral in its intent, but adversely affects members of a protected group (*e.g.*, religious groups). The consistent application of such a rule, practice or qualification adversely affects a subset of people because of their membership in a protected group. Where adverse impact exists, it must be determined if the employer can accommodate the employee(s) so affected without undue hardship to the organization. In this case, the Supreme Court reasoned that though Mondays were particularly busy days, the Alberta Dairy Pool had procedures to deal with employee absences on Mondays due to illness or vacations. Therefore, it decided that the Pool could deal with Mr. Christie's absence on Easter Monday without undue hardship.

Of more importance than the facts of this particular case was the Supreme Court pronouncement that employers have a duty to accommodate (short of undue hardship) even though the human rights legislation governing the employer did not explicitly have a provision requiring accommodation. The *Central Alberta Dairy Pool* decision reversed an earlier Supreme Court decision made in 1985. In the fall of 1985, on the same day, the Supreme Court released two decisions dealing with accommodation. Both cases involved accommodation of religious beliefs. One case was *Ontario (Human Rights Commission) and O'Malley v. Simpsons-Sears Ltd.*,[2] involving the Ontario *Human Rights Code*.[3] The other was *Bhinder v. C.N.R.*,[4] which was heard under the *Canadian Human Rights Act*.[5] The two pieces of human rights legislation differ in that the Ontario statute specifically required a duty to accommodate while the federal law did not. So, in 1985, the Supreme Court made different rulings in these two cases. Simpson-Sears was required to accommodate Ms O'Malley while CN was not required to accommodate Mr. Bhinder. The *Central Alberta Dairy Pool* decision reversed the *Bhinder* decision since in both cases the *Canadian Human Rights Act* was involved. The *Central Alberta Dairy Pool* decision said that an implicit guarantee of all human rights legislation is to be free of adverse impact and, therefore, employers must accommodate employees belonging to protected groups, short of undue hardship.

### What exactly does the duty to accommodate involve?

In its most basic sense, the duty to accommodate means that equitable treatment does not mean identical treatment. Rather, employees (and applicants) must be treated as individuals. Accommodation can be required for:

- Applicants during the selection process;
- Employees regarding the terms and conditions of employment;
- Employees regarding how a job is performed.

### What kind of accommodation might be needed by applicants during the selection process?

Applicants could need accommodation in the interview, in testing or other selection processes. For example, one employer, who gave a written, essay test, was asked by an applicant with dyslexia if he could use a computer to write the answers. An individual with a speech impediment might need a longer time for an interview or the opportunity to write answers instead of responding verbally. The purpose of accommodation is to give the applicant the full opportunity to demonstrate her/his abilities to fulfil the requirements of the job so that they can compete on an equal footing with other candidates.

### What kind of accommodation might be needed regarding terms and conditions of employment?

Accommodation of terms and conditions of employment has involved alternative work locations, adapting equipment, flexible starting times, hours of work (part-time work), time off for religious holidays, adaptation of safety equipment, distribution of work assignments and allocation of parking spaces. For example, one employee who used a wheelchair requested two accommodations from the employer. The first was to have a parking spot close to the plant entry; such parking spots normally were assigned on the basis of the organizational hierarchy. The second accommodation was to punch in and out ten minutes earlier than coworkers, to make getting to and from the work site less difficult. A common accommodation is time off for religious holidays. This could involve a few specific days per year, such as Easter Monday in Mr. Christie's case, or Rosh Hashana and Yom Kippur for Jewish employees. Alternatively, it could mean to avoid scheduling an employee, who is a Seventh Day Adventist, to Friday evening or Saturday shifts.

*What kinds of costs are we talking about?*

A study covering the period from July 1, 1984 to December 31, 1986, showed the following breakdown of costs of accommodations for employees with disabilities:[6]

### TABLE 8-1

| COST OF ACCOMMODATION FOR EMPLOYEES WITH DISABILITIES | | |
| --- | --- | --- |
| Cost of accommodation | Per cent of employers spending this amount | Cumulative percentage |
| No cost | 31% | 31% |
| Between $1 and $50 | 19% | 50% |
| Between $50 and $500 | 19% | 69% |
| Between $500 and $1,000 | 19% | 88% |
| Between $1,000 and $5,000 | 12% | 100% |

Source:    Adapted from "Evaluation Report Executive Summary," Morgantown, WV: Job Accommodation Network, April 1987, p. 3.

Many accommodations have little or no cost associated with them, such as allowing someone to punch in and out ten minutes early. Others could have a non-monetary cost on employees who are treated differently (*e.g.*, those who do not get a parking space close to the entrance). Some examples of accommodations for persons with disabilities with a low to minimal cost are:

- Putting four bricks under the legs of a desk to raise it up to accommodate an employee using a wheelchair;
- Making print information available in alternative formats such as tape or braille, or providing a reader;
- Translating auditory information into visual or tactile modes;
- Adapting some equipment or providing some special devices or supports (one employer found it cost three dollars to change a foot peddle into a hand lever);
- Allowing some or all of the work to be done at home and providing the necessary equipment to link home and office (*e.g.*, computer modem).

*What kind of accommodation might be needed regarding how work is performed?*

To assess accommodation regarding job tasks or performance of job duties, one needs to identify the following:

- The essential and non-essential aspects of the job;
- What specific accommodation a particular individual needs; and
- What constitutes undue hardship.

The discussion which follows is based on the Ontario Human Rights Commission's *Guidelines for Assessing Accommodation Requirements ...* published in 1989.[7] Because Ontario human rights legislation has explicitly included the duty to accommodate they have developed more communication in this area than have other jurisdictions.

### What are non-essential duties of a job?

It is necessary to distinguish between essential and non-essential job duties because the latter must be accommodated while the former may not have to be. In the performance of many jobs there are typically some activities which are critical or key (essential) to the job and some which are tangential or non-essential. For example, it is typical for lawyers, salespersons, shippers/receivers and social workers to photocopy papers during the course of their day. However, photocopying is not essential to the performance of these jobs. Photocopying would be an essential part of some clerical jobs and, certainly, in the job of photocopy operator. An essential part of the job of receptionist requires verbal communication over the phone and in person; such communication could be non-essential for a file clerk. Firefighters need to be physically mobile to do their job, a corporate accountant does not.

Non-essential aspects of work *must be* accommodated. Accommodation may be achieved by reassigning these duties or by permitting the employee needing accommodation to use an alternative method to fulfil the non-essential duties.

### Do essential duties have to be accommodated?

Accommodation of essential duties *must be explored*. If such duties can be accommodated without undue hardship to the employer (discussed below), then accommodation must be made. However, if accommodating essential duties would cause an undue hardship then accommodation is not required.

### What constitutes undue hardship?

In assessing undue hardship one must consider:

- The *current* situation of the person requiring the accommodation;
- The *current* accommodation required; and
- The cost of the accommodation and its impact on health and safety.

Assessment of the current situation means that a determination that an undue hardship exists *cannot* be based on speculation or presumption of what could happen. For example, if a person with a disability can be accommodated today without undue hardship, then, even if it is likely that this person's particular disability will deteriorate, requiring further accommodation in the future, this speculation cannot be used to make a decision now of undue hardship. The future reality is unknown. Another example of what cannot be done is to avoid hiring women of child-bearing years, anticipating that they will need to be accommodated in the future. The assessment of undue hardship must be based on the present situation, not speculation about the future.

What might constitute undue hardship is not definitive. In the *Alberta Dairy Pool* case the Supreme Court of Canada did not deal with the issue of undue hardship in any detail, but it did list some possible criteria: cost, disruption of a collective agreement, problems of morale among other employees, interchangeability of work force and facilities, and safety. The Ontario Human Rights Commission has provided more specific information on possible assessment of undue hardship. They have stated that undue hardship could be due to cost or health and safety (each of which is discussed later).

Two things cannot be used in the assessment of undue hardship. The first is customer preference. The second is the collective agreement. *Renaud v. Central Okanagan School District*[8] involved a Mr. Renaud who was a janitor for the Central Okanagan School District No. 23. Mr. Renaud was a Seventh Day Adventist who could not work the scheduled workweek because it involved working on Friday evening, which infringed on the observance of his Sabbath. The School Board was willing to change his schedule so that he could work from Sunday to Thursday. The union, Canadian Union of Public Employees (CUPE), was unwilling. Mr. Renaud was terminated. The Supreme Court, in the fall of 1992, ruled that Mr. Renaud should be reinstated. The Court decision said that the School Board was correct in their willingness to accommodate Mr. Renaud. They were wrong in terminating him under threat of a grievance from the union. The union was wrong in not accommodating Mr. Renaud. Both the employer and the union had to pay damages.

### What is the cost standard to determine undue hardship?

In the Ontario guidelines on accommodation, the cost standard reads:

> Undue hardship will be shown to exist if the financial costs that are demonstrably attributable to the accommodation ... would alter the essential nature or would substantially affect the viability of the enterprise responsible for accommodation.[9]

Costs, to represent an undue hardship, must be:

1. Quantifiable;
2. Related to the accommodation; and
3. (a) So substantial that the organization would be unable to carry out its purpose; or
   (b) So significant that the organization would cease to exist.

Clearly, the application of this cost standard differs for organizations of different size and financial viability. It is important to note that it is the existence of the entire organization which must be threatened (in (3) above), not just a unit of the organization, for undue hardship to be present. The guidelines state:

> [T]he appropriate basis for evaluating the effect of the cost is the company as a whole, not the branch or unit in which the person ... works or to which the person has made application.[10]

Costs may include capital and operating costs, cost of additional staff time and any other quantifiable and demonstrably related cost. Costs cannot be mere speculation, and they must be directly related to the actual accommodation needed. For example, if the addition of a wooden ramp would provide the needed accommodation, the cost of reconstructing the entire front entry of the building would not be considered to be directly related. Increased insurance costs or sickness benefits would be included as operating costs if they are quantified in terms of actual higher rates and are not in violation of human rights legislation.

The costs are net costs; costs less any grants, subsidies or loans from the federal, provincial or municipal government or other sources which could offset the costs of accommodations. In Box 8-1 some sources of funds for accommodation of persons with disabilities are listed. Any additional savings available as a result of the accommodation would be subtracted to arrive at the net cost. These may include:

- Tax deductions and other government benefits;
- Improvement in productivity, efficiency or effectiveness;
- Any increase in the resale value of property, where it is reasonably foreseeable that the property might be sold; and
- Any increase in clientele, or potential labour pool.

### What is the health and safety standard to determine undue hardship?

Health and safety concerns are expressed in laws, regulations, rules, in a collective bargaining agreement, or through an informal practice. The

---

## Box 8-1

### SOME SOURCES OF FUNDS FOR ACCOMMODATION

**Canada Employment and Immigration (federal) – Program for the Employment of the Disadvantaged**
- Physically, mentally disabled and other severely employment disadvantaged persons.
- Pay 85% of gross wages for three months, 50% for six months and 25% for six months.
- Up to $5,000 per business establishment for restructuring workplaces or acquiring special equipment to accommodate persons with disabilities.

**Vocational Rehabilitation Services (VRS) (Ontario) Ministry of Community and Social Services**
- Can hire VRS client for trial work periods of up to four weeks during which time VRS pays wages.
- If training is necessary, VRS will provide 50% of wages for up to 12 months.
- For permanent jobs, financial assistance is available to modify workplace and/or to purchase technical aids for persons with disabilities.

**Workers' Compensation Board (provincial)**
- Financial assistance in retraining of workers for up to 12 months during which time the employer takes over an increasing share of the employee's wages.
- Funds for modification of workplace.

**Technical Aids and Systems for the Handicapped (TASH)** Ajax, Ontario – Markets, services and encourages the manufacture of aids for persons with disabilities unavailable through other means.

**Ontario Training Adjustment Board (OTAB)** – A number of funding arrangements in the province will be changing when OTAB becomes the umbrella organization which will administer various funding programs for persons with disabilities and other groups.

---

Supreme Court of Canada has decreed that human rights legislation prevails over other legislation, including health and safety. This does not mean that health and safety issues are no longer a concern when accommodation is needed. Rather, in each situation the risks and benefits of waiving health and safety requirements must be considered. Such a risk-benefit analysis will determine if undue hardship exists. The benefit of enhancing equality must be compared to any remaining risk if the accommodation was made. Benefits of equality include the benefits to the individual employee, to family and friends, to co-workers, and to the general public. Where a health and safety risk is so significant that it outweighs the benefits of equality, an undue hardship exists.

Health and safety issues can arise when accommodation is required for persons with certain disabilities, for members of some religious groups and for some women. Examples include:

- A deaf person cannot hear a fire alarm.
- A man who is a baptized Sikh cannot wear a hard hat over or under his turban.
- A woman using safety equipment designed for a man.

These situations cannot be considered in the abstract. The particular work circumstances, the required accommodation and the following issues need to be considered in assessing the risk-benefit trade-off between equity and safety. Three issues must be examined according to the Ontario accommodation guidelines:

1. *The willingness of a person with a disability to assume the risk in circumstances where the risk is to her or his own health or safety.*[11]

Where, even after accommodation, there is still an element of risk *to the individual employee*, then that employee, on having the risk fully explained to her/him, is the one to make the decision as to whether or not she/he is willing to take the risk. For example, it is common practice in some organizations for groundskeepers to wear hard hats and safety glasses when operating tractor lawnmowers. Although slight, there is a risk of a stone being thrown up and causing a head or eye injury. A man who is a baptized Sikh would not be able to wear a hard hat in this situation, given his religious obligation to wear a turban. A Sikh applicant, after discussing the risks and past experiences with someone in the organization who is familiar with them could decide whether to continue pursuing the job or not. Accommodation may or may not be required, for instance, it could be decided that:

- The risk is minimal and is clearly outweighed by the benefits of employment.
- An accommodation is needed to compensate for the fact that a hard hat cannot be worn. Such an accommodation may involve installing a "wind shield" screen on the tractor lawnmower.
- His turban provides adequate head protection and so no accommodation is needed nor is any additional risk encountered.

2. *Whether the modification or waiving of the requirement is reasonably likely to result in a serious risk to the health or safety of individuals other than the person requiring the accommodation.*[12]

Where the health and safety of co-workers, clients/customers or the general public is involved, the assessment of risk and benefits cannot be made by the individual requiring the accommodation. The seriousness of the risk needs to be determined using the following four factors:

1. The nature of the risk: What could happen that would be harmful?
2. The severity of the risk: How serious would the harm be if it occurred?
3. The probability of the risk: How likely is it that the potential harm will actually occur? Could it occur frequently? Is it a real risk, or merely hypothetical or speculative?
4. The scope of the risk: Who will be affected by the event if it occurs?

The determination of risk must be objective rather than impressionistic. A moderate probability that harm could come to a large number of people; or a low probability that severe harm could come to a few may outweigh the benefits of equality. But a low probability of minor risk to many probably would not.

3. *The other types of risks found within an organization or within society as a whole.*

There are certain risks everyone encounters at their workplaces, homes, on the streets, anywhere they may be. Individuals who need to be accommodated should not be denied the right to assume comparable risks. Often a person with a disability is denied an opportunity because he or she risks further impairment. Everyone has the right to balance the benefits of employment against potential risk; this is referred to as the dignity of risk. Everyone assumes certain risks in the course of many non-work activities, such as crossing a street, taking a bath, driving a car, cooking a meal. While the workplace should be as safe as possible, people should not be denied the benefits of employment just because they have to incur some risk. For instance, for women working the night shift, putting lights into a parking lot or escorting women to and from their cars does not eliminate all the safety risks, but it does a reasonable job.

## How can the kind of accommodation needed be determined?

Each accommodation is likely to be different because it is based on the job requirements and the situation of the person being accommodated.

Obviously, a discussion between someone who knows the job and the person who requires the accommodation to do the job is needed so that each can share their information. The actual accommodation may be obvious or it may require creativity and exploration of available options. A service designed to provide information about possible accommodations needed for persons with disabilities is provided by the Job Accommodation Network (JAN). Their toll-free number in Canada is 1-800-526-2262. Their hours of operation are 8:00 a.m. to 8:00 p.m. eastern time.

### Do employees have any responsibility with respect to accommodation?

Yes. Employees or potential employees are responsible for making their needs for an accommodation known in a timely fashion. For example, employees whose religious observances differ from the statutory holidays know the schedule of their holidays well in advance. Time off for religious observance must be made known in a reasonable period of time for scheduling. Applicants who need accommodation during the selection process must ask for it in enough time for it to be arranged. This assumes that applicants know all the components of the selection process that he/she will go through. Therefore, there is a responsibility on the employer to make this information known. In the *Central Alberta Dairy Pool* decision regarding accommodation for religious observance, the Supreme Court said that in order to prove that an organization discriminated the *employee* must accommodate the employer as far as possible (*e.g.*, requesting time off for a religous holiday is sufficient time).

Employers can facilitate the accommodation process by encouraging employees to communicate their needs. As examples: in an advertisement or job posting, applicants who may require accommodation can be encouraged to inquire about all the components in the selection process. Supervisors or those responsible for scheduling staff can remind employees to advise them about any scheduling requirements due to religion. As part of new employee orientation, employees should be told that employers have a duty to accommodate and they should be given the name of the person who can help them with any accommodation requests.

### How exactly does an organization fulfil its duty to accommodate?

The key to accommodation is individuality and flexibility. The process is one of balancing the job which needs to be done with the ability/needs of the employee. The employer is obligated to work with the employee(s) to ensure that they are accommodated in a manner which meets their needs, ensures that the job gets done, and that the organization does not experience undue hardship. Potential employees are not required to inform the organization about their accommodation needs prior to hiring (except with respect to facilitating the selection process), since an organization cannot make a decision not to hire someone because they require an accommodation.

It is important that human resource professionals and supervisors do not make assumptions about the kind of accommodation an employee may need. Talk to the person. For example, some people who use wheelchairs can drive a car but cannot walk at all; others can walk a short distance but may not be able to drive a vehicle; others can do both while still others can do neither. Not communicating with the person requiring the accommodation can lead to unnecessary accommodation. For example, one employer accommodated a visually impaired employee by purchasing a very large computer screen. However, the new employee's visual abilities constited of seeing only part of the screen at one time. A standard size screen with large type would have been the appropriate accommodation.

A key accommodation for persons who are disabled is the organization's ability to purchase technical devices expediently. For example, an organization wanted to make an offer of employment to an outstanding candidate with a disability. The person needed a piece of equipment which was reasonably priced and well within the means of the department's budget. However, the bureaucracy involving purchasing would delay the arrival of the equipment for at least three months after the person could begin work. Consequently, the organization was faced with the choices of (1) having someone on the payroll for three months before they could begin to perform the essential duties of the job, (2) taking the second best candidate, or (3) asking the candidate to wait before starting work and risk losing the person. The inability to make an accommodation within a reasonable period of time can itself be an employment barrier – the very thing EE is trying to overcome. To avoid this situation, some large organizations have set aside a fund for accommodations; other organizations have expedited purchases needed to accommodate employees.

Accommodation for the four designated groups is required in the Ontario legislation. However, the importance of accommodation for persons with disabilities is highlighted in the draft regulations. The following must be set out in the EE plan:

1. The procedure to be followed by employees and applicants with disabilities when requesting an accommodation, and
2. The procedure to be followed when a request for accommodation is received.

Further, section 20(2) specifically sets out four kinds of accommodations for persons with disabilities. These are:

- Communication and human support services
  (*e.g.*, job coach when learning the job, communications in forms other than print, lights for fire alarms, stress management support, readers/notetakers)
- Technical aids and devices
  (*e.g.*, Telephone Device for the Deaf (TDD)/hearing devices, specialized computers, large print)
- Job design, including work hour flexibility and work restructuring
  (*e.g.*, flexible hours, regular part-time work, job-sharing, working from home,[13] reduction of driving as job component)
- Workstation modifications and physical access to the workplace
  (*e.g.*, ramps, elevator indicators)

The draft regulations also state (section 20(1)) that the accommodation under EE needs to be compatible with what is required under the Ontario *Human Rights Code*.

### Isn't accommodation a lot of work?

It may or may not be. One of the most difficult aspects of job accommodation is adjusting the organizational mindset toward the issue. Traditionally, unions and management have defined fairness as being consistent – treating everyone the same. Accommodation involves a different kind of fairness – treating everyone in terms of who they are.

Accommodation is always a balancing of the job to be done and the situation of the person. There must be a match, though accommodation can mean that the manner in which the job is done may be changed. For example, an individual without legs was able to effectively perform a job which routinely required a foot peddle. For less than three dollars the foot peddle was transformed into a lever which could be operated with the elbow.

### A classic accommodation case.

The Royal Canadian Mounted Police, like all law enforcement agencies, require their officers to wear a uniform. The uniform regulation concerning head gear was inconsistent with the religious requirements for baptized Sikh men who are required to wear a turban. *In anticipation* of successful Sikh candidates the RCMP changed the regulations. Rather than looking at this as a legal issue, let's examine it from the perspective of the organizational needs. What are the reasons for the RCMP uniform? Three potential reasons come to mind:

1. Creating a sense of authority.
2. Identification as an RCMP officer.
3. Tradition.

## FIGURE 8-1

### LAW ENFORCEMENT UNIFORM:
### TRADITIONAL AND FOR SIKH OFFICER

Photo courtesy of the Metropolitan Toronto Police Department

Are these three reasons job-related? The answer would be "yes" to the first two and "no" to the third. Tradition is another way of saying "this is the way we have always done things". Traditions, in and of themselves, are often challenged by EE. However, if there is a valid reason behind the tradition – something which must be done for the successful performance of the job – then the practice can stand. So the wearing of the traditional head gear provides RCMP officers with an image of authority and allows for identification.

In thinking about accommodating Sikhs the question to be asked is: Is there a way in which authority, identification and the wearing of a turban can be combined? The answer is "yes". Figure 8-1 shows a picture of the Metropolitan Toronto Police law enforcement uniform as worn by a number of officers, including a male Sikh. Note that the uniform which includes a turban with the badge in the centre fulfils the need for identification. Further, the turban, like the traditional head gear, provides a sense of authority.

# VALUING DIVERSITY

## *What does diversity mean?*

Diversity refers to differences between people. These differences can be gender, race, disability status, plus many other characteristics such as age, religion, ethnicity, parental status, sexual orientation and so on.

Different kinds of people have always been found within organizations, of course. Today, the reference to "diversity" is really about increased diversity and a change in attitude toward diversity within work organizations. It used to be that when one joined an organization one was expected to fit into the organization, to assimilate – without questioning. Increasingly now, and more so in the future, there will be adaptation on both sides – employees will adapt to their organization, but work organizations will also adapt to their employees. This mutual adaptation will enable organizations to better utilize the human resources available to them. In the past, because of greater homogeneity within the labour force, work organizations could be designed to fulfil the needs which held for the majority of their employees. This meant that these workers did not have to ask the organization to accommodate them. For example, statutory holidays include Good Friday, Easter, and Christmas, the most important Christian holidays. This means that Jews, Hindus, Moslems and members of other religions – but not most Christians – have to request accommodation of their religious needs. Another example is the rigidly defined workweek – nine to five, Monday through Friday. This makes the assumption that husbands/fathers who go to work have a wife/mother at home to care for children and the home. When both mothers and fathers are employed, this rigid workweek can cause problems. Further, the assumption that only full-time workers are committed and loyal to their employers and that only they deserve or need benefits denies the reality that some people are fully productive for part of the workweek, and need and deserve benefits. Some mothers of young children and some persons with disabilities are likely to want and/ or need to work part-time during at least some of their working career.

Work organizations in Canada have been structured to fulfil the needs typically associated with white, Christian, able-bodied, men. This makes sense since, until recently, the vast majority of the work-force shared these characteristics. Over the last 20 years this homogeneity has given way to increased diversity and to a change in values. Today, people want their differences to be acknowledged, rather than being expected to totally assimilate into the mainstream culture. While this new value of recognizing differences is found elsewhere, such as the United States and Britain, Canada is unique in having made multiculturalism the official policy of the country in 1971. In 1988, the federal government restated the legal right of all Canadians to preserve their cultural heritages in the Preamble to the *Multiculturalism Act*,[14] which reads in part:

> ... Government of Canada recognizes the diversity of Canadians as regards race, national or ethnic origin, colour and religion as a fundamental characteristic of Canadian society and is committed to a policy of multiculturalism designed to preserve and enhance the multicultural herit- age of Canadians while working to achieve the equality of all Canadians in the economic, social, cultural and political life of Canada;

Now diversity is becoming a workplace issue.

### Isn't diversity contrary to good business practice?

No. There are two reasons for organizations to be concerned about diver- sity:

1. Because they will have to; and
2. Because there are benefits when diversity is valued.

The work-force is changing, and it is changing permanently as dis- cussed in Chapter 3. Diversity is the future reality for most work organi- zations if they are not yet experiencing it. Some of the potential benefits to valuing diversity include:

- Competitive advantage in attracting and retaining those in the in- creasingly diverse workforce.

- Better utilization of an organization's human resources.
- Better ability to deal with increasing worldwide competition in a diverse world.
- Greater flexibility and ability to deal with continued change.
- Greater innovation and synergy. Creativity comes about by seeing a problem from a different perspective. Synergy is the ability to get more than the sum of the parts and results through the interaction of the parts and the different perspectives which a diverse workforce brings about.
- Improved productivity as more employee effort is directed at accomplishing tasks and less energy spent managing interpersonal conflict and cultural clash.

As Roosevelt Thomas, president of the American Institute for Managing Diversity says: "[C]ompanies must make it a priority to create the kind of environment that will attract the best new talent and make it possible for employees to make their fullest contribution."[15] Acceptance of diversity is the beginning to obtaining a greater contribution from all employees.

### What does it mean to value diversity?

Valuing diversity means recognizing that people are different, but, rather than minimizing these differences, building on their strengths toward a common goal. In the past, diversity has typically been approached with one of two attitudes:

1. Yes, there are differences; and the mainstream way of doing things is right and any other way is wrong.
2. No, there are no important differences between people – we are all members of the human race.

Both these attitudes have denied organizations creativity, variability and synergy. The first one has put down non-mainstream people while the second one denies their very existence. Valuing diversity recognizes that differences exist and that each perspective has something to offer.

The terms "managing diversity" or "valuing diversity" are being heard more and more. Managing diversity is a comprehensive managerial process for developing an environment that works for all employees.[16] All employees include white, able-bodied males and those who have Aboriginal origins, people of colour, persons with disabilities, and women. The challenge to realizing the benefits of valuing diversity is to simultaneously blend greater differentiation with a clear focus on the common ground. "[C]ommon ground ... is a shared set of assumptions that provide the basis for all cooperative actions ... [I]ncludes shared goals, rewards, mutual respect and understanding, mutual commitment to fairness and shared vision of the future."[17]

### What has been the traditional way of dealing with diversity?

The typical assumptions about diversity in work organizations have been noted by Loden and Rosener[18] as:

1. "Otherness" is a deficiency.
2. Diversity poses a threat to the organization's effective functioning.
3. Expressed discomfort with the dominant group's values is oversensitivity.
4. Members of all diverse groups want to become and should be more like the dominant group.
5. Equal treatment means the same treatment.
6. Managing diversity requires changing the people, rather than the organization culture.

In the past it was felt that the best way was to ignore differences. This meant that everyone was treated in a manner which was most appropriate for those in the mainstream. Valuing differences recognizes and respects differences and treats people according to these differences.

### What are some examples of organizational culture which may have to change when diversity is valued?

The way an organization is structured and run is based on a set of assumptions. These assumptions, plus the values and norms of the organization, form an organization's culture. Culture is learned. For example, in mainstream North American culture the lunch-hour, typically, is between 11:30 and 1:00. This is not the typical lunch-hour, for all other ethnic groups. We do not think about our culture too much – it is simply "the way things are done around here". Culture becomes problematic when we do not recognize that there are often many ways to accomplish the same outcome. Some may be better than others, but many are equally good.

"Our company is like a family" is a common cultural value found in North American work organizations. Some of the underpinnings of this value require examination.[19] The idea of the organization as a family is usually interpreted to mean creating a positive, caring environment. But a family has other underlying assumptions. For example, a family has traditionally had a paternalistic climate where "father" (the boss) knows best and the "children" (the employees) should do exactly what father tells them, without talking back. Further, families are a place where sons have traditionally inherited the business, while mothers and daughters are expected do the housework. Flowing from the "family" concept is a rigid definition of loyalty as childlike obedience. Employees are expected to obey the manager, in return, they expect that this behaviour will be rewarded. Putting in long hours shows commitment to the organization (family). It also assumes that there is someone at home cooking the meals and doing the laundry.

## What happens if diversity is not valued?

If people of increased diversity are brought into organizations designed for only one kind of people then the following occurs:[20]

- High turnover among diverse employees.
- Low morale among those remaining because of persistent culture clash.
- Limited innovation and overreliance on "tried and true" methods. Sometimes the problems identified by groups other than those in the mainstream identify problems for mainstream groups also – but problems which may not have been easily seen from the perspective of the mainstream. For example, women, members of racial minorities persons with disabilities an Aborginal Peoples can identify that they are not getting the career development support they require. It often does not take long to determine that this is also true for white, able-bodied men. However, this issue is not always as easily seen, given the stereotype that men manage their careers well enough on their own.
- Lagging productivity as mainstream employees and others remain locked in intergroup conflicts that impede their ability to work together and impair their effectiveness in dealing with diverse customers.
- Growing inability to recruit the best and the brightest new workers.

## What can be done to value diversity?

The first thing is to realize that the manner in which organizations are structured and run is not divinely inspired. That is, the way organizations are currently structured is not the only way they can operate successfully. It is one way. It is a way which, in general, works better for white, able-bodied men than for other groups. For the most part, white, able-bodied men have been designing organizational structures for other white, able-bodied men. While this kind of structure has not been too problematic in the past, it is a poor strategy for the present and the future. In the future organizations must work for white, able-bodied men, for Aboriginal Peoples, persons with disabilities, racial minorities, women and so on.

Roosevelt Thomas in his book[21] on diversity lists four steps in the process of managing diversity, these are:

1. Examine an organization's corporate culture and make it explicit. [It is easy to take culture for granted.] That is, to assume that your organization does not have a culture, but that it is simply operating in the only appropriate way. Making the culture explicit helps everyone see what it is and what it is not. Once the culture is known it is possible to examine which groups have compatible cultures and which groups are likely to experience a culture clash.
2. Identify those elements of the culture that are fundamental, the "roots" from which corporate behaviours spring.
3. Determine whether the roots support or hinder the aspirations for managing diversity.
4. Change the culture roots that are hindrances.

From these steps it can be seen that valuing diversity is not about a total overhaul of an organization's culture, but about changing those values, practices and habits which are incompatible with the valuing of diversity. The organizations which do not do this may have trouble surviving when they face a labour shortage and over 80 per cent of the new entrants to the labour force are from the four designated groups, as is predicted to be the case by the year 2000.

Some of the cultural values that have to be examined in the process of valuing diversity are:

- Time
- Competition versus co-operation
- Norms of fairness
- Expectations as to how organizational loyalty will be demonstrated
- Appropriate rewards
- Appropriate dress for work
- Use of language
- Assimilation versus respect for diversity

Changing employment systems and the people that use them so that they truly value diversity is a long term process – Roosevelt Thomas, the President of the American Institute for Managing Diversity, says it could take 15 to 20 years. It requires a willingness to change, a willingness to learn and a recognition that mistakes will be made. The change required is not easy, since it means changing some of the core assumptions and values upon which work organizations are founded – some of which we often feel are essential to what a work organization is. But valuing diversity does mean not abandoning the mission of the organization; it involves changing how that mission is accomplished. For example, Marilyn Loden and Judy Rosener, writing about diversity argue that in too many organizations people are judged in terms of how many hours they "put in" rather than on what they really accomplish. This is based on the cultural norm found in many organizations that "we work really hard around here". "Working really hard" is translated into working long hours. Working long hours can be problematic for those who have family responsibilities. So the cultural norm of "long hours" and family care responsibilities clash.

Valuing diversity, in this case, would force us to ask the question: Is there a direct relationship between putting in time and the amount of work that gets done? All of us can think of a time when the answer is "yes": when the new inventory system was introduced; when that report had to be written; when the big shipment had to get out, and so on. But in many organizations, over the long-run, people put in time because it is expected (and rewarded) even though it may mean that they are not being as efficient as they can be. A cultural norm of "we really work smart around here" could translate into an effective and efficient operation – but one where long hours are not valued in and of themselves. Assessing performance, rather than time, is totally consistent with the mission of the organization and will facilitate greater flexibility for those with family care responsibilities, and workers who are disabled and need to work at home or part-time.

Valuing diversity is also about avoiding stereotypes and assumptions about people because they belong to a particular group. Rather, it means recognizing and utilizing their unique, individual characteristics. Often people react to others in stereotypical ways ignoring actual similarities. It is important to remember that differences between individuals are often greater than differences between groups. For example, let's look at a factual difference between men and women – height. On average, Canadian men are 5 feet, 9 inches tall and Canadian women are 5 feet 4 inches tall. But information about average heights does not provide the whole picture. Figure 8-2 shows that while men are taller, on average, there is a great deal of overlap (double hatched area). Many women are as tall as many men and many are taller. Knowing average height does not provide any information about the height of any particular man or woman. Still, height is like many stereotypes – since men, on average, are taller than women, people feel safe in assuming that *all* men are taller.

One of the best ways to appreciate how limited stereotypes are is to think about the stereotypes associated with a group to which you belong. Think of the ethnicity, religion, gender , or race of this group. Now think about the stereotypes associated with this group. Now think about the people you know who belong to this ethnic, religious, gender, or racial group. See how the stereotypes do not fit? When we think of all those who are in the same group as ourselves, we see the diversity, not the similarity, suggested by stereotypes.

FIGURE 8-2

**COMPARISON OF AVERAGE HEIGHTS OF CANADIAN MEN AND WOMEN**

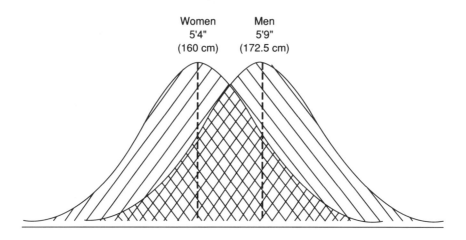

*What are some specific things which can be done to value diversity?*

This book cannot provide a full description of the complex process of
valuing diversity. Instead it's purpose is to give a general sense of what
is needed. More complete sources are provided in the reference sections
at the end of the chapters.

Some of the factors which help in valuing diversity are explained below:

- Establish a clear statement of the *mission* of the organization. This
  mission will facilitate the assessment of specific current practices
  and requests for accommodation. For instance ask:

  > Is there a compelling business reason for
  > _____(current practice)?
  > Does the nature of the work require
  > _____be done this way? Why?

  By answering these questions explicitly it is possible to ascertain
  whether or not the adaptation the organization is being asked to
  make is feasible. Recall the example of the baptized, male Sikh
  who had to wear a turban and the RCMP's traditional uniform
  requirement. An assessment showed that the true purpose of the
  organization could be served by someone wearing a turban.
- Cross-cultural awareness training enables people to become aware
  of their own culture so that they can better understand cultural
  differences, rather than making judgments about other cultures –

usually that everyone else's ways of doing things are wrong or strange. This training can highlight the organization's current culture and where it supports and clashes with aspects of other cultures.

- Practise good, open communication. Withholding judgment while seeking information is helpful – do not make assumptions about others' cultures.
- Identify a common ground on which to build relationships of trust and mutual respect.
- Leaders of the organization – its managers and supervisors – need to set an example. They must reinforce values of diversity and celebrate differences.
- Reward, in a concrete way, those who value diversity.
- Show examples of diversity when EE is NOT the issue. For instance, including pictures of designated group members in recruiting materials is a good EE strategy. Including pictures of designated group members in the annual report or other material not directly related to EE shows a commitment to integrate designated group members within the organizational context.
- Realize that mistakes will be made. View cultural clashes as an opportunity to learn rather than as a mistake.

### What happens when organizations try to value diversity?

Valuing diversity is difficult and cultural clashes will occur. Cultural clash is conflict over basic values that occur between groups of people with different core identities.[22] Such clashes are disruptive and often are personally discomforting. Cultural clashes can be threatening and confusing but they also offer the opportunity for organizational enhancement. How the cultural clashes are dealt with is a measure of how well the organization is valuing diversity.

Those who feel threatened by the clash are likely to engage in avoidance and isolation, termination of the interaction or the relationship, defensiveness and hostility. Those who are confused can either avoid this issue or seek further information or a new way of looking at the problem. Often this focuses on sharing information about expectations, about style and about what is perceived to be important. If the clash is taken as an opportunity for enhancing organization effectiveness then there is increased awareness, sharing of information, and willingness to adapt and change.

Dr. S. Kanu Kogod[23] suggests dealing with cultural clash using the following four steps:

1. Listen: Actively listen to everything the other person has to say, including all expressions of feelings. Then respond to *what* is being said, not *how* it is said. Stay calm, confident and open to all information.

2. Evaluate: Determine the cause of the problem, [could it be due to]: Violation of expectations? Intrusion from an external source? Lack of role clarification? Avoid expressing anger, shock or amusement.
3. Negotiate: Agree with the other person's right to hold her/his opinion, and explain your own perspective. Offer options, and allow the person to choose any option that does not cause harm to any party.
4. Accommodate: Explain pertinent organizational values and assumptions ... explain and demonstrate, if necessary, the action that will be taken.

Diversity can bring about many good things. It will always require doing things differently. This will take time and may cause frustration (hopefully only for a period of time, not forever).

### Isn't communication key?

Yes, it is. But this is one of the challenges, since there are clear differences in communication styles between groups which can create a great deal of confusion as the various groups try to communicate with each other. Communication problems arise between individuals from the same culture, so it is likely they will arise between people who are different. For example, communication issues can arise between those from different ethnic communities, between men and women, and between persons who have speech and/or hearing impairments.

It would be easier if communication involved only the spoken or written word. People are less conscious of the many other aspects of communication which have significant meaning. These include such things as grammatical structure, physical gestures, posture and body language, timing, stress and intonation of speech, the sense of physical space and body contact, eye contact or lack of contact, facial expressions and the strength of a handshake.

Communication always involves both a sender and a receiver of information and cultural differences can affect either, or both, of these functions. Since the purpose of communication is an exchange of ideas, both the sender and the receiver are responsible for ensuring that the communication exchange occurs. Complaints of "You just don't listen to me" or "I cannot understand you" require work on the part of both the sender and the receiver. The first thing to do is to admit that communication is not occurring, without placing blame. Do not avoid conflict by simply ignoring the problem. To help identify where the mis-communication occurred, one may try to repeat what the other person said in their own words. Avoiding sarcasm, idioms, and humour which is not shared can help minimize the communication problem. Sometimes getting a third party involved can help. Active listening is not as well-developed a skill for most people as talking.

Become sensitive to language that is appropriate or inappropriate in communicating with diverse groups, as was noted in Chapter 3. Though the words may change, the basic principles are to use language which is inclusive rather than exclusive, and to show respect for all groups.

Some concrete suggestions on cross-cultural communication are provided in The McDonald Series publications. Some of these suggestions are as follows. Patience when talking to those in groups other than one's own, including allowing more time to establish rapport. Listening carefully. Testing of one's understanding of what has been said by repeating, in different words, what one thinks the other person said and asking for confirmation. Being aware that different cultures have different norms about directness. Further, there are differences in the length of time deemed appropriate between asking a question and getting a reply. For instance, in mainstream Canadian culture there is almost no pause while in some other cultures a pause can last up to 15 seconds. In some cultures the important information is put at the beginning of a sentence while in other cultures, it comes at the end.

In all cultures much information is communicated non-verbally – however, the non-verbal signals vary across cultural groups. For example, in some white cultures people who are listening to another in conversation tend to look at the speaker; the person talking will tend to look around, making eye contact with the listener only periodically. In some Black cultures the pattern of eye contact is just the opposite – the speaker looks at the listener, while the listener makes only periodic eye contact. Some other subtleties in communication differ between cultures, such as norms concerning the proper physical distance between people when having a conversation, saying "no" or using other negatives, and rules about politeness to those in positions of authority.

Sometimes it is useful to involve "translators" – others who know both cultures or have struggled with cross-cultural communication problems before.

### How will you know if diversity has been successfully valued?

All the employment systems will naturally work well for everyone. When they do not, the organization will be open to exploring options and making the necessary changes.

## NOTES

1. [1990] 2 S.C.R. 489, 72 D.L.R. (4th) 417.
2. [1985] 2 S.C.R. 536, 12 O.A.C. 241, 23 D.L.R. (4th) 321, 9 C.C.E.L. 185, 7 C.H.R.R. D/3102.
3. R.S.O. 1990, c. H.19.
4. [1985] 2 S.C.R. 561, 23 D.L.R. (4th) 481.
5. R.S.C. 1985, c. H-6.
6. The study was conducted by Job Accommodation Network (JAN) and published in "Evaluation Report Executive Summary". A copy can be obtained from JAN at 809 Allen Hall, West Virginia University, P.O. Box 6123, Morgantown, West Virginia, 26506-6123.
7. *Guidelines for Assessing Accommodation Requirements for People with Disabilities*, Ontario Human Rights Commission, Toronto, 1989. Reproduced with the permission of the Ontario Human Rights Commission.
8. (1992), 71 B.C.L.R. (2d) 145, [1992] 6 W.W.R. 193, 141 N.R. 185 (S.C.C.).
9. *Supra* note 7, p. 8.
10. *Ibid.*, p. 10.
11. *Ibid.*, p. 13.
12. *Ibid.*
13. Many of the same accommodations as are needed to balance work and family which is discussed at the end of Chapter 7.
14. R.S.C. 1985, c. 24 (4th Supp.).
15. R. Roosevelt Thomas, Jr., *Beyond Race and Gender: Unleashing the Power of Your Total Work Force by Managing Diversity*, New York: American Management Association (AMACOM), 1991, p. 4.
16. *Ibid.*, at p. 10.
17. Marilyn Loden and Judy B. Rosener, *Workforce America! Managing Employee Diversity as a Vital Resource*, Homewood, Ill.: Business One Irwin, 1991, p. 138.
18. *Ibid.*, at pp. 27-28.
19. *Supra* note 15, at pp. 52-53.
20. *Supra* note 17, at pp. 220-221.
21. *Supra* note 15, at p. 14.
22. *Supra* note 17, at p. 121.
23. S. Kanu Kogod, *A Workshop for Managing Diversity in the Workplace*, San Diego: Pfeiffer & Company, 1991, p. 64.

# REFERENCES

John P. Fernandez, *Managing a Diverse Work Force*, Lexington, Mass: Lexington Books, 1991.

David Jamieson and Julie O'Mara, *Managing Workforce 2000: Gaining the Diversity Advantage*, San Francisco: Jossey-Bass, 1991.

S. Kanu Kogod, *A Workshop for Managing Diversity in the Workplace,* San Diego: Pfeiffer & Company, 1991.

Marilyn Loden and Judy B. Rosener, *Workforce America! Managing Employee Diversity as a Vital Resource*, Homewood, Ill.: Business One Irwin, 1991.

The McDonald Series, *Managing Diversity*, Winnipeg: Cross Cultural Communications International, Inc.

R. Roosevelt Thomas, Jr., *Beyond Race and Gender: Unleashing the Power of Your Total Work Force by Managing Diversity*, New York: American Management Association (AMACOM), 1991.

# CHAPTER 9

# Staffing: From Recruitment to Orientation

Staffing is the process of getting the right people into jobs – and retaining them. Staffing involves both initial hires and promotions. In this chapter, staffing is considered in its broadest terms to include outreach recruitment, selection, and orientation. "Outreach recruitment" is the term used to refer to recruitment efforts necessary to ensure that members of the four designated groups are within the pool of candidates to be considered for jobs. The selection process includes all the means an organization uses to collect information on candidates and to make a hiring decision. Tests, interviews and reference checks are all part of selection. Orientation of new employees is concerned with facilitating retention.

Both outreach recruitment and selection must be based on bona fide job requirement. A common myth surrounding EE is that it results in the hiring of unqualified people. This should not occur. This chapter begins with a discussion of job qualifications within the context of EE.

## QUALIFICATIONS

*What are the EE issues around qualifications?*

Employment equity *never* means hiring unqualified people. To do so would be detrimental to the organization, the individual hired and EE efforts. Rather, EE requires that:

- Job qualifications be assessed to ensure they are expressed in terms of what is needed to *begin* the job.
- Recognition be given for qualifications acquired in non-traditional ways.
- The image of who, traditionally, is expected to do particular jobs is made explicit.

*What is meant by job qualifications "needed to begin the job"?*

First it means:

Job requirements must be job-related.

This statement sounds naive and obvious. But it is key to EE. To clarify its meaning it should be stated as follows:

Job requirements must be expressed in terms of
those needed to begin the job.

Setting job requirements is an art, not a science. Typically, many factors, some of them irrelevant, have influenced the establishment of job requirements. Many requirements are added because "they would be nice to have", or because "those are the qualifications of the current incumbent". Others reflect "the qualifications of the boss". Some requirements are known to be excessive but are added because, at a particular time, the organization could "get people with these requirements". Employment equity principles require, for jobs where there is an inadequate representation of designated group members, that job requirements be only those actually required to begin the job. Setting higher requirements which prevent designated group members, *who are capable of performing the job*, from being hired is inconsistent with the achievement of EE.

The qualifications held by someone beginning a job are unlikely to be the same as those held by someone leaving the job. The latter has the experience of actually doing the job. They have learned from performing the job. That learning may have been formal or informal, come from co-workers, supervisors or training programs, been obtained on or off the job. The new employee needs to have the qualifications to take advantage of this learning to become fully competent in the job.

One of the biggest issues related to job requirements is the concern that people in entry-level jobs have the qualifications to be promoted. Many organizations say: "This entry-level job does not require five years of experience, but for someone to get promoted they must have it." What happens when organizations are not just looking for someone to fill an entry-level job, but are looking for someone who can move up in the organization? This situation needs to be analyzed in terms of:

1. How many of the people promoted will have started in the entry-level job? (Of all the people in the higher level job, what proportion would have been employed in the entry-level job originally?)
2. How many of the people in the entry-level job will be promoted? (Of all the people in the entry-level job, what proportion will be promoted – rather than remaining in the entry-level job or quitting the organization?)
3. What are the minimum requirements needed to begin the higher level job?

It is true that organizations that promote from within need to have people who can move into higher level jobs. But, does everyone who gets promoted begin in the entry-level position? (Question 1). Even if the answer to this question is "yes", it does not mean that everyone hired into the entry-level job must have the ability to be promoted. One must look to Question 2 – What proportion of people in the entry-level position get promoted? It could be that all the people promoted into a higher level job have worked in the entry-level job, but that only 20 per cent of the people who work in the entry-level job actually get promoted. The other 80 per cent of the people hired into the entry-level job either remain in this job, move laterally, or quit. So, it is unnecessary that everyone hired into an entry-level job be promotable. In fact, since only a small proportion of people get promoted, hiring everyone with the potential to be promoted, while having one advantage, can have a significant disadvantage. The advantage is that there is a large pool of people from which to promote. However, if only a small proportion will actually be promoted, but everyone has the potential to be promoted, then dissatisfaction and higher turnover can result. If only a small proportion of people are likely to be promoted then it is particularly important not to exclude from entry-level positions those who have the qualifications to successfully perform the entry-level position, even if they do not appear to have the potential to be promoted.

Question 3 is What are the minimum qualifications to begin the higher level job? Specifically, how much of the skills and knowledge needed for promotion is gained from performing the entry-level job? How else can the qualifications be gained? Must the person have those qualifications before beginning to work in the entry-level job (*e.g.*, licence)? It is important to determine whether a job candidate must begin the entry-level position with the actual skills and knowledge to perform in higher level positions, or whether he or she must simply demonstrate the potential to learn (either on or off the job) what is needed for higher level jobs.

### *What does it mean to recognize that there are different ways to gain qualifications?*

Many job requirements are expressed in terms of degrees and diplomas or years of experience. But these are used as a shorthand way to express a level of skill and/or kind of ability needed on the job. Employment equity principles require organizations to consider what is required to do the job and realize that there is often more than one way to obtain this knowledge, skill, ability or talent. (Exceptions include requirement for licences (*e.g.*, drivers), trades ticket, or medical certification (*e.g.*, M.D.) where these are required by law to perform certain duties of the job.)

For many jobs, paid work is not the only way to acquire skills. Many individuals have gained useful skills through volunteer work. Running a household can also provide good work-related skills. Where, or how, one learns a skill is less important than the fact that one has learned it. Interview questions that allow candidates to share skills gained in non-work settings, in addition to paid employment, are good. For example, an employer who needed people familiar with basic tools (*e.g.*, hammers, screwdrivers) asked the question: "Have you worked in construction?" This question would screen out many women who are capable of doing the job but have not worked in a construction job. The question was changed to: "Have you done any home repairs?" Responses to this question would supply the information needed to assess the candidate's – both female and male – qualifications. This question recognizes that it does not matter if a person uses tools around the home or on the job – once he/she knows how to use them the skill is available in a work environment.

### Why should organizations make explicit their images of who can or should perform each job?

Often, people unconsciously associate images or pictures with particular occupations. The common image of a nurse differs from the image of a police officer; the image of an engineer differs from a librarian. Generally, there is a strong association between many occupations and gender. Sometimes images associated with certain occupations have an ethnic component. None of these images are likely to incorporate someone with a disability. Such images can be a powerful influence. If someone being interviewed does not "look like" the type of person who typically does this job, the interviewer may judge the candidate's answers differently from someone who fits the image. A candidate's application may even be eliminated because it does not show the career expected pattern. For example, a university faculty of accounting was considering a female applicant and the search committee had decided to reject her. When they were questioned why, the committee noted its concern that she was not committed to the field. The search committee had come to this conclusion because her career path did not fit the standard mould. Most male candidates either had gone straight through school to get their Ph.D.s or had worked as accountants before getting their Ph.D.s. This female candidate had spent time in another field before getting her Ph.D. in accounting. What exactly had she been doing? – teaching math. Upon reflection the search committee realized that having left another career to pursue a Ph.D. in accounting demonstrated her commitment and that high school teaching was a valuable background for a faculty position. By making explicit the image of the type of person associated with a particular job, those making selection decisions can be vigilant to ensure that such an image does not influence their hiring decisions.

### Does EE mean we cannot hire the most qualified person?

Employment equity challenges organizations to assess what is meant by "most qualified". First, it should be recognized that "most qualified" does not mean the best person in the whole world for this job. Rather, it means the person those making the hiring decision perceive to be the best person from among those who applied and whose talent is recognized. In other words, if the truly "most qualified" person does not apply, or, if that person is not perceived to be the best qualified, then true talent is being lost.

Many people are concerned that there is a conflict between qualifications and the hiring of designated group members. Many people assume that EE is the antithesis of hiring qualified persons. This reaction is based on the following four assumptions:

1. Merit is the only determinant in a hiring decision.
2. If designated group members were qualified they would be hired/ promoted without EE.
3. Gaining qualifications is an individual's responsibility.
4. The most qualified person can be identified and such identification is independent of race, gender, or perceptions of physical or mental disability (beyond what is actually required to do a job).

With these assumptions in mind, an examination of how job candidates are evaluated is in order. Potential employees are typically judged on three criteria:

1. Task capability (merit, job-related qualifications)
2. Organizational citizenship
3. Organizational fit

Task capability relates to ability, talent, knowledge and skills. The ability to do the technical aspects of the job. A truck driver must know the rules of the road and how to drive a truck. A professor must know the course material and how to teach effectively. A secretary must know wordprocessing and how to set up letters, tables, reports, etc. But the term "most qualified" is not based solely on task competence.

The second criteria measures whether or not the candidate is perceived to be a good organizational citizen. No job description spells out everything that is expected of employees. It is understood that everyone is expected to be concerned for safety, to handle equipment appropriately, to call in when sick or otherwise unable to come to work, to be civil, etc. In addition, employees are expected to co-operate and to give freely of their ideas. Sometimes an organization will trade-off technical competence for good citizenship. For instance, hiring someone who is perceived to be willing to play by the organizational rules and not "rock the boat". Generally, there is an assumption that technical competence is more important.

Organizational fit is the third criteria. Fit refers to how similar or dissimilar candidates are to the people who are already in the work unit. If the candidate "fits in" then everyone is likely to feel comfortable and, it is presumed, will work well together. Organizational fit is also related to trust and commitment to the organization. Fit affects how new employees will be accepted into the informal network. Through this network vital information is passed from one part of the organization to another, perhaps via casual conversation in an elevator or a person from one department may call another after meeting at a party.

While task competence is assessed formally through the selection process, assessment in terms of organizational citizenship and fit are assessed informally during the interview. This assessment is often based on stereotypes (*e.g.*, "members of this group are usually late, I bet this person will not be at work on time"); or it may simply be based on appearance (*e.g.*, "this person does not look like the other people working here"). Though these assessments are less explicit than the assessment of task competence, they influence the perception as to who is the "best qualified".

Qualified designated group members may not be perceived so because they do not fit the image of those typically filling the job, or because equally qualified individuals who are different are not judged the same. Studies demonstrating how equally qualified members of different races are not treated the same was mentioned in Chapter 1. Another study focusing on gender also illustrates this point. Six resumes were sent to human resource professionals, along with a job description. The human resource professionals were asked to rank the six candidates in terms of their qualifications for the job. All the human resource professionals received identical resumes – with one exception. On one resume, sent to half of the professionals, the candidate's first name was "John" and on the other resume, sent to the other professionals, the first name was "Jane". The resumes were otherwise identical. Consistently, both female and male human resource professionals ranked Jane as less qualified than John for the job in question. Since the qualifications of the two were identical – only the gender of the applicant was different – this may have been due to vague notions that Jane would not want to travel or would not be as committed to her job. It could not have been her qualifications since they were the same as John's.

Employment equity never means hiring unqualified people. It does require an honest assessment of job qualifications to ensure that they are neither inflated nor irrelevant. It also requires recognition of qualifications regardless of where they have been acquired. Finally, EE requires acknowledging that hiring decisions have been influenced by images of the kinds of people who have traditionally filled certain kinds of work; such images can block out recognition that those who differ from the image can be qualified for the work.

## OUTREACH RECRUITING

*What is outreach recruiting?*

The purpose of recruiting is to create a pool of applicants from which an organization will hire the people it needs to do its work. Outreach recruiting refers to efforts to ensure that the pool of candidates includes members of designated groups not traditionally considered for the particular position being filled.

Outreach recruiting means going to where designated group members are rather than more generalized recruiting. Outreach recruitment is needed because traditional recruiting practices have not always been equally welcoming. This was demonstrated in a research study conducted in Toronto in the mid-1980s which found that racial minority applicants were treated poorly – even though they had the same qualifications as white applicants – when they applied to jobs advertised in the major Toronto newspapers.[1] Members of the designated groups have learned that traditional job advertisements and other traditional recruiting sources do not always include them. For example, the Canadian Civil Liberties Association has conducted five studies in the last 15 years. They have called employment agencies pretending to be an employer asking the agency to send them only mainstream candidates. The results have all been similar. In the 1992 study, seven out of ten, and in the 1991 study, 13 out of 15 employment agencies agreed to discriminate in terms of the types of people they would refer.

The very essence of outreach recruiting is to make it clear that an organization is truly interested in hiring members of the four target groups. This is done by issuing a specific "invitation" to these groups to come and apply. This may involve posting a notice in Indian Friendship Centres, advertising in community papers serving various racial minority communities, or sending job announcements to women's groups or agencies working with persons with disabilities.

Being open to hiring designated group members, *if* they apply, is not enough. Placing advertisements in mainstream newspapers and publications with the intention that the organization will consider any qualified candidate who applies is not enough. Each organization needs a reputation for being a good place to work for Aboriginal Peoples, persons with disabilities, racial minorities, women and white, able-bodied men. In order to gain this reputation with respect to each of these groups, it is necessary to recruit, hire and retain designated group members. Where there is an underrepresentation of designated group members or if they are not found throughout the organization then active, targeted outreach recruitment efforts are needed. Recruitment will have to be conducted in ways which have not traditionally been used.

### Is word-of-mouth recruiting a problem?

To the extent that recruitment (and selection) is based on who one knows, those who are on the outside will remain so because they are less likely to have the necessary contacts. This is why word-of-mouth recruiting is considered systemic discrimination. Though it is often inexpensive and effective, if an organization does not have racial minorities or Aboriginal Peoples in the work-force already it is unlikely that the friends, relatives and neighbours of the current work-force will increase the representation of these two designated groups. Further, unless it is clear that the organization will accommodate persons with disabilities it is unlikely that the disabled friends, relatives or neighbours of the current employees will be encouraged to apply. Finally, unless it is clear that the organization welcomes women into non-traditional jobs, few in the current work-force are going to think of mentioning non-traditional jobs to the women they know.

### What are the typical outreach recruiting sources used?

Recruiting sources should be analyzed to determine if they are a barrier to designated group members. Some of the internal recruiting sources are:[2]

**Notices on bulletin boards or in organizational publications:** Are the notices accessible to everyone (*e.g.*, those in remote locations or out of the office much of the time)?

**Seniority:** If there are few designated group members or if all are new employees then seniority can act as a barrier. More is said about seniority in Chapter 4.

**Next-in-line:** Vacancies are sometimes filled simply by promoting the individual perceived to be next-in-line in the hierarchy. If feeder positions have no designated group members, nothing will change.

**Skill inventory:** Skill inventories solicit voluntary information from all employees about career interests and skills (regardless of where obtained). Inventories which are collected on all employees, kept up to date and factual allow an organization to search among current employees for those who have the necessary skills.

**Previous applications:** Retaining applications for a short time may be useful if it is likely that similar jobs will soon become vacant or if, historically, there has been a high turnover rate. It is a good idea to inform candidates how long their applications will be kept, so that they will not assume the organization will continue to consider them after their applications have been discarded.

**Tapped on shoulder:** When there is a job opening often the hiring manager will ask her or his colleagues within the organization who would be a good candidate for the job. This can be an obvious barrier if only mainstream candidates are recognized.

External sources include:

**Newspapers (provincial, local, ethnic, national, trade):** Consider sources other than the mainstream press (*e.g.*, community papers or industry newsletters that target specific groups such as the *Women in Engineering* newsletter). Deadlines for many newspapers and trade publications make it difficult to make advertisements timely. For that reason, a general advertisement for the positions your organization typically needs may be more effective in the long run.

**Walk-ins:** Effectiveness of walk-ins depends on where an organization is located and how many of the designated group members are likely to "walk by".

**Unsolicited resumes:** It is important not to rely solely on these applications, unless they have been reviewed to ensure that they contain a reasonable proportion of designated group members.

**Schools:** Pick schools which have a good representation of designated group members.

**Professional associations:** Some professional associations provide employment advertising and candidate referral services for their members. It is important that an organization makes it clear that they are anxious to see a diverse group of candidates and that they follow EE principles.

**Union hiring halls:** Some unions (*i.e.*, carpenters) are working to increase their number of designated group members. Unions need to continue to do more in this area.

**Employment agencies/Temporary help agencies:** Employers should inform any agency they deal with that they are an EE employer and want to see a diversity of candidates. It may be best to seek out employment agencies which specialize in working with designated group members.

**Government agencies or other non-profit:** Organizations such as Canada Employment Centres (CEC), YM/YWCA, Women in Trades Association, Native Friendship Centres, Canadian Institute for the Blind and many others are available as recruiting sources.

**Referrals from associations or employees:** Word-of-mouth recruiting is never sufficient unless an organization has achieved its EE goal of full representation.

*What are some outreach recruiting strategies?*

Various outreach recruiting strategies are described below:

- Specialized recruitment visits to schools and colleges (*e.g.*, career days, youth motivation programs, or job fairs).
- Write-ups in trade and community papers. Try to get coverage in the papers and in the sections that minorities and women read (*e.g.*, the "Women's Section") for maximum impact. Minority-oriented radio stations, television stations, or magazines can be used regularly for public relations efforts.
- Establishment of internships with local colleges and universities. Consider a program modeled on the Native Internship Program run by Canada Employment and Immigration.
- Communicate with local groups involved with Aboriginal Peoples, persons with disabilities, racial minorities and women about what the organization does, the types of workers it employs, and its commitment to EE.
- Co-operate with other organizations in the area or the same industry interested in outreach recruiting.
- Advertise in community newspapers through organizations, schools and media which attract specific groups such as women or Aboriginal Peoples. If reading knowledge of English/French is not necessary to begin a particular job, advertise in the language of the target communities, in minority publications, community centres or on minority language television or radio programs.
- Include designated group members in all publicity and advertising efforts and materials. Employ designated group members as recruiters for their community.
- Contact community groups associated with the designated groups.

Recognize that the community group and organizations may have different cultures. Study the community, but also be aware when approaching them that there is a lot to learn. Initially distrust of organizations is a common reaction. Frustrations at encountering barriers in the past may be expressed by members of the community even though the organization is trying to change things. It takes time for trust to be established. Remember respect of both mainstream culture and the culture of the designated group community is important.

- When placing an advertisement ensure that all qualifications listed are job-related and written in language that is clear and at a vocabulary level suitable for the language used on the job. Ensure the advertisement is not cluttered with descriptive words (*e.g.*, expert, advanced, thorough, etc.) which may not have the same meaning to everyone.
- Advertise in general help-wanted categories with the phrase "Aboriginal Peoples, persons with disabilities, racial minorities and women particularly encouraged to apply" at the bottom of the advertisement. Seek out publications read by designated group members and contact local community leaders.
- Always stress the policy of hiring qualified candidates, regardless of race, sex, age, or physical/mental ability.
- Contact national, regional and local chapters of professional and technical organizations associated with designated group members.

### What are some sources for identifying outreach recruiting targets?

Ask your current designated group employees what organizations they think would be helpful. Contact an EE network group – there are groups in Halifax, London, Ottawa, Toronto, Winnipeg, and Saskatchewan. (The London group has compiled a resource book for its community.)

The phone book is a potential source. For organizations near a First Nations reserve – call them. Listings related to Aboriginal Peoples might be under "Indian," Native" or "Aboriginal". Groups working with persons with disabilities are numerous, call a vocational services office (often part of provincial government) or a provincial Office of Disability Issues to get a listing. Look under "women" in the phone book of most major cities and you are likely to find some resources. Call the women's bureau or women's directorate associated with the federal, provincial or territorial government. Many provincial or municipal governments will have implemented EE before private sector organizations, call them or other organizations that have been dealing with EE and ask them for the outreach recruiting sources they have used. Check to see if there are any employment services specifically directed at members of designated groups; Employment Connection and Hiring Ability are two recruitment agencies working with persons with disabilities in Toronto.

## SELECTION

### *What is involved in selection?*

Selection is about gathering information on job candidates in order to make a hiring or promotion decision. Supervisors and human resource staff have knowledge about the job. Each applicant has knowledge about her/himself. The objective in selection is to obtain the information to identify the person or persons who can fulfil the needs of the organization. When putting together a set of selection procedures it is essential that each procedure be job-related. That is, each should help distinguish successful job holders from those less likely to be successful. It is the ability of the person to perform the duties of the job on day one that is to be assessed. When considering a selection mechanism, the following questions should be considered:

- What will this reveal about the candidate's skills and abilities for performing the job or their relevant work habits?
- Is this the best way to gain this information? The best way is the one which provides the most reliable information in a cost effective manner.

Information is collected formally (*e.g.*, written tests) or informally (*e.g.*, first impression). Typical information-collection mechanisms include:

- Application form or resume
- Written, work sample or other kinds of tests
- Interview
- References

**Application form or resume:** Some EE professionals advise requiring all candidates to complete an application form rather than accepting resumes. This ensures that candidates do not include information that is irrelevant to the selection decision but that is often included on a resume, such as health and marital status. Requiring use of the organization's application form also ensures that decision-makers have the same information in the same format on all candidates. This facilitates a consistent assessment of the information to be obtained from applications.

Obviously, application forms must be consistent with human rights requirements and must not include any illegal questions. All questions should be job-related. Organizations employing a broad range of jobs may find that they need more than one application form (or that different questions are to be completed by those applying for different jobs). In deciding what questions to include on an application form, the following queries should be made:

- How will the information gained from this question help assess the candidate's qualifications against the job requirements?
- Is this information needed from an applicant or is it information which is needed about an employee (someone who is hired)? If the answer is from an employee then do not ask for the information on the application form, ask for it after the person is hired.

Appendices 1 and 2 to this chapter provide material from the Ontario Human Rights Commission regarding what questions can be asked on an application form and a sample application form.

**Written, work sample or other kinds of tests:** Tests of any kind should measure either:

- Skills and abilities needed to begin the job; and/or
- Potential to learn the skills required on the job.

Tests measuring performance easily learned on the job are a waste of time.

Testing is the most technically sophisticated area in selection. This is because tests must be reliable and valid. Reliability means that the person would score the same on the test each time he/she took it. Validity means that the test is measuring what it is intended to measure and that this is job-related. Using tests which do not provide information as to how someone would do on the job will result in incorrect hiring decisions.

Designing valid tests is a science and is difficult to do without the assistance of a specialist in test design (*e.g.*, an industrial psychologist). The more a test resembles relevant work samples, the better the test is. For example, typing tests have been used for decades to determine how fast and accurately candidates can type. Given wordprocessing technology found in most organizations today, a simple typing test – even if it is given on a wordprocessor – does not provide good information about job skills required. A work sample involves asking someone to set up a document and would allow them to demonstrate their knowledge of formatting, "bolding" and underlining, moving a paragraph, etc. Valid work sampling tests require candidates do something which they will actually do on the job. Simulations fabricate work-like situations, for example, landing an airplane can be simulated on a computer.

There are different kinds of tests. Some measure a person's level of skill (*e.g.*, welding or editing). Others measure aptitude (*e.g.*, computer programming or decision-making). Others measure specific ability such as a (strength) or general ability (verbal, numerical or mechanical tests).

There are a number of ways to validate tests. Three types of validity are consistent EE principles – content, concurrent, or predictive (see Box 9-1). It is a good idea to have another type, face validity – this means that the test appears to be relevant to the job for which applicants are applying. However, just having face validity is never enough since it is only about whether the test appears to be appropriate, not whether it is or not. Validity is established by either purchasing validated tests *and* using them in the appropriate situation with the appropriate population, or validating a test within an organization. The latter is better because it ensures that the test works in the actual situation in which it is being used. This should be done with the aid of a specialist in testing. In the United States test validation became an important part of the affirmative action process.

Validation is technical and can involve a great deal of work. However, whether one is concerned because of EE reasons or not, it would be harmful to give a test which is not adequately related to the job. It is important to remember that testing is used to determine if someone is able to begin the job or to learn what they will need to learn on the job, not whether the person is currently proficient on the job.

Types of tests which have been used in employment situations include:

Skill tests (*e.g.*, dexterity, spatial ability)
Aptitude tests
Intelligence tests
Personality inventories or interest inventories
Strength tests
Work simulation or sampling
Skill assessment centre
Role playing or presentation

Regardless of the type of test being considered, many tests have been found to be cultural biased. That is, those who score high are not necessarily better at performing the job than those who score low – they are just more familiar with the culture. For example, one intelligence test for children developed in the United States asked a question about the kind of equipment a "conductor" would work with. While the question referred to a symphony conductor, many inter-city children tried to answer the question in terms of the conductor with which they had had contact – a streetcar conductor.

---

**Box 9-1**

**KIND OF VALIDITY**

Face validity:
Selection device looks like it measures what it is supposed to measure.

Content validity:
The content of the job is defined. Representative samples of this content are put into the test.

Concurrent validity:
Use relationship between performance of current employees on the test and on the job to assess if the test can identify those who can do the job. The problem with this method is that since current employees already are on the job they are likely to test differently from those who have not performed the job.

Predictive validity:
Give the test to a set of typical applicants, but do not use it to make a hiring decision. Hire a group of applicants and after a period of time on the job correlate test scores with performance and determine if test scores were able to predict performance.

---

**Interview:** Some organizations use tests and some check references, but virtually every organization interviews candidates. Even before EE became an issue, academic researchers criticized the interview process because of its potential for bias and ineffectiveness. Studies have shown that interviewers make à decision to hire or not within a few minutes of the start of the interview. Interviews also need to be valid – how a candidate does in the interview should be related to how that person would perform the job.

Some of the specific problems with interviews are:

* Their susceptibility to distortion and bias;
* Not being job-related;
* Too flexible – leading to inconsistencies between candidates;
* Tendency for interviewer to look for qualities that he/she prefers rather than what is job-related.

The one consistent finding of research on interviewing is that structuring the interview increases its reliability and validity.

A set of job-related questions are asked of all candidates in a structured interview. Questions may be of three types:

1.  Situational questions (may be hypothetical).
    These questions do not prompt an obvious answer. Rather than asking "Can you work under pressure?" the following question can be asked: "Tell me about a situation, either at work, school, home, or on holiday, where you had to deal with pressure." Alternatively, a hypothetical situation can be set up "What would you do if you had to finish an important report and your boss's boss asked you to take on a rush task?"
    Situational questions are often designed to assess non-technical work skills such as: communication skills, interpersonal skills, enthusiasm, good organizational citizenship and persuasiveness or aggressiveness. As noted below, assessment of these characteristics needs to take into account cultural differences.
2.  Job knowledge questions.
    These questions assess job knowledge which is essential to job performance and which must be known prior to entering the job. Asking factual questions in a written test, rather than in the interview, is often a better use of time. This assumes that reading skill is needed on the job, otherwise the organization is requiring skills in the selection process which are not needed on the job.
3.  Worker requirement questions.
    Assess an applicant's willingness to work in various environmental conditions and/or to discuss an accommodation which may be needed.

Questions must be unambiguous since having to clarify questions during the interview reduces standardization and can introduce bias. The language level of the questions should not exceed that required on the job. Questions should be strictly and clearly job-related. Further, the interviewer should spend most of the interview time on the important aspects of the job. The structured interview overcomes one of the biggest problems with interviews – interviewers who talk too much. Interviewers should only do 10 per cent to 20 per cent of the talking, since this is an opportunity to collect information from the candidate. The structured interview should also consider the diversity of candidates who are likely to be interviewed so that the questions can be designed to elicit from all candidates the information needed to make a selection decision.

Another major problem with interviews is that only about 7 per cent of the information received during an interview is based on the verbal answers given to questions. About 38 per cent of the meaning is deduced by the way the answer is communicated vocally, and 55 per cent comes from non-verbal communication. Non-verbal communication such as eye-contact, posture, accent and dress are interpreted and given more weight than the actual answers to the questions. Non-verbal communication differs between men and women, among persons who have different kinds of communicating ability (*e.g.*, hard of hearing, visually impaired) and people with different cultural backgrounds. For example, in different cultures the means of showing respect for authority differ; there are various cultural norms about bragging or selling oneself and assertiveness is displayed differently between men and women. None of this would be worrisome, except that people have a tendency to make broad, conclusive judgments from a single piece of information. For instance, what does a weak handshake mean? What does it mean if a candidate does not want to talk about her/his qualifications because they are outlined in detail on the application form? Those of one culture will interpret these behaviours differently than those of another culture.

To prepare for interviews with diverse candidates, The McDonald Series recommends providing all candidates with information about what to expect during the interview process. This should include the number of interviewers, how interviewers should be addressed (by first name or by title), the physical arrangement, examples of questions and the kinds of answers sought. Interviewers should be trained in the cultural and language differences of the potential interviewees. For example, interviewers should be alerted that in some Aboriginal cultures it is typical to pause longer than in the mainstream culture before answering a question; that it is permissible to discuss someone's disability within the context of what is needed to perform the job; and that it is not permissible to discuss child care arrangements. Interviewers should be familiar as to which cultures are boastful (*i.e.*, mainstream North American) and which are not (*i.e.*, Asian and Aboriginal).

**References:** References must be related to the job for which the applicant is applying. A serious problem with most reference checks is that they involve open-ended questions such as:

Was he/she a good employee?

This is problematic if the previous job was dissimilar from the one the candidate is applying for or if an organization and the person giving the reference place different emphasis on different aspects of the same job. For instance, one organization may emphasize the interpersonal aspect while another organization may emphasize the technical aspect of the same job. References are not about the individual candidate but about the person-job match. Before asking any questions about performance, it is best to ask about the job that the person performed for the other organization. Then it is appropriate to ask how they performed in those aspects of the job relative to those in the job the candidate is applying for. Unfortunately, if not conducted properly, the information obtained may say more about the person giving the reference (*e.g.*, whether they are a lenient or severe evaluator) than about the candidate for whom the reference is being given.

### How should the selection mechanisms be structured?

The answer to this question will depend on the job for which an organization is hiring. The number of selection mechanisms used should be related to base rate, cost of training, cost of making selection error, cost of each selection device, and the amount of testing reasonable for the level of the job. The base rate is the proportion of people in the population who can do the job. More people have the ability to be a cleaner than to be a brain surgeon. The effect of base rate on selection is demonstrated by the following two selection processes. In the Appalachian mountains when it is time to pick tomatoes, the entire recruiting and selection process involves someone from the canning company driving around in a jeep announcing from a loudspeaker that work is available picking tomatoes. Anyone who shows up is hired. At the other end of the continuum is a string quartet which, when hiring a violin player, requires candidates to rehearse and perform with the group.

A selection decision must be based on the individual being considered and not on stereotypes of the group to which the person belongs. To ensure this some organizations require that a second look be given to any designated group candidate at each point in the selection process if the person is being turned down. Those doing the hiring must make explicit the basis for their judgment. This second look is a good example of how differential treatment is required to ensure equality. Mainstream candidates do not require a second look because there is no reason to believe that stereotypes would interfere in their assessment during the selection procedure. Because this is not true with designated group candidates, a second look, making explicit why someone was not selected, accomplishes two things. One, it ensures that nothing was missed and that the candidate was not judged on stereotypes rather than on individual skills and abilities. It allows a second assessment as to whether a presumption that the person would not fit in, rather than qualifications, was the deciding factor. Two, this second look may provide ideas on how to improve recruiting efforts in the future in order to identify a pool of designated group members who are more likely to be selected.

### Focus on selection of persons with disabilities.

Up to this point this chapter has been general in its orientation. Within EE it is necessary to be aware that while the four designated groups are all disadvantaged, each faces unique barriers. Thus, each group raises unique issues which must be addressed. To highlight this, this section focuses on selection of persons with disabilities. Even within this group there is great heterogeneity, so that different barriers are faced by those with different kinds of disabilities.

Earlier it was stated that the objective of the selection process is to obtain information from job candidates so that a hiring decision can be made. Sometimes it is necessary to discuss a person's disability and any required accommodation. This can be done during the interview. Information as to disability status should not be asked on the application. Employment equity requires that organizations consider individuals and not make decisions based on stereotypes. Since it is possible that two individuals with the same disability can have different abilities it is impossible to obtain full information on an application form. Further, most people are unfamiliar with the potential of persons with disabilities, so it is common for employers to make erroneous assumptions and exclude persons who could perform jobs. Those who are unfamiliar with a particular disability tend to see it as "either-or". For example, either one can see or one is blind. In reality there is always a continuum. For example, a person can be legally blind and still have some sight. It is impossible to know where a particular individual is on this continuum simply by knowing their disability status.

During an interview, one should not avoid obtaining the information necessary to assess someone's qualifications to perform the job. Yet, many interviewers are influenced by the social norms that it is not polite to call attention to someone's disability. When one is interviewing a person who has a disability and there is a question in the interviewer's mind as to the interviewee's capacity to fulfil the essential requirements of the job, the interview provides the opportunity to gain this information. It provides the opportunity to begin discussion of any necessary accommodation. The important thing to remember is that the interviewee with a disability has information which the interviewer needs in order to make a fair assessment of the candidate.

The best way to approach this in the interview is to take a problem-solving approach. The interviewer has information about the job, while the interviewee has information about her/his capabilities. An exchange of information is needed to determine the correct selection decision. An opening for this kind of discussion might be:

I see (or I understand) that you are (have) _____. I am unfamiliar with this condition in general and your specific situation. I am aware that it is common for those unfamiliar with a particular disability to make erroneous assumptions about it and I want to avoid doing that by learning from you about your capabilities with respect to _____ (position for which candidate is being interviewed). Please forgive me if I seem insensitive or ignorant at times, I just want to ensure, as I do with all the candidates I am interviewing, that I fully understand your capabilities with respect to this job. This discussion will also provide me with an opportunity to supply you with information about the job. And, of course, I will be happy to answer any additional questions you have. Further, this discussion will let me know if I will need to re-search further any accommodation which may be needed if you are the successful candidate.

The interview will then continue with a discussion of each of the essential activities in the job:

• Begin with the most essential and key part of the job.
• Ensure that the candidate understands what is involved in this activity.
• Be open to the fact that jobs can often be accomplished in different ways, not just the way it is currently being performed by able-bodied individuals.
• Obtain from the interviewee her/his suggestions as to how the tasks may be accommodated (but do not assume this is the final answer, accommodation often has to be discussed further after both the organization and the candidate know more).

Some tips for interviewing applicants with certain disabilities are found in the Box 9-2.

One device which has been used to aid in the assessment of candidates for particular jobs is a physical demands analysis (PDA). This is a form to record the physical demands of jobs developed by the Ontario Ministry of Labour, see Figure 9-1. Used as an addendum to a narrative job description it describes the job in terms of strength, mobility, sensory/perceptual requirements and the work environment. The PDA provides a starting point for a discussion as to whether a person can perform a job or not – given the way the job is currently being performed. One danger with the PDA is that it may not be flexible enough to recognize that there may be other ways the job can be done. For example, if a PDA were done for the job of baseball pitcher it would imply that two hands are needed. Yet, Jim Abbott is a one-handed pitcher in the major leagues. In fact, Abbott is one of only a handful of baseball players who have gone from playing college ball into the major leagues without going through the minor leagues. The PDA is simply an aid, it does not replace the need to consider accommodation.

Use of the PDA to remove bias is enhanced when used as follows:[3]

---

**Box 9-2**

**TIPS FOR INTERVIEWING**

*Speech Impaired Persons*
- Do not hesitate to ask a speech-impaired person to repeat a statement that is unclear to you.

*Deaf/Hearing Impaired Persons*
- Obtain the attention of a deaf person who must lip-read before speaking to him/her.
- Face a deaf/hearing-impaired person who is lip-reading.
- Speak slowly and distinctly when addressing a lip-reader, but not to the extent of exaggerating your lip movements.
- Position a signing interpreter properly.
- Some deaf people are "non-verbal", others speak.
- To make it easier for a lip-reader, it is best to avoid having a bright or glaring light behind you.
- Speak in a normal tone to a deaf person.
- If a deaf person does not have an interpreter, most likely they can lip-read so that communication with them is possible.

*Blind/Visually-Impaired Persons*
- Speak in a normal tone and directly to a blind person.
- A dog guide is a tool or aid used by a blind person. It is not a pet; therefore, do not pet or play with it or you will distract the dog from its task as a working animal.
- When you enter a room where a blind person is present, announce your presence.
- If you are discussing a form or passing out material, describe these to a visually-impaired person and ensure that a copy is given to him/her.

*Developmentally-Disabled Persons*
- Keep sentences short and to the point when interviewing a developmentally-disabled person. Use clear and understandable language.
- Ask for their feedback to make sure that they understand important points, just as you would with any other applicant.

---

- Provided to all applicants routinely so that those with disabilities are not placed in the position of having to ask.
- Considers only physical demands of essential aspects of the job.
- It is understood that the way the job is currently performed is not the only way it can be done.

# FIGURE 9-1

Ontario
Ministry of
Labour

Centre for
Disability
and Work

**Physical Demands Analysis**

| Position Title | | Contact |
|---|---|---|
| Department | Date | Phone |

| | Physical Demands | | Weight | | ★Frequency | | | | Comments |
|---|---|---|---|---|---|---|---|---|---|
| | | Check if Performed | Maximum | (Usual) | 1 Seldom | 2 Minor | 3 Required | 4 Major | |
| **Strength** | 1 Lifting | | | | | | | | |
| | 2 Carrying | | | | | | | | |
| | 3 Pushing | | | | | | | | |
| | 4 Pulling | | | | | | | | |
| | 5 Fine Finger Movements | | | | | | | | |
| | 6 Handling | | | | | | | | |
| | 7 Gripping | | | | | | | | |
| | 8 Reaching — Above Shoulder | | | | | | | | |
| | 8 Reaching — Below Shoulder | | | | | | | | |
| | 9 Foot Action — 1 Foot | | | | | | | | |
| | 9 Foot Action — 2 Feet | | | | | | | | |
| | 10 Throwing | | | | | | | | |
| **Mobility** | 11 Sitting | | | | | | | | |
| | 12 Standing | | | | | | | | |
| | 13 Walking | | | | | | | | |
| | 14 Running | | | | | | | | |
| | 15 Climbing | | | | | | | | |
| | 16 Bending/Stooping | | | | | | | | |
| | 17 Crouching | | | | | | | | |
| | 18 Kneeling | | | | | | | | |
| | 19 Crawling | | | | | | | | |
| | 20 Twisting | | | | | | | | |
| | 21 Balancing | | | | | | | | |
| **Sensory/Perceptual** | 22 Hearing — Conversation | | | | | | | | |
| | 22 Hearing — Other Sounds | | | | | | | | |
| | 23 Vision — Far | | | | | | | | |
| | 23 Vision — Near | | | | | | | | |
| | 23 Vision — Colour | | | | | | | | |
| | 23 Vision — Depth | | | | | | | | |
| | 24 Perception — Spatial | | | | | | | | |
| | 24 Perception — Form | | | | | | | | |
| | 25 Feeling | | | | | | | | |
| | 26 Reading | | | | | | | | |
| | 27 Writing | | | | | | | | |
| | 28 Speech | | | | | | | | |
| **Work Environment** | 29 Inside Work | | | | | | | | |
| | 30 Outside Work | | | | | | | | |
| | 31 Hot/Cold | | | | | | | | |
| | 32 Humid/Dry | | | | | | | | |
| | 33 Dust | | | | | | | | |
| | 34 Vapour Fumes | | | | | | | | |
| | 35 Noise | | | | | | | | |
| | 36 Moving Objects | | | | | | | | |
| | 37 Hazardous Machines | | | | | | | | |
| | 38 Electrical | | | | | | | | |
| | 39 Sharp Tools etc. | | | | | | | | |
| | 40 Radiant/Thermal Energy | | | | | | | | |
| | 41 Slippery | | | | | | | | |
| | 42 Congested Worksite | | | | | | | | |
| **Conditions of Work** | 43 Travelling | | | | | | | | |
| | 44 Work Alone | | | | | | | | |
| | 45 Work Independent but in group | | | | | | | | |
| | 46 Deadline Pressures | | | | | | | | |
| | 47 Interact with Public | | | | | | | | |
| | 48 Operate Equipment/Machinery | | | | | | | | |

Accessibility to person using wheelchair ☐

**Human Rights Considerations★★**
Essential Duties

1918 PO 05 (06/90)

★★Review duties before interview.
Discuss reasonable accommodation at interview.
Cette grille est aussi disponible en français.

★**Frequency** (The frequency of maximum weight should be shown without brackets and the frequency of usual weight, within brackets.)

1 — Seldom Perform, Not Daily
2 — Minor Daily Activity, Less than 1 Hour
3 — Required — Frequent Repetition, for 1-3 Hours Daily
4 — Major Job Demand, Maximum ability required, Frequent Repetition for more than 3 Hours Daily.

Reprinted (at reduced size) by permission of the Centre for Disability and Work, Ontario Ministry of Labour.

- Used to begin exploration of potential accommodation, not to screen people out.
- Focuses on outcomes or results desired from activity, rather than on physical demands of how the job is being performed.
- Creatively, being open to problem-solving about accommodation.

An issue related to PDA is the use of medical examinations as a selection procedure. Pre-employment physicals have often been used in the past as a general assessment of an applicant's health *unrelated to the job*. That is, a physical was given without the physician having any knowledge of the job for which the candidate was applying. Today, like any selection device, physical examinations must be job related. In contrast to past practice some human rights commissions (*e.g.*, Ontario) have recommended that physical examinations be required only for candidates who have a job offer.

Regarding orientation issues related to persons with disabilities – should the supervisor and co-workers be informed about a new employee's disability? Consultation with the new employee is required to decide. Talk to the person just hired. They know what makes them feel the most comfortable and what may be the most effective means of integration. Also two individuals with the same disability may have different wishes regarding their introduction to the work unit.

### How do you help readily qualifiable designated group members develop?

Many designated group members will have the necessary job qualifications, sometimes packaged differently from mainstream candidates. It is also true that many designated group members will not have all the necessary qualifications but will be close. As many organizations find themselves facing skill shortages, dealing with readily qualifiable candidates – both designated group members and mainstream candidates – will become increasingly important. That is, organizations will have to be able to identify potential and then train employees or sponsor the necessary training. This process requires three steps:

1. A clear identification of the minimum qualifications a candidate must have to begin the job.
2. A good assessment of each candidate's current skills and abilities.
3. A development plan to fill-in any deficiencies between (1) and (2).

Some means of accomplishing step (3) are:

- Bridging positions so that individuals can gain the experience necessary to move up in the organization;

- Specialized or remedial training (*e.g.*, for women moving into trades and technology positions);
- Internship programs;
- On-the-job training at a learner's rate of pay;
- Scholarships for education;
- Mentoring.

## ORIENTATION AND RETENTION

### *Why is orientation important?*

Many supervisors, managers and human resource staff congratulate themselves (as they should) when they have been successful in locating and hiring designated group members into jobs they have not held in the past. However, they often think that EE has been achieved once the job offer has been accepted. This is a serious mistake.

### *What are some of the special issues designated group members face?*

By definition, designated group members are likely to stand out in jobs they have not traditionally held. While these new employees are technically qualified their success is dependent on a number of other factors, such as their acceptance by their co-workers. Further, their supervisors and co-workers may find it difficult to behave "naturally" towards the first designated group members in a work unit. This inability to behave naturally is not necessarily due to resentment that the person was hired. It may be a recognition of differences without the knowledge of how best to deal with them – so people withdraw. For example, some supervisors are concerned that any negative feedback will be perceived as being prejudicial against the designated group member, so no feedback is given. This denies the designated group member valuable information needed to succeed. Designated group persons who find they are the first of "their kind" are often treated like a token (discussed later).

Orientation is often needed for supervisors, co-workers and the designated group members. Everyone likes to feel competent. When people are put into a new situation or when a familiar situation changes and the "right way" to behave is unknown people feel uncomfortable. The purpose of orientation is to facilitate feelings of comfort and competence as soon as possible. It is impossible to provide supervisors and co-workers with all the information they would need to instantly feel comfortable interacting with the other gender, members of all ethnic groups and persons with every conceivable disability. Further, different individuals who are members of these various groups will want to be treated individually. Orientation should foster an appreciation of diversity and an ability to communicate with others who are different so that everyone can learn to work well together.

### What does it mean to be treated like a token?

The first designated group members moving into non-traditional jobs tend to be treated as tokens. That is, the person serves as a representative of all Aboriginal Peoples, or persons with disabilities, or racial minorities or women. This is not fair, nor right, but it happens. Being a token is uncomfortable for the new designated group member, but it is unavoidable. Someone has to be the first.

While designated group members serving as tokens for a period of time cannot be avoided, tokenism should be. Tokenism is a policy of making only a superficial effort or symbolic gesture toward the goal of full representation of designated group members and non-designated group members throughout the organization. Designated group members cease being tokens once there is a critical mass of each particular designated group. For instance, the fact that approximately 75 per cent of the banking industry is staffed by women does not decrease the token status of those women who are pioneers into the technical or executive ranks.

It is useful to understand the experiences typical of tokens so that designated group members in this role can receive the help and support they need. Knowledge about the experience of tokens is based on the work of Rosabeth Moss Kanter.[4] She has found that when a particular kind of people (*i.e.*, people of colour) are in small numbers among people who share a different characteristic (*i.e.*, Whites) that certain things happen to those who are in small numbers. This phenomenon is *not* only based on race, gender and disability status. A few Americans finding themselves at a party of Canadians will experience the same phenomenon. The phenomenon is that of being different. What is interesting is that while there may be many similarities between individuals in the different groups (*i.e.*, people of colour and Whites who are accountants), the focus on differences (*i.e.*, race) predominates, at least initially.

Tokens experience three phenomena:

1. Being spotlighted.
2. Being noticed for the wrong things.
3. Being expected to represent all members of their group.

For instance, women in construction trades stand out. They are noticed. It is easy to observe them and note differences. There tends to be a lot of gossip about these one or two women. Because of greater public scrutiny, their mistakes are noticed more. Often a particular woman feels that she is carrying the banner for all the women who ever wanted to get into construction trades. If Doug makes a plumbing mistake it is attributed to Doug (drank too much last night, did not think it through). But if Sally makes a mistake it is taken as evidence that women cannot do this kind of work. An additional strain is the double standard often applied to tokens. On the one hand, women must prove that they are as good at construction trades as the men. On the other hand, they have to do this without losing their femininity. This can become a no-win situation since the traditional definition of femininity is the antithesis of what is required in many jobs (*e.g.*, dirty, manual labour or showing leadership).

Such high visibility is draining. Yet, while designated group members are feeling the negative aspects of being spotlighted, there is sometimes jealousy from those who traditionally perform the job, since they are not getting any extra attention. Another way designated group members are spotlighted is that they are expected to provide the designated group's perspective. For instance, the recognition that Aboriginal Peoples have a different perspective and that it is sought out is good. However, when there are only one or two Aboriginal People in an organization, they often find that acting as a spokesperson for all Aboriginal Peoples becomes time consuming and exhausting – besides being impossible.

Finally, the presence of a token affects the behaviour of the majority group. One or two women working in a unit are likely to find their male co-workers emphasizing their maleness. The presence of women makes the men more conscious that, whatever their individual differences, they all share being men in common and this distinguishes them from the women. Further, the men now have to think about their behaviour and how it is perceived by their female co-workers.

Typical strategies designated group members employ to deal with the added pressures of being a token are to:

- Try to be perfect.
- Operate like non-designated group members (that is, ignore their own designated group status).
- Remain in a lower level position in the organization which has historically been typical for someone from their group, avoiding the spotlight and everything else which goes with it.

While each of these may be an appropriate short-run solution it can be tough to maintain in the long run. Trying to be perfect is tiring (and impossible).

While it is true that to some degree members of the designated groups may operate "like white, able-bodied men" in a white, able-bodied, man's world, if taken to an extreme this requires denying what is unique and good about being Aboriginal, being a person of colour, being disabled or being a woman. Further, such behaviour often isolates designated group members from each other. A woman who is accepted by men because she is seen as different from other women ("You think like a man") may feel that any identification with other women is a betrayal to her male colleagues. This is a reason why women and other designated group members supporting each other is seen as threatening to some in the mainstream group – it is a question of loyalty – "Are you like us or are you a designated group member?" The underlying assumption is that one cannot be both.

Remaining in a lower level position within the organization is another option. For instance, employees from designated groups are more likely to be perceived as employed in an assisting, rather than managing, capacity. Assisting is the right job for those who find the assistant job challenging and fulfilling. However, it may be denying the organization some needed skills if designated group members are not moving up because they find it too stressful or because of a lack of self-esteem.

Some things organizations can do to help minimize the strain on token employees are:

- Set reasonable expectations. Remember that tokens have all the demands required of anyone doing the job plus the demands of being a pioneer.
- Facilitate support groups for designated group members in positions where they have historically been underrepresented.
- Help designated group members integrate into the non-designated group networks and help these networks adapt to meet the needs of all.
- Avoid overloading designated group members as representatives of their designated groups.

*Some general hints to facilitate retention.*

- Create support systems to anticipate any special considerations of designated group members. For example, removing calendars and other pin-ups so that the first women hired will not have to make an issue of it if it bothers them.
- Establishing a communication mechanism to ensure that any issues which were not anticipated (and it is impossible to anticipate all of them) can be discovered and addressed.
- Set performance standards which ensure that all employees are judged against the most objective assessment possible so that everyone will know that members of designated groups and mainstream employees are qualified for the jobs they are doing.
- Ensure equality of opportunity for training and development.

# APPENDIX 1

## QUESTIONS PERMITTED ON AN APPLICATION FORM

Taken from "Human Rights Employment Application Forms and Interview" prepared by The Ontario Human Rights Commission, Toronto, November 1991, ISBN 0-7729-74748, pp. 6-9.

### Employment Interviews

At the interview stage of the employment process, the employer may expand the scope of job-related questions if necessary to determine, for example, the applicant's qualifications or his/her ability to perform the essential duties. Inquiries in relation to the "Exceptions", outlined below, are also appropriate at the interview stage. Examples of permissible interview questions follow:

|  | Permissible Questions | Prohibited Questions |
|---|---|---|
| Race Colour Ancestry Place of Origin Ethnic Origin | • Inquiries by a service organization working with a particular community as to membership in the group served, if such membership can be justified as required to do the particular job. | • All inquires which do not fall into the "Special Interest Organizations" [noted below]. |
| Creed | • Inquiries by a denominational school as to religious membership, if the job involves communicating religious values to students ... | • All inquiries which do not fall into the "Special Interest Organizations" [noted below]. |
| Sex | • Inquiries as to gender, if it is a reasonable and genuine requirement for a particular job, such as where employment is in a shelter for battered women. ... | • All other inquiries concerning the applicant's sex. [See Special Employment below.] |

|  | Permissible Questions | Prohibited Questions |
|---|---|---|
| Disability (Handicap) | • Inquiries directly related to the applicant's ability to perform the essential duties of the job and the nature of any accommodation which may be required. | • All other inquiries concerning the applicant's handicap or disability. |
| Age | • Inquiries as to age if the employer serves a particular age group and/or if age requirements are reasonable to qualify for employment. | • All other inquiries as to age. [See Special Employment below.] |
| Marital Status | • Inquiries as to marital status if the employer serves a particular group (identified by marital status, e.g. single woman) and/or if marital status is a reasonable requirement for employment. | • All other inquiries as to marital status. [See Special Employment below.] |

...

Special Interest Organizations (*Code*, Section 24)

A religious, philanthropic, education, fraternal or social institution or organization that is primarily engaged in serving the interests of persons identified by race, ancestry, place of origin, colour, ethnic origin, creed, sex, age, marital status or handicap, is allowed to give preference in employment to persons similarly identified, if the qualification is a reasonable and genuine one because of the nature of the employment: section 23(1)(a). Inquiries about such affiliation may be made at the employment interview stage.

Special Employment (*Code*, Section 23)

In some instances, because of the nature of the employment, age, sex, ... or marital status may be a reasonable and genuine qualification for the particular job: section 23(1)(b). In such instances, inquiries with regard to the particular qualification may be made at the employment interview stage.

# APPENDIX 2

## APPLICATION FOR EMPLOYMENT

Adapted from "Human Rights Employment Application Forms and Interview" prepared by The Ontario Human Rights Commission, Toronto, November 1991, ISBN 0-7729-74748, pp. 11-12.

| Position being applied for | Date available to begin work |
|---|---|
| | |

PERSONAL DATA

Last name          Given name(s)

---

Address     Street     Apt. No.          Home Telephone Number

---

City     Province     Postal Code     Business Telephone Number

---

Are you legally eligible to work in Canada?          ——— Yes ——— No

---

Are you 18 years and more and less than 65 years of age? ——— Yes ——— No

---

Are you willing to          ——— Yes          Preferred
relocate in Ontario?     ——— No          Location

---

To determine your qualification for employment, please provide below and on reverse, information related to your academic and other achievements including volunteer work, as well as employment history. Additional information may be attached on a separate sheet.

SECONDARY SCHOOL___ BUSINESS, TRADE OR SECONDARY SCHOOL___

Highest grade          Name of course          Length of course
or level completed

---

Type of certificate          License, certificate or diploma awarded?
or diploma obtained          ——— Yes ——— No

COMMUNITY COLLEGE___                    UNIVERSITY___

Name of Program   Length of Program   Length of course
                    Degree awarded   ——— Yes ——— No
                    ——— Pass ——— Honours

---

Diploma received ——— Yes ——— No     Major subject

---

Other courses, workshops, seminars          Licenses, Certificates, Degrees

Work related skills

Describe any of your work related skills, experience, or training that relate to the position being applied for.

EMPLOYMENT

Name and Address of present/last employer          Present/last job title

Period of employment   Present/last salary
From    To:

Name of Supervisor       Telephone

Type of Business                Reason for leaving

Functions/Responsibilities

Name and Address of former employer          Present/last job title

Period of employment    Present/last salary
From    To:

Name of Supervisor          Telephone

Type of Business                Reason for leaving

Functions/Responsibilities

Name and Address of former employer          Present/last job title

Period of employment    Present/last salary
From    To:

Name of Supervisor          Telephone

Type of Business                Reason for leaving

Functions/Responsibilities

For employment references we may approach:
Your present/last employer?          ———— Yes ———— No
Your former employer(s)?          ____ Yes ____ No
List references if different than above on a separate sheet.

Personal interests and activities (civic, athletic, etc)

I hereby declare that the foregoing information          Have you attached an additional
is true and complete to my knowledge.          sheet?____Yes ____ No
I understand that a false statement may disqual-
ify me from employment, or cause my dismissal.

Signature          Date

## NOTES

1. Francis Henry and Effie Ginzberg, "Who Gets the Work? A Test of Racial Discrimination in Employment", Toronto: The Urban Alliance on Race Relations and The Social Planning Council of Metropolitan Toronto, January, 1985.
2. Adapted from, "This Job Requires... A Planned Approach to Recruitment and Selection" A joint project of The Ontario Women's Directorate and Computing Devices Company, Toronto, September, 1990, Module 3, pp. 17-20.
3. Adapted from "A Need Analysis on the Ontario Public Service Use of Physical Demands Analysis" Toronto: Centre for Disability and Work, Ministry of Labour, 1992.
4. Rosabeth Moss Kanter and Barry A. Stein, *A Tale of "O": On Being Different in an Organization*, New York: Harper & Row, Publishers, 1980.

# REFERENCES

"Avoiding Sex Bias in Selection Testing", *Equal Opportunities Review*, 21, 1988, 20–21.

"This Job Requires ... A Planned Approach to Recruitment and Selection" The Ontario Women's Directorate and Computing Devices Company, Toronto, 1990.

F.C. Edwards, R.I. McCallum and P.S. Taylor (eds.), *Fitness for Work: The Medical Aspects*, Oxford: Oxford University Press, 1988.

M.E. Giffin, "Personnel Research on Testing, Selection, and Performance Appraisal", *Public Personnel Management*, 18:2, 1989, pp. 127–37.

Francine S. Hall and Maryann H. Albrecht, *The Management of Affirmative Action*, Santa Monica, CA.: Goodyear Publishing Co, Inc., 1979.

John A. Hartigan, Alexandra K. Wigdor (eds.), *Fairness in Employment Testing, Validity Generalization, Minority Issues and the General Aptitude Test Battery*, Washington, D.C.: National Academy Press, 1989.

Frances Henry and Effie Ginzberg, "Who Gets the Work? A Test of Racial Discrimination in Employment", Toronto: The Urban Alliance on Race Relations and The Social Planning Council of Metropolitan Toronto, January 1985.

M.A. Hughes, R.A. Ratliff, J.L. Purswell, et al. "A Content Validation Methodology for Job Related Physical Performance Tests," *Public Personnel Management*, 18:4, 1989, pp. 487–504.

Harish C. Jain, "Anti-Discrimination Staffing Policies: Implications of Human Rights Legislation for Employers and Trade Unions", Ottawa: Department of Secretary of State, 1985.

Rosabeth Moss Kanter and Barry A. Stein, *A Tale of "O": On Being Different in an Organization*, New York: Harper & Row, Publishers, 1980.

C. Less, "Testing Makes a Comeback", *Training*, 25:12, 1988, pp. 49–52, 56–59.

The McDonald Series, "Interviewing Aboriginal Peoples", Winnipeg: Cross Cultural Communications International, Inc. (undated).

S.L. Martin and L.P. Lehnen , "Select the Right Employees through Testing", *Personnel Journal*, 71:6, 1992, pp. 46, 48–49, 51.

M.A. Nester, "Employment Testing for Handicapped Persons", *Public Personnel Management*, 13:4, 1984, pp. 417–434.

L.M. Rudner, "Pre-employment Testing and Employee Productivity", *Public Personnel Management*, 21:2, 1992, pp. 133–150.

# CHAPTER 10

# Harassment-Free Environment

*Why is harassment an issue?*

First, harassment is illegal under federal and provincial human rights laws. The four EE designated groups are included among the groups protected by all human rights legislations. So harassment based on race, disability status and gender are all illegal. Second, harassment in the workplace has negative effects on productivity, turnover and absenteeism. Harassment costs money. In Ontario, harassment leading to extreme stress has been found to be compensable under workers' compensation.

*What is harassment?*

Harassment is any action which is unwelcome or should be known to be unwelcome that is irritating, annoying and vexatious and which is predicated on the victim being a member of a protected group under human rights legislation. Harassment tends to make the person being harassed feel humiliated, insulted or degraded.

It is generally recognized that there are two kinds of harassment. These are:

1. **Poisoned environment harassment:** The work environment, due to behaviour of supervisors or co-workers, is made intimidating, hostile or offensive to the extent that it substantially interferes with a person's work performance or causes the employee to leave her/his job.

   A poisoned atmosphere can exist even if there is no specific employment consequence (*e.g.*, loss of a salary increase), although, the harassing behaviour must be repetitious. However, specific behaviour which on its own would not be harassing becomes harassing because of the cumulative effect (*e.g.*, hearing racially derogatory jokes from a number of co-workers). The source of such harassment might be one's supervisor, someone in another position of authority, co-workers, or a customer or supplier.

2. *Quid pro quo* **harassment:** This kind of harassment is unique to sexual harassment. Here job security, salary, benefits, promotions, etc., are offered in exchange for sexual favours.

   The source of such harassment are those who have the power to give rewards or withhold punishment – typically, those in positions of authority. The unique aspects of sexual harassment are discussed at page 265.

## What are some examples of harassing behaviour?

Harassment can be exhibited in many forms – physical, psychological, or verbal. Examples of behaviour which can constitute harassment include, but are not limited to, the following:

**Harassment based on race, gender or disability status:**

- Physical or verbal abuse,
- Derogatory or offensive jokes or teasing,
- Insults, taunting or slurs,
- Unwelcome physical contact of any nature,
- Suggestive looks (leering or staring) or suggestive gestures,
- Display or circulation of written materials or pictures which are derogatory,
- Unwarranted and unfounded charges and complaints brought against another with intent to discredit, harass, or in any way harm that employee.

**Sexual harassment only:**

- Unwelcome and unsolicited sexual advances,
- Requests for sexual favours used as a condition of employment or affecting any decisions, such as hiring, promotion, transfer, performance appraisal and compensation,
- Employment opportunities or benefits granted to one individual over another qualified individual as a result of submission to, or rejection of, sexual advances.

## What are the most typical bases of harassment?

Harassment on the basis of gender and race are most typical. There have been cases where persons with disabilities and Aboriginal Persons have been harassed. Sexual harassment is disproportionately directed against women of colour and women with disabilities.

## Why does harassment occur?

Harassment can occur

- as an exercise of power,
- out of spite or dislike,
- because of frustration, and
- sometimes, it is unintentional.

## What if the harassment was unintended?

What if someone is just joking and they do not mean to humiliate or degrade another person? The definition of harassment is helpful in understanding the issue of intent related to harassment. The definition refers to conduct which is "unwelcome" or "unwanted" or "should be known to be unwelcome or unwanted".

Some actions are clearly unwanted and inappropriate within an employment context. These behaviours "should be known to be unwelcome". There are other behaviours which one can know are unwelcome only if one is told. That is, there are some behaviours which would be unwelcome by some but not to others. Figure 10-1 helps demonstrate this.

**Figure 10-1**

**Acceptability Continuum of Behaviours**

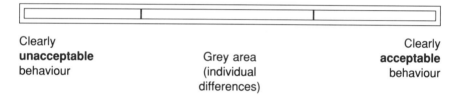

| Clearly | Grey area | Clearly |
| **unacceptable** | (individual | **acceptable** |
| behaviour | differences) | behaviour |

Figure 10-1 shows a continuum from clearly acceptable behaviours (on the right) to clearly unacceptable behaviour (on the left). For example, shaking hands is acceptable touching in a work environment. At the other end of the continuum, a clearly unacceptable behaviour is touching someone's crotch, buttocks or a woman's breast. No one has to indicate that this kind of touching is unwelcome – it is assumed. There are some behaviours which fall into the middle, grey area. In that area are behaviours that some people would find unacceptable but others would find acceptable. For example, one employee may not mind a supervisor or co-worker putting their arm around the employee's shoulder, while another employee may find it very uncomfortable.

It is about behaviours in this grey area that communication is required. A person is *not* harassing another if the behaviour is not clearly unwelcome *and* the person who finds it irritating has not informed the person who is engaging in this conduct. In other words, that is, individuals who find something uncomfortable or unpleasant have an obligation to inform the person of their feelings when it is not obviously unacceptable. However, such communication may not always be a direct verbal statement. Because of status and power differences, ethnic differences and gender differences, the message sent is not always the message received. For example, someone who comes from an ethnic group which where touching is common outside of intimate relationships may not realize that a co-worker might find an arm around the shoulder uncomfortable. The employee, who does not like this behaviour, may feel that moving away or stiffening up would communicate their sense of unease. In today's organizations, awareness of potentially harassing behaviour, even unintentionally harassing behaviour, needs to be increased. This means that those who feel harassed have an obligation to be as clear as they can that another's behaviour is irritating; and those whose behaviour others might find to be harassing have an obligation to become sensitive to non-verbal and/or subtle communication that something is unwelcome. Anti-harassment training is a mechanism to increase such communication. For example, if a person stiffens or pulls away when an arm is put around their shoulder they are communicating that the behaviour is unwelcome. Someone who looks uncomfortable when sexist, racist or ethnic jokes are being told may feel harassed after hearing a number of them.

### Can jokes really be harassing?

Yes. Humour can either make us feel good or can be used effectively to degrade and insult. A human rights case brought by an individual of Polish background found that put-down jokes about his ethnic group were harassing. "Blonde" jokes which demean women are another example. But remember, to be harassing the behaviour has to be unwelcome. In some work environments everyone feels free to tell jokes about groups to which they and others belong. If everyone feels this is good fun then it is not harassing. However, the work group has to be sensitive to others who may not feel the same way. The courts employ the "thin skin" doctrine. If there are ten people in a work unit and nine are comfortable with put-down humour but the tenth person feels uncomfortable, the courts have ruled that the "thin-skin" of the tenth individual should be the standard for the entire work group.

Joke tellers can get into the habit of asking "Want to hear a joke about _____?" If the answer is "no" they should refrain from telling the joke. One way to test for harassment is reciprocity. If people feel they can tell jokes about the groups others belong to but do not want to hear put-down jokes about the group they belong to, then the situation is a potentially harassing one. Alternatively, someone who is concerned about hearing put-down humour can take some control. When someone asks, "Do you want to hear a joke?" those who do not want to be exposed to certain jokes can ask: "Is it racist or sexist?" If the answer is "yes" then the person who does not want to hear this kind of humour can leave or ask that the joke not be told in their presence.

*Isn't telling people that they cannot tell jokes at work against rights of free speech?*

One is not telling the joke-teller that they cannot tell the joke; rather, they are saying that the joke-teller cannot tell the joke to them. This is consistent with the fact that there are a number of restrictions placed on our behaviour at work. For example, appropriate dress for the workplace is different from the way most of us choose to dress on weekends. Employers have a responsibility to create a work environment which is harassment-free. Put-down humour can be harassing as can "pin-ups". Neither is needed at the work site.

*Why is harassment an organizational problem; shouldn't individuals take care of it on their own?*

First, the Supreme Court of Canada has ruled that an organization is liable for harassment if an employee who feels harassed has informed someone in authority and nothing is done to investigate the situation, and correct it if necessary. Second, the Workers' Compensation Board in Ontario has compensated an employee for stress directly related to sexual and racial harassment.

The Supreme Court ruling was made in *Robichaud v. Brennan*[1] in 1987. Bonnie Robichaud was the first women in her work unit promoted to the position of cleaning supervisor. She was still in her probationary period when her boss, Dennis Brennan, requested that Mrs. Robichaud engage in sexual activity with him in order to pass her probationary period. While Mrs. Robichaud did as she was asked at first, she felt coerced and later refused. She also told someone in authority at the National Department of Defense, her employer, that she was being sexually harassed. Nothing was done. Mrs. Robichaud filed a human rights complaint. Initially, the lower court ruled that Mrs. Robichaud had not been sexually harassed because one does not engage in sexual activity with another person against their will. This ruling was overturned by higher courts. Further, the Supreme Court decision made it clear that the employer was liable for the sexual harassment because someone in authority had been informed but did not investigate the situation.

In the Workers' Compensation Board hearing, a black woman, working for Colgate-Palmolive, was racially and sexually harassed by co-workers for six years. The harassment was a contributing factor to her attempted suicide. Based on the poisoned atmosphere in which she worked, the Workers' Compensation Board compensated her for work-related stress.

***What should an organization do to ensure a harassment-free environment?***

Five things are required:

1. Institute an anti-harassment policy;
2. Communicate the anti-harassment policy;
3. Train supervisors on how to maintain a harassment-free environment;
4. Enforce the anti-harassment policy;
5. Establish an investigative procedure and follow through quickly when there is a complaint.

Everyone agrees that dealing with harassment is difficult for all concerned. Dealing with sexual harassment is particularly difficult. This is often due to:

- A perception that the person feeling harassed is overly sensitive ("Making a mountain out of a mole hill.")
- A disbelief that the alleged harasser meant to harass the person. ("They are just teasing and having fun. Can't you take a joke?")
- Conflicting stories as to what happened.
- The fact that the issues do not get raised until the situation reaches a certain level. ("The straw that breaks the camel's back.")
- Feelings of embarrassment when talking about specific issues in some sexual harassment incidents.

For these reasons, it is important to have an anti-harassment policy and investigative process which is well communicated. Further, someone within the organization should be trained specifically to deal with harassment issues. This person can aid supervisors in ensuring a harassment-free environment and can help those feeling harassed who want to deal with the situation without a formal complaint.

***What should an anti-harassment policy contain?***

This section provides the elements of an anti-harassment policy and an example of each element in the Boxes. An anti-harassment policy should:

State a commitment to a harassment-free environment.

---

**Box 10-1**

Our Company is committed to a work environment free of harassment.

Harassment is considered to have taken place if a person knows, or ought reasonably to know, that their behaviour is unwelcome.

The company prohibits any form of harassment by employees, co-workers, supervisors and managers and views such action as extremely serious misconduct. Violations of this policy will result in disciplinary action, including possible discharge.

---

Define the basis of harassment covered by the policy.

---

**Box 10-2**

Harassment on the following bases are prohibited: race, ancestry, place of origin, colour, ethnic origin, citizenship, disability or handicap, religion or creed, sex, sexual orientation, marital or family status, age, or record of provincial offenses.

---

Give a definition of harassing behaviour.

---

**Box 10-3**

Harassment, on any of the bases outlined above, is any unwelcome action that humiliates, insults or degrades creating a hostile, offensive or intimidating work environment. Harassment in any form - physical, psychological or verbal - is prohibited.

---

Give some examples of harassment.

---

**Box 10-4**

Behaviour which can constitute harassment includes, but is not limited to, the following:

• Physical or verbal abuse,
• Derogatory or offensive jokes or teasing,
• Insults, taunting or slurs,

---

---

### Box 10-4 (Cont'd)

- Unwelcome physical contact of any nature,
- Suggestive looks (leering or staring) or suggestive gestures,
- Display or circulation of written materials or pictures which are derogatory,
- Unwarranted and unfounded charges and complaints brought against another with intent to discredit, harass, or in any way harm that employee.
- Unwelcome and unsolicited sexual advances,
- Requests for sexual favours used as a condition of employment or affecting any decisions, such as hiring, promotion, transfer, performance appraisal and compensation,
- Employment opportunities or benefits granted to one individual over another qualified individual as a result of submission to, or rejection of, sexual advances.

---

Define what is covered by the policy.

---

### Box 10-5

The workplace is not confined to the offices, buildings and work sites of our Company. It also includes company cafeterias, washrooms, locker rooms, vehicles and any other location where the business of the company is being conducted.
Harassment which occurs outside the workplace but that has repercussions in the work environment, adversely affecting employee relationships, may also be defined as workplace harassment.

---

Encourage employees to talk about potentially harassing situations with their supervisor, human resources or someone else in a position of authority.

---

### Box 10-6

If an employee feels that he/she is experiencing behaviour which is inappropriate within a work setting, they are encouraged to discuss the matter with someone with whom they feel comfortable. This might be their supervisor, someone in the human resources department or anyone else in a position of authority.

(Name of sexual harassment officer) has been named as the sexual harassment officer for our company. Employees who would like to discuss what constitutes harassment and how to deal with it may contact this person.

---

Indicate responsibilities of various parties.

---

### Box 10-7

It is the responsibility of each employee to ensure that these prohibited activities do not occur. Workplace harassment is unpleasant and intimidating. Fear of retaliation, embarrassment or feelings of guilt may persuade employees to withhold their complaints. However, it is essential that all employees take the necessary steps to stop harassment.

Supervisors, particularly, are responsible for the climate of their work unit. However, if anyone in a position of authority is informed about harassment (on the prohibited grounds noted above) they must take immediate action to ensure the issue is investigated and resolved.

---

Indicate investigation process.

It may be helpful to name a number of individuals (*e.g.*, a man and a women, someone who is from a racial minority group and someone who is white) who can be approached to discuss harassment issues or to file a complaint.

---

### Box 10-8

The exact nature of the investigation will depend on the particulars of the allegation. However, all investigations should involve getting full information from the person who feels harassed, from the alleged harasser and, possibly, from other relevant individuals. To the greatest degree possible the investigation should be confidential. The investigation should be conducted in a timely manner and, if necessary, the resolution should be implemented as soon as possible.

---

State consequences of harassing behaviour.

---

### Box 10-9

Violations of this policy will result in disciplinary action, including possible discharge.

Retaliation against anyone who makes a good faith complaint is, in itself, a violation of this policy.

---

### To whom should the anti-harassment policy be communicated?

All employees need to be informed that an anti-harassment policy is in place. However, unlike some other policies which can simply be sent to people, an anti-harassment policy requires training. Because harassment will not be tolerated it is vital (and only fair) that everyone fully understand what is considered harassing. Recent human rights cases have broadened the definition of harassment. In *Shaw v. Levac Supply Co. Ltd.*[2] in Ontario, a woman was awarded $48,000 because she was exposed to behaviours which some people might think of as teasing rather than harassing. A male co-worker lampooned and insulted the female employee simply because she was a woman. He commented negatively on her work, appearance, weight, the way she dressed, often dozens of times each day. The harassment went on for 14 years. Since the president of the company knew about this behaviour and did nothing to stop it, the employer, and the individual who did the harassing, were fined.

The rules as to what is acceptable behaviour in the workplace are changing. It is only fair to ensure that everyone knows these new rules. Training can help reduce harassment in three ways. One, it will prevent some people from behaving in ways that they do not mean to be harassing but that they have come to realize, through training, others might feel are harassing. Two, training can enable those feeling harassed to speak up sooner and more clearly, thus stopping unintentional and/or mildly offensive behaviour before it escalates into harassing behaviour. Three, it can sensitize people at work that some of their behaviours may be irritating to others and enable them to understand, often from non-verbal clues, when their behaviour is unwelcome.

### What kind of anti-harassment training is needed?

For unionized workers, joint union-management training is best. This will communicate the joint commitment of the union and the employer to a harassment-free environment. It ensures that both workplace parties are defining harassment consistently. Further, it should minimize the potential of the union being in the middle between one member who is alleging harassment against another member.

Three groups need training. Some of the training is the same for each group and some is different, as outlined below. These groups are:

1. Those in positions of authority including supervisors, managers and those in the human resources department. These individuals are most likely to be informed about allegations of harassment or approached to talk about how to deal with a situation which has a harassing element. Since the organization is liable if some-

one in authority is informed about harassment, these individuals need to understand that they must act immediately on an allegation of harassment.

They must also know how to counsel (or to whom to refer) those who want to talk about a potentially harassing issue.

2. Those who might be accused of harassing behaviour.

Since intention is never the issue, anyone within the organization may be perceived by someone else to be engaging in harassing behaviour. Training should cover harassment on the basis of race, disability status and gender, in addition to sexual harassment.

The objective of training is two-fold. First, just as those in authority have to know what constitutes harassment, so do all employees. Second, employees must become more sensitive to both verbal and non-verbal indications that something they do may be unwelcome by someone else. Training employees on what harassment is supports the second objective. Further anti-harassment training provides all employees with a better vocabulary with which to express discomfort. Finally, the training program facilitates communication between employees about potential or actual harassing experiences.

3. The potential victims of harassment. Potentially, any employee could be harassed or be made to feel uncomfortable because of their race, gender or disability status. However, separate training for people of colour, persons with disabilities and women, will usually be more beneficial since they are more likely to be the targets of harassment. Further, the socialization of these groups can make it particularly difficult for them to express their distaste when they are made uncomfortable. Some individuals do not feel that they have a right to tell others, particularly those in authority, to stop inappropriate behaviour. Training for these groups focuses on empowering individuals to deal with situations early on, before they escalate into more difficult situations, and how to use the system to deal with harassment, if necessary. Role-playing is a very useful way to provide people with the skills they need to deal with harassing situations. It helps them define what is bothering them, to ask that the behaviour stop without blaming (or assuming bad intentions) of the other person.

### How might employees, feeling harassed, choose to deal with the situation?

If one is feeling harassed there is a continuum of reactions. Some people want to keep what is happening a secret. The reasons for this are discussed later. Others reach a stage where they need to talk to someone as a "reality test". That is, they are feeling uncomfortable but they may feel that they are being over-sensitive, or they may need to know if others are being treated the same way. Employees are more likely to talk to co-workers or friends away from work at this stage, since they are still sorting out, what, if anything, they want to do to change the situation. An employee is likely to approach someone in authority within their workplace to:

- Talk about how to deal with the situation her/himself. Helping someone deal with the situation on their own can change that situation from one where an employee feels victimized to one where they feel empowered. Persons in authority should follow-up after about a week to ensure that the employee was able to resolve the situation on her/his own.
- Inform the organization about the situation (but not to file a complaint). The person in a position of authority should talk to the individual about their options. From doing nothing to filing a complaint. It is important that the person in authority follow-up.
- Communicate willingness to be part of a group complaint. People who knowingly harass as an exercise of power, typically harass more than one person. An individual may be willing to be part of a group complaint, but unwilling to file an individual complaint. It is useful to confer with former employees in the same or similar position to the person feeling harassed to determine if others have had the same experience.
- File an individual complaint. The investigation should begin immediately.

The person who is feeling harassed may not know exactly which of these steps they want to take when they decide to talk to someone in authority – this will be decided as a result of the discussion with the person in authority.

*How should a person in authority counsel someone who wants to talk about a potentially harassing situation?*

When approached by an employee for help with a potentially harassing situation, managers and supervisors are advised to:

- Listen and accept the employees' reality.
- Help the employee assess the situation. Is it likely this situation can be dealt with informally or should a formal complaint be filed immediately?

- Empower them to handle the situation themselves, if possible.
- Encourage the employee to keep a diary recording
    what happens,
    dates and times,
    location,
    who is present.
- Follow up within a short time period to determine if the situation has been resolved or if there is something that needs to be done.
- Encourage the employee to file a complaint if the harassment cannot be dealt with any other way.

## *How should an allegation of harassment be investigated?*

Investigation should take place immediately. Supervisors and other managerial employees should inform human resources or someone in the anti-harassment function, if there is one. Some organizations have found it helpful to have an "advisor", separate from an "investigator" (particularly where the allegation concerns sexual harassment). The role of the "advisor", who maintains strict confidentiality, is not to take action or to make recommendations to the complainant, but to provide information and explain options. For example, as to time limits to file a complaint with the Human Rights Commission.

Advisors are not advocates for the person who feels harassed or for the alleged harasser. Their job is to facilitate a harassment-free environment. Advisors do not investigate an allegation of harassment, though they might mediate between the individuals involved to try to resolve the situation.

Some questions to be asked in investigating harassment:[3]

- Confirm the name and position of person complaining.
- Ascertain who allegedly harassed the employee.
- What occurred? Try to get as many details as possible, even though this may be uncomfortable for the complainant. Ask open-ended, non-judgmental questions.
- How often did the harassment occur?
- On what dates and at what times did the harassment take place?
- Where did the incidents of harassment take place?
- Who, if anybody, witnessed the incidents of harassment?
- How did the complainant feel about the harassment at the time it occurred?
- Does the complainant feel the same way now? If not, what is different about how the complainant now feels, and what brought about the difference?
- How did the complainant respond to the harassment? Did he or she make any effort to bring it to a halt?

- Did the complainant tell anyone else about the incidents of harassment? If so, get the details concerning who, what, when, where, and the response, if any.
- Does the alleged harasser (or retaliator, if they are different people) have control over the compensation, working conditions, or future employment of the complaint?
- Has the alleged harasser (or retaliator, if they are different people) made or carried out any threats or promises in connection with the alleged sexual harassment?
- Does the complainant know or suspect that there are other victims of harassment by the same person?
- To what extent were managing partners or others in control made aware of the situation?
- What action would the complainant like to have taken?

Some tips for investigators:

- Avoid "why" questions, such as "Why didn't you do something about this before?" Such questions are likely to be perceived as being judgmental.
- Do not ask leading questions, such as, "Would you want to continue working here if he continues his behaviour?"
- Avoid asking multiple choice questions, such as "Were you touched on the arm, shoulder, or face?" Instead ask "Where did the person touch you?" or "Can you be more specific about how the person touched you?"

Assuming that the person feeling harassed wants an investigation (they are filing a formal complaint) then it is necessary to begin as soon as possible. When informing the alleged offender of the need to talk about this complaint, he/she should be informed that they can have someone else present at the meeting, if they so choose. Through an interview, it is necessary to find out from the alleged offender her/his side of the story. In addition, gather all the pertinent evidence from witnesses or others in a manner which provides as complete a picture as possible, while attempting to maintain confidentiality.

Some suggestions for an internal organizational review process are:[4]

- Ensure that employees know they can make an allegation of harassment to someone other than their supervisor.
- Speed is of the essence – respond immediately and complete the investigation as quickly as possible, preferably within 90 days.
- Involve the union if the person alleging harassment or the person accused of harassment is represented by a bargaining agent.
- Let the person making the complaint know they have the right,

beyond the internal process, to file a complaint with the Human Rights Commission or agency.

- Records should be kept of all information provided by either party and all witnesses consulted in the investigation.
- Confidentiality must be maintained wherever possible. Though, if there is a need to speak with potential witnesses or former employees this becomes difficult.
- Investigators should be sensitive and knowledgable about human rights and harassment.
- Ensure protection against reprisal of those participating in the investigation including: complainant(s), person(s) complained against, witnesses, advisers, investigators and decision makers.
- Those responsible for investigating complaints should be independent and removed from the parties involved. For example, investigations should not be conducted by anyone who has any direct influence on the career advancement of either party.
- The investigator should report to someone with the authority to make decisions and ensure settlement is carried out.

If the complaint is substantiated then the outcome should ensure that the person making the complaint is treated as they should have been had the harassment not occurred. The person who has been found to be harassing should be disciplined in a manner which is consistent with the severity of the offense. Others, in positions of authority, who, by their behaviour, condoned or did not carry out their responsibility to maintain a harassment-free environment should also be disciplined in a manner consistent with either their error of co-mission or omission. If the allegation is unfounded then a determination should be made as to how such a misunderstanding occurred and what can be done to prevent it from happening. If it is found that an employee has lodged a complaint maliciously then disciplinary action is required. Records of disciplinary action should be put into an employee's personnel file; otherwise, information should be kept confidential.

After an investigation of harassment it is useful to assess if training or communication is needed to facilitate an environment free of harassment for all employees.

### *Isn't it best if we do not have many reports of harassment?*

It depends on whether harassment is occurring or not. Table 10-1 shows the possible combinations of whether harassment is occurring and whether it is reported.

The ideal situation is that harassment is not reported because it is not occurring; this is cell A. Cell C is where harassment is occurring and

## TABLE 10-1

### OCCURENCE VERSUS REPORTING OF HARASSMENT

| | | Sexual harassment is reported | | |
|---|---|---|---|---|
| | | **No** | **Yes** | |
| Sexual harassment occurs intentionally | No | A<br>Preferred situation | B1<br>Misunderstanding | B2<br>Malicious complaint |
| | Yes | D<br>Encourage reporting | C<br>Take corrective action against harasser | |

being reported. This is "desirable" because it enables the organization to deal with the reality. Dealing with allegations of harassment is not easy or pleasant, but, if harassment is occurring and is not dealt with then the negative consequences outlined later are likely to occur.

There is a fear that harassment will be reported when it is not occurring. There are be two reasons this could occur. The most typical reason is a misunderstanding (cell B1). The person on the receiving end feels that the behaviour is irritating and intimidating. The person who is engaging in this behaviour does not mean it to be harassing. The behaviour is in the grey area. While the person receiving the behaviour finds it unacceptable, the person behaving in this manner feels it is acceptable. Communication is needed to correct this situation. The one engaging in the behaviour needs to be told that this particular individual finds this particular behaviour unwelcome.

The possibility that harassment will be reported maliciously, when it is not occurring, is unlikely. If this occurs, it is a type of harassment and can be dealt with under the anti-harassment policy. It is much more likely that there is a difference in people's definition of acceptable and unacceptable behaviour.

### What are the consequences of not investigating an allegation of harassment?

If a harassment is not investigated internally, the organization faces a number of legal risks. One is financial liability for lost wages and damages. If an employee quits because of the harassment, the organization could be sued for constructive dismissal because it did not fulfil its legal obligation to maintain a harassment-free environment. If an employee suffers stress-related illness as a result of the harassment, a successful workers' compensation claim could result in increased assessments for the employer. Additionally, negative publicity can result from complaints which are not properly investigated. Finally, the lack of investigation is a contributing factor to harassment and there is evidence of lower productivity, increased absenteeism and turnover due to harassment and, of course, lower morale.

### *What are some of the unique aspects of sexual harassment?*

Everything which has been said to this point is true for all types of harassment. However, there are some unique aspects of sexual harassment which should be addressed.

One does not have to talk about sexual harassment for too long before someone will smile and say "I wish I was sexually harassed more often." (No one ever says that they wish they were racially harassed more often.) Why would anyone say they want to be harassed? The confusion is due to focusing on the word "sexual" rather than "harassment". With the phrase "sexual harassment" it is best to always envision it as follows:

# Sexual **Harassment**

That is, sexual harassment is about harassment – NOT sexual attraction. It is harassment, first and foremost; it is harassment exhibited in terms of touching or other sexually oriented behaviours, gestures, looks (*i.e.*, leers) or jokes. Sexual harassment is critically different than sexual attraction. Occasionally, a person who honestly finds another attractive may engage in sexual harassment because they do not accept that the other person does not reciprocate their feelings. It is common for someone to use harassment as an instrument of power or to be insensitive to the fact that their teasing is unwelcome.

### *What about sexual attraction within the workplace?*

Sexual attraction always has and always will occur within the workplace. But the difference between attraction and harassment goes back to the definition of harassment as "any unwelcome action". Reciprocated attraction is not unwelcome. When attraction is not mutual and the "I'm not interested in you" signals are respected, then it is not harassment.

### What are the negative consequences of sexual harassment?

Because of the nature of sexual harassment its consequences are even more severe than other types of harassment. It is not uncommon for a harassed person to become ill and miss work. Low morale results. The most common reaction to harassment is to quit. This leads to increased staff turnover costs. An increasingly common reaction to harassment is to file a human rights complaint with the appropriate human rights commission.

Increasingly, sexual harassment cases are making the news. For example, the sports writer, Lisa Olson, was harassed by a naked football player while she was interviewing another player after a game. Another example, is the extensive coverage given to Anita Hill's allegations of sexual harassment against Clarence Thomas during Thomas' confirmation hearings for the U.S. Supreme Court. Recently, as mentioned earlier at page 258, the Ontario Human Rights Commission awarded a woman $48,000 for harassment by a co-worker. Because the president of the company knew about the harassment but did nothing about it, the organization was liable for part of the fine.

### Is harassment likely to increase in the future?

In the next few years there could be an increase in harassment complaints from members of all the target groups. As EE succeeds, some people who resent or disagree with the policy may exhibit their backlash through harassment. This is why it is important that organizations deal with the issue pro-actively rather than taking an ostrich-like approach and pretending there is no problem.

## NOTES

1. [1987] 2 S.C.R. 84, 40 D.L.R. (4th) 577.
2. (1990), 91 C.L.L.C. 17,007 (Ont. Bd. of Inquiry).
3. From the American Bar Association Commission on Women in the Profession, "Lawyers and Balanced Lives: A Guide to Drafting and Implementing Workplace Policies for Lawyers, Part III Sexual Harrassment Policies," (undated), p. 12. Reproduced with the kind permission of Levin & Funkhouser, Ltd., Chicago, 1993.
4. See Ontario Human Rights Commission, *Guidelines for Internal Human Rights Complaints Resolution Procedures* (1991), pp. 3–4.

# REFERENCES

Arjun P. Aggarwal, *Sexual Harassment in the Workplace*, Markham: Butterworths, 1992.

Alliance Against Sexual Coercion, *Fighting Sexual Harassment*, Boston: Alyson Publications, Inc., 1981.

Kenneth C. Cooper, *Stop it Now*, St. Louis: Total Communication Press, 1985.

Joel Friedman, Marcia Mobilia Boumil and Barbara Ewert Taylor, *Sexual Harassment*, Deerfield Beach, Fla.: Health Communication Inc., 1992.

Catharine MacKinnon, *Sexual Harassment of Working Women*, New Haven: Yale University Press, 1979.

Amber Coverdale Sumrall and Dena Taylor (eds.), *Sexual Harassment: Women Speak Out*, Freedom, CA: The Crossing Press, 1992.

Susan L. Webb, *Step Forward: Sexual Harassment in the Workplace*, New York: Mastermedia, 1991.

# CHAPTER 11

# Monitoring and Evaluation

## WHAT IS INVOLVED IN MONITORING AND EMPLOYMENT EQUITY EVALUATION?

Employment equity is like many organizational strategies. Goals are set and initiatives identified to actualize the goals based on the best available information at the time. Then it is necessary to monitor and evaluate the outcome of the initiatives in terms of how effective they have been in actually achieving the goals. Typically, it is then necessary to reassess and revise the initiatives for another year to further advance the goals. Each set of initiatives should move the organization closer to the desired target. The same process is true with EE. The ultimate goal is a representative work-force with a workplace which works for all employees. Internal monitoring and evaluation involves:

1. Reviewing goals and timetables.
2. Collecting information on all EE activities and operational employment systems.
3. Assessing the relationship between the actual and expected accomplishments.
   - What has lead to desired results?
   - What has blocked desired results?
4. Deciding on future activity: What initiatives should be continued, what should be changed, what should be added?
   - What is the continuing or new role for:
     Senior management
     Middle managers and supervisors
     Human Resource professionals
     Co-workers
     Unions
   - What on-going or new resources are needed?
5. Who should be informed of progress and/or consulted about revisions?
   - Employees
   - Government
   - Stockholders
   - Designated group communities
   - General public

6.   What are the specific initiatives and their timetable for the next 12-month period?

**Review of goals and timetables:** Monitoring will be done quarterly for some goals and at least annually for all. In order to monitor, it is necessary to know what the desired results were – these are set out in the goals and timetables. What was scheduled to be accomplished over the period? In addition to formal goals, it is typical for some informal projects to be established. For example, the goal of reviewing the selection procedure for an entry-level job may have lead to the need to investigate and develop a strength test. All the initiatives identified to advance EE goals – whether carried out or not – should be reviewed at this time.

**Collect information on all EE initiatives and activities:** Information needs to be collected on all the planned goals and initiatives. In addition, there may be other activities related to EE which have occurred and should be monitored. For example, there have been a number of requests for company representatives to speak on the organization's involvement in EE. This information is needed to evaluate the organization's EE progress. Information to be collected includes:

- A description of all EE initiatives and activities;
- Up-to-date stock and transaction data;
- Information from sources such as exit interviews, employee attitude surveys, focus groups of employees and/or supervisors and feedback from support groups for the various designated groups.

Other information needs to be collected for monitoring rather than evaluation. This is the continuous scanning of the environment for issues and ideas related to EE. Examples include: monitoring of government legislation and regulations, monitoring of designated community groups and other organizations involved in EE for new ideas and issues and meeting with other organizations to talk about alternatives to achieve EE. A number of associations have evolved such as the Toronto Employment Equity Practitioners Association (TEEPA) and similar groups in Halifax, London, Ottawa and Winnipeg, or various industry-related associations such as municipal, and college and university EE networks.

**Assess the relationship between the actual and expected accomplishments:** Information on goals provide information on the desired target; information on initiatives, activities and stock and flow data provide information on what has actually happened. Evaluation involves comparing the two. The impact of all initiatives and activities needs to be evaluated. For example, it was expected that outreach recruitment would lead to more applications from the designated group members. Has this happened?

Work-force analysis and availability data are critical to the evaluation. The discussion of how to analyze this data was presented in Chapter 5. For the purposes of monitoring and evaluation it is important to remember that it is often the flow (transaction) data which is most helpful.

When evaluating EE progress one needs to be sensitive to interpretation. Sometimes, the outcome may appear to be negative. For example, many organizations find that after they introduce an anti-harassment policy and training that the number of harassment complaints increases. While this may appear "negative" it is really a positive, assuming that the reporting of harassment has increased, and not the incident of harassment. By knowing about harassment, the organization and union can do something about it. Alternatively, sometimes what looks like a positive advantage may have negative consequences. For instance, assume that the organization has been successful in outreach recruiting in that many more members of the designated groups have applied for jobs. However, no one has made it through the selection process. This may discourage people from the designated groups from applying in the future. The organization needs to review the selection process to ensure it is job-related and valid. If not, it must be changed. If the selection process is acceptable then the recruiting needs to be changed so that it is better targeted to those who can do the job.

As suggested by the Ontario Women's Directorate,[1] there are three areas to evaluate:

1. Changes in the corporate environment – the climate and culture of the organization.
2. Changes in employment systems – are the policies and practices naturally working for everyone?
3. Changes in the employment status of the designated group members – their distribution and representation throughout the organization.

One important issue associated with organizational climate is backlash, discussed later. As discussed in Chapter 9 under orientation, it is very important that the climate *in each work unit* be welcoming and supportive of diversity. As noted in Chapter 6 on systems review, this is an on-going process. During monitoring and evaluation is the time to assess if the changes made in employment systems have lead to the desired results. It is unlikely that all the needed changes will be identified in the first review of employment systems, nor is it likely that all the changes will work without, at least, some fine tuning.

In evaluating the changes in employment status of designated group members it is important to "get behind" the numbers. Are the people who have moved into non-traditional jobs feeling comfortable, are they being listened to, is there a revolving-door problem? Evaluation gets behind the numbers to answer some questions. Two questions should be constantly asked in the evaluation process:

1. What has lead to desired results?
2. What has blocked desired results?

This information will be helpful in the next step – deciding on future activities.

**Deciding on the future activities:** From the evaluation phase, decisions should be made as to what should be continued because it is working well or what needs to be changed because it is not working, or because changes indicate that what has worked well in the past will not be appropriate in the future. It is also necessary to determine what initiatives or goals should be added. Be aware that each EE success can lead to new concerns. For example, the success of getting a critical mass of persons from a designated group into the organization will eventually lead to the issue of promotion of designated group members into supervisory positions – requiring new goals and initiatives.

In evaluating what needs to be done, careful consideration should be given to the roles of the various stakeholders: senior management, middle managers and supervisors, human resource professionals, co-workers, and unions. Who has been a help in the past? Who has been a hindrance? One of the most effective ways to get people on-side is to use EE to help them solve an existing problem. For instance, rather than saying "You must hire more persons from the designated groups!" it is better to identify designated group members as an untapped source for a job for which recruiting is difficult.

What additional resources are needed to meet the EE challenges? Resources include money, staff and commitment. What exactly is needed should be based on the monitoring and evaluation process.

**Who should be informed of progress?** Organizations and unions want to have a good reputation with respect to equity. Thus, one consideration in the monitoring and evaluation phase is how best to communicate EE successes. Such communication goes beyond the reporting of data required by governments under the federal *Employment Equity Act*,[2] and Contractor's Program and the Ontario employment equity legislation. Communication to other audiences is a good idea – if there are EE successes to be highlighted. Employees, who should have been told about the organization's commitment to EE and who were surveyed about their designated group status, should be kept informed about what EE has meant in actual practice. Some private sector corporations keep their stockholders informed through their annual report. Government and organizations serving diverse communities find it useful to inform their constituencies of EE results. If contact has been made with designated group communities, then informing them of both successes and problems is appropriate feedback in exchange for their help.

**What are the goals and timetables for the next 12 months?** Based on the evaluation of what has been accomplished and what still needs to be accomplished, EE goals and initiatives should be re-established every 12 months.

Goals should be revised every 12 months even though those operating under Ontario law are required to have a three-year EE plan. According to the draft regulations, the plan revision is to be based on ascertaining if any of the four designated groups are underrepresented in any of the occupational groups. If underrepresentation exists then qualitative measures to address this problem must be included in the revised plan. While the draft regulations require that the plan be reviewed and revised every three years, annual assessment of goals and timetables are needed to get the job done effectively. A three-year planning horizon is simply too long given the number of changes which will occur.

The draft regulations specifically require that the process by which the employer intends to monitor the development and implementation of the goals and timetables be set out in the EE plan. Further, the plan must state who is responsible for this monitoring. For jobs which are unionized, the review and revision of the EE plan is a joint union-management responsibility. For jobs which are not unionized, unrepresented employees must be consulted with respect to reviewing and revising the plan.

## *What is backlash?*

Backlash refers to the negative reaction against persons from the designated groups when they begin making inroads into employment areas where they have been underrepresented. Backlash typically comes from those who are not members of a particular designated group; it can also come from designated group members. Backlash usually results from feelings that others are getting an unfair advantage.

Among non-designated group members, individuals may engage in backlash because:

- Discrimination is not perceived to exist, consequently EE is perceived to be inappropriate.
- Redress for past discrimination through special measures is not

considered necessary as long as present discrimination is discontinued.
- EE initiatives are perceived as having gone too far.
- Advantages to their group will be eliminated by EE.
- Personally threatened by EE – the next promotion will go to a person from the designated groups.
- Change of any kind is disliked.

It is also important to remember that backlash comes from different people on different issues; while still others feel everything about EE is wrong.

Backlash often comes from fear and misunderstanding. Some of the specific fears are likely to be:

- Being denied a job or promotion because of EE.
- Employment equity resulting in unqualified people being hired and promoted.
- Uncomfortable feeling about working with people who are different; particularly people who have traditionally had lower status.
- Being personally blamed for discrimination.
- Sense of unfairness because others are getting special privileges.

Backlash from some designated group members is often based on their feelings that, since they struggled to get where they are, others like them should have to struggle too. Additionally, they may feel that special programs for designated group members implies that they, as a member of a designated group, cannot make it on their own merits. Backlash from designated group members comes in the form of:

- Not helping others from designated groups. Sometimes they will do less for members of target groups than for those in the mainstream.
- Holding designated group members to higher standards.
- Hampering other designated group members because they enjoy being unique in the mainstream culture.

Some backlash is typical – there is always resistance to change. However, it is the responsibility of the organization to deal with backlash rather than putting this additional burden on designated group members. Backlash is often exhibited through:

- Excessive testing of new employees.
- Harassment on the basis of gender, race or disability status.
- An unwillingness to work with co-workers from designated groups

or not providing them with informal training ("tricks of the trade") routinely shared with new employees.
- Treating designated group members as if the only reason they have the job is because they are a member of a designated group; behaving toward the person as if they are unqualified.

### How can we deal with backlash?

Dealing with backlash is not easy. Further, depending on the cause and the specific circumstances, backlash needs to be dealt with in different ways. Some means to address it are:

- Clear signs of senior management and union commitment to EE;
- Allowing people to express their concerns so that their issues can be addressed;
- Communication and education;
- Honest feedback of what is actually happening.

Statements of commitment to EE and education on the subject should emphasize facts and figures that explain why the target groups are disadvantaged. Also, individuals who are following EE principles should be rewarded. This might be a manager who has succeeded in creating a more diverse work unit or ensuring that a man who used parental leave comes back to a good assignment. Further, it needs to be demonstrated that changing demographic trends necessitate the adoption of EE policies. The goal of EE – a representative work-force – should be communicated in a manner which enables employees to understand that persons from the designated groups are not the only ones who are being hired and promoted. Communicate to employees what is actually happening, such as how many designated group persons and non-designated group persons were hired and promoted over the last year. Communicate how EE has lead to better human resource policies and practices for all employees. Listen to employees – what are their fears and concerns? Hire only qualified people and hold everyone to the same performance standards.

To help in the communication process, four of the most typically asked questions related to EE, and their answers, are given below.[3]

1. Isn't EE reverse discrimination?
   - Employment equity ensures organizations meet with the objective of EE – equitable hiring. It also ensures that all those who are qualified are recognized.
   - It focuses on redressing the effects of past systemic discrimination

and is a kind of "catch-up". That is, it is not enough to simply stop systemic discrimination, organizations must also engage in behaviour which speeds up the full utilization of human resources.

- Employment equity forces organizations to do things differently, to change perceptions, to accommodate differences so that organization policies and practices work for all organizational members, not just those who have historically comprised the majority of the work-force.
- Employment equity never means hiring unqualified people. Rather, it means ensuring that job qualifications are those needed on the first day of the job and recognizing all qualifications that people have, even if they were acquired in non-traditional ways.
- The assumption that EE is "reverse discrimination" assumes that discrimination against persons from the designated groups has occurred and that those who have previously benefited from an unfair advantage do not want done to them what they believe has been done to others. In other words, claiming "reverse discrimination" acknowledges the fact that persons from the designated groups have been discriminated against. Employment equity seeks to end all forms of discrimination by redressing the effects of past discrimination until a level "playing field" is achieved.
- Employment equity may appear to be reverse discrimination because current systems have been designed by white, able-bodied men. It is not surprising for those in the majority to design systems from their own perspective. Now organizations must take many different perspectives into account and only one of these is that of white, able-bodied men. Because this has been the only perspective considered in the past, Whites, men and the able-bodied must now start to share.
- Employment equity acknowledges the changing demographics of the work-force. This cannot be ignored if organizations are going to be able to successfully utilize the talent available in the Canadian labour force.

2. Is there really a difference between quotas and goals?
   - Employment equity requires goals, not quotas.
   - Quotas are externally imposed and state exactly what kinds of people have to be hired. If the quota cannot be filled then the job vacancy is left open. Quotas are only numerical.
   - Quotas are inflexible and do not allow the circumstances of a particular organization from being taken into consideration.
   - Goals can be both numerical and qualitative in nature. They are derived by workplace parties based on circumstances unique to

the organization (*e.g.*, growth in one area but decline in another). Goals can be reassessed and methods of achieving the goals can be varied so that the desired results are achieved.

3.  If work-force demographics are changing, why bother with EE? Won't the situation fix itself?

    *   Yes, over the long term EE principles would eventually be incorporated into human resources practices because of changing demographics. But this would take a long time and there would be costs to the organization. For example, the high incidence of women starting their own businesses is credited, in part, with the typical work organization's attempt to make them fit into the male model — it does not work.

    *   Implementing EE is now a matter of timing. The talent of many Aboriginal Peoples, persons with disabilities, racial minorities and women is being lost by organizations today.

    *   It is a matter of fairness to remove the barriers of systemic discrimination now, rather than ignoring the disproportionate negative impact of some employment practices of persons from the designated groups. Why should the employment system work well for white, able-bodied men and not for anyone else. They should work for white, able-bodied men and all other groups too.

    *   Employment equity is a good strategy for organizations. It will take a long time to remove all the systemic barriers found in employment systems and to capitalize on the benefits of a diverse work-force. The organizations which begin sooner rather than later will be in a better position to attract and retain the best among the diverse pool of human resources and well positioned for the predicted skill shortage.

4.  Even if there has been discrimination in the past, aren't individuals responsible for their own employment success?

    *   This question is asking if personal choices or employer discrimination is to blame for the disadvantages of designated group members. This question is both complex and irrelevant.

    *   This question is complex because personal choice is not separate from opportunity. If members of particular groups believe there is no opportunity for them then they will not make certain choices. For instance, look at the tremendous increase in the numbers of women in medicine, law and business over the last two decades. Different personal choices are being made because there are now different opportunities available.

    *   This question is irrelevant because correction of systemic discrimination is not concerned with the issue of blame. Change is required, but no one needs to be blamed for the current situation.

## *What are the costs of EE?*

A U.S. study found that the cost of developing EE programs was usually less than 1 per cent of the average firm's annual capital investment and that there was a 50 per cent return on its investment.[4]

## *What are some of the common pitfalls to watch for when engaging in EE activities?*

Rosabeth Moss Kanter has identified some common pitfalls.[5]

**Not taking EE seriously:** Many organizations become involved in EE only to keep the government "off their backs" (a focus on compliance only). Employment equity is intimately connected with good human resource practices. The same initiatives which work for EE are also needed to prepare for the predicted skill and labour shortage.

**Tokenism:** Tokenism is dangerous, both to the individuals involved and to the organization. Placing one token from a designated group into a work environment designed for white, able-bodied men or women will not work. There has to be change on both sides.

**No follow through:** Official statements are important as a starting place but if resources are not committed to EE, employees, and eventually the public, learn that change is not truly desired. Once you lose credibility with the various target groups it is difficult to recapture it.

**Emphasizing the individual model:** This pitfall assumes that each individual is *totally* responsible for her/his success. This model ignores the effects of systemic discrimination. The individual model either lays the blame at the feet of those in power because they are consciously holding others down, or it puts the blame on individuals from the designated groups because of the choices they have made or because they are not qualified. On the other hand, the systemic model recognizes that systems were designed by those in power at a time when most of the people working were similar to those in power and that what has changed over time is the composition of the labour force which now makes these systems obsolete. It is the systems which must change.

**Promoting unqualified people:** This helps neither the individual nor the organization since both experience failure. What sometimes happened in the United States as part of affirmative action was that women or black people who had the capabilities to be supervisors at that point in time were promoted to middle management. While they would have been very good supervisors, they were mediocre managers. Organizations should avoid the numbers game of simply putting people into jobs to make the data look good. Rather, they should find qualified people and develop them even further.

**Promoting people because of their designated group status:** Related to the previous point is the insidious self-doubt which affects a person who thinks he/she has been given an advantage because of factors other than competence. It is true that non-competence issues have long been a part of hiring and promotion decisions (*e.g.*, which university one attended) but if the general attitude is "she got that job because she is a woman" – this allows others to dismiss her and causes the individual to doubt her real abilities.

## CONCLUSION

Employment equity is a challenge. It can be difficult. It is an opportunity for creativity. By looking at employment systems differently, they can be made to work better for all employees. By being open to talent, regardless of how it is packaged, the organization will be staffed with better people. By building on diversity, organizations will be stronger. The future of the workplace is different than the past and the present. Equality in employment is part of that future.

# NOTES

1. Ontario Women's Directorate, "Organizational Change and Organizational Impact" in *Managing Employment Equity* series, Toronto, March 1989, p. 16.
2. R.S.C. 1985, c. 23 (2nd Supp.).
3. The first three questions and answers were developed by the author from the discussion of the membership of the Toronto Employment Equity Practitioner's Association meeting on 29 October, 1991.
4. Cruz, "Is Equal Employment Opportunity Cost Effective?" *Labour Law Journal*, Vol. 31, No. 5, May 1980, p. 295.
5. Rosabeth Moss Kanter, in Joyce M. Young, "Affirmative Action Strategies", *The Human Resource*, August/September 1985, p. 12, at 13-14.

# Statistics

## LABOUR FORCE AND POPULATION FIGURES

When looking at any data it is important to know exactly what the data represents. When considering the availability of designated groups to an organization (discussed in detail in Chapter 5) there are three possible sets of figures which can be reported. These are:

1. Total population
2. Working age population
3. Labour force

Total population figures are not particularly relevant for an organization to ascertain if it has a representative work-force. Total population figures include everyone, regardless of age. Using population figures would not be problematic if all the various groups had similar proportions at each age group. However, this is not true. For instance, more than half of all Aboriginal Peoples are under 24 years of age, while only 37 per cent of non-Aboriginal Peoples are in this age range. Further, among older people there is more likely to be a higher proportion of persons with disabilities.

The working age population provides a good estimation of the upper limit of available workers. The working age population is defined as those 15 years of age or older. Fifteen may seem a little young today, but this definition of the working age population has been around for a long time; a time when people got less schooling than they do today.

The labour force has a very specific definition. It is *not* just those who are employed. Rather, the labour force includes those who are employed and unemployed. Those who are not in the labour force are not available for work at a particular point in time. They may be preparing for the labour force (students); not available to work (those in prisons); while others would work if there were jobs available (discouraged workers). "Able and looking for work" is the definition of someone who is unemployed. If someone has become discouraged about their chances of finding employment they may give up even trying to find work. The "discouraged worker" effect is common during times of recession. Even during more prosperous times some workers may become discouraged because they keep experiencing barriers when they look for work. It is likely that, all things being equal, a higher proportion of designated group members will be discouraged workers who would join the labour force if they felt they had a chance of finding work. Data for the labour force provides information on those 15 years of age or older who are in the labour force – either employed or unemployed.

Table A-1 provides the data on the composition of the *labour force* which is shown in Chapter 1, Figure 1-3. This data is based on the 1986 census. The data from the 1991 census is not available at the time this book is being written though it is expected out in the fall of 1993. It is likely to show an increase in the proportion of designated group members in the labour force. It is estimated that the availability for the four designated groups, based on the 1991 census, will be approximately: 2.5 per cent (up from 2 per cent) for Aboriginal Peoples, 6 per cent (up from 5 per cent) for persons with disabilities, 8.5 per cent (up from 6.3 per cent) for racial minorities, and 45 per cent (up from 44 per cent) for women (approximately 37 per cent for white, able-bodied women).

## TABLE A-1

### COMPOSITION OF CANADIAN LABOUR FORCE
(Data used for Figure 1-3)

|  | Availability in the Canadian Labour Force* | |
|---|---|---|
|  | Number | Percentage |
| White able-bodied women | 5,245,000 | 38.0% |
| White able-bodied men | 6,693,000 | 48.0% |
| Visible minority women | 406,000 | 2.9% |
| Visible minority men | 467,000 | 3.4% |
| Women who are disabled | 314,000 | 2.3% |
| Men who are disabled | 439,000 | 3.2% |
| Aboriginal women | 133,000 | 1.0% |
| Aboriginal men | 161,000 | 1.2% |
| TOTAL | 13,858,000 | 100% |

Source: Adapted from Statistics Canada, 1986 data. Combination of information from Employment Equity Availability Data Report, Tables 6 and 13 (provided by Employment Immigration Canada) which is based on data from 1986 Census and 1986 Health and Activities Limitation Survey (the latter provides data for persons with disabilities).

* Labour force is comprised of all those 15 years of age or older who are employed or are looking for work (are unemployed).

Table A-2 shows the composition of the *working age population* in Canada. This data is shown in Chapter 1, Figure 1-4.

Figure A-1 shows the proportion of people within each group who are in the labour force. This is referred to as the labour force participation rate (LFPR). (Where Tables A-1 and A-2 show the distribution of the various groups within the labour force, Figure A-1 shows the proportion within each group which is in the labour force.) For instance, 65 per cent of all racial minority women in Canada are in the labour force. This compares with a 55 per cent LFPR for women in general and an 80 per cent LFPR for visible minority men. Seventy-seven per cent of men are in the labour force.[1]

TABLE **A-2**

**COMPOSITION OF CANADIAN WORKING AGE POPULATION**
(Data shown in Figure 1-4)

| | Availability in the working age population in Canada* | |
|---|---|---|
| | **Number** | **Percentage** |
| White able-bodied women | 8,631,000 | 44% |
| White able-bodied men | 8,277,000 | 42% |
| Visible minority women | 589,635 | 3% |
| Visible minority men | 563,000 | 3% |
| Women who are disabled** | 572,000 | 3% |
| Men who are disabled** | 549,000 | 3% |
| Aboriginal women[2] | 235,000 | 1% |
| Aboriginal men[2] | 217,000 | 1% |
| TOTAL | 19,634,000 | 100% |

Source: Adapted from Statistics Canada, 1986 data. Combination of information from Employment Equity Availability Data Report, Tables 8 and 14 (provided by Employment Immigration Canada) which is based on data from 1986 Census and 1986 Health and Activities Limitation Survey (the latter provides data for persons with disabilities).

\* The working age population is comprised of those over 15 years of age.

\*\* Figures for persons with disabilities takes into account 10% of population which is institutionalized.

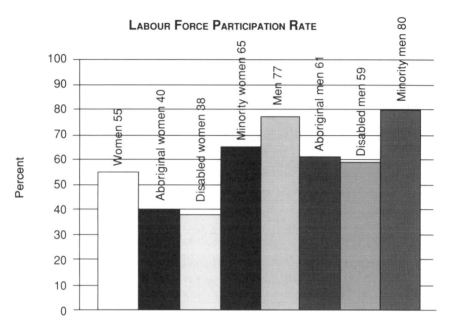

**Figure A-1**

**Labour Force Participation Rate**

Source: Adapted from Statistics Canada, 1986 data.

## EXTERNAL AVAILABILITY DATA

It has been stated that one of the ultimate goals of EE is that an organization's work-force will mirror the community from which it recruits. In order to do this it is necessary to know what the external availability of each designated group is. Four maps are presented providing availability information for each of the four designated groups for Canada, each province and some of the major cities (with the exception of persons with disabilities). This data is taken from Table 3 of the 1988 EE report provided by the federal government and based on the 1986 census.[3]

Figure A-2 shows the 1986 external availability statistics for Aboriginal Peoples; it is 2 per cent in Canada. With the exception of the territories, availability for First Nations people ranges from 1 per cent to 5 per cent. In the Yukon it is 17 per cent and 45 per cent in the Northwest Territories.

Figure A-3 shows the availability within the working age population for persons with disabilities, which is 7 per cent in Canada. (The proportion in the labour force is 5 per cent.) The Atlantic provinces have a higher proportion of workers with disabilities (8 per cent to 10 per cent) while the territories have a lower proportion (4 per cent each). Central and western Canadian provinces have 7 per cent to 8 per cent.

Geographic location makes the most difference in availability of racial

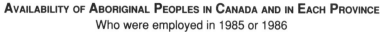

FIGURE A-2

AVAILABILITY OF ABORIGINAL PEOPLES IN CANADA AND IN EACH PROVINCE
Who were employed in 1985 or 1986

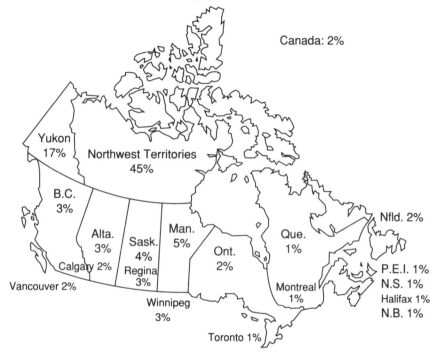

Source:    Adapted from 1986 Census, Employment Equity Availability Data Report, Table 3.

minorities as shown in Figure A-4. While the external availability is 6.3 per cent in Canada as a whole, British Columbia (10 per cent) and Ontario (9 per cent) have the greatest proportion, while the Atlantic provinces, the territories and Saskatchewan only have 1 per cent to 3 per cent. There is also a rural-urban difference as to where members of racial minorities are likely to live. All major cities listed have a higher proportion of racial minority workers than the province in which they are located. Vancouver and Toronto have the highest proportion, 16 per cent each.

The proportion of women who are employed is consistent across the country, ranging from 42 per cent (Newfoundland) to 47 per cent (Regina); availability is 44 per cent at a national level as shown in Figure A-5.

# EVIDENCE OF DISADVANTAGE

The four designated groups are disadvantaged in employment and need EE initiatives. Groups which are disadvantaged show:

## Figure A-3

### Availability of Persons with Disabilities in Canada and in Each Province*
Working Age Population

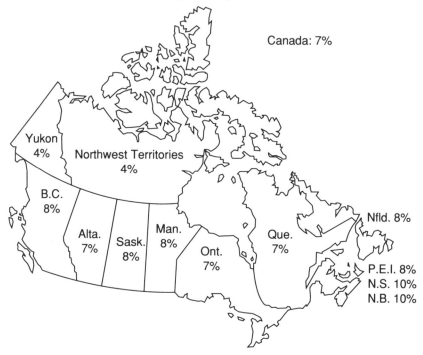

Canada: 7%

Yukon 4%

Northwest Territories 4%

B.C. 8%

Alta. 7%

Sask. 8%

Man. 8%

Ont. 7%

Que. 7%

Nfld. 8%

P.E.I. 8%
N.S. 10%
N.B. 10%

Source:   Adapted from 1986 Census,  Health Activity Limitation Survey, in EE Availability
          Data Report, Table 10.

*Data unavailable for cities.

- Higher levels of unemployment and underemployment;
- Lower pay for equal qualification; and
- Lower participation in positions of authority (*e.g.*, management).

*Higher levels of unemployment and underemployment.*

People who are unemployed are able to work and are looking for work but have not found a job. Figure A-6 shows the 1986 unemployment rates for the various groups. Men have the lowest unemployment rate (9 per cent) which is slightly lower than women (10 per cent) and minority men (10 per cent). Typically, with the exception of Aboriginal men,[4] men in each group have a lower unemployment rate than women. Figure A-7 shows the unemployment rates of men and women in Canada between 1975 to 1989. Consistently, with the exception of late 1981 into 1983,

FIGURE **A-4**

AVAILABILITY OF RACIAL MINORITIES IN CANADA AND IN EACH PROVINCE
Who worked in 1985 or 1986

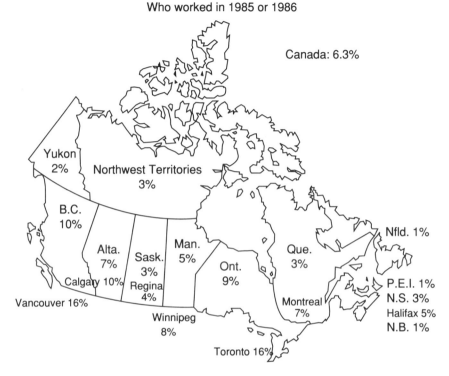

Source:   Adapted from 1986 Census, Employment Equity Availability Data Report, Table 3.

women always have a higher unemployment rate. The slightly higher unemployment rate of men during a recessionary time (1981 to 1983)
is not unusual since when a bread-winning husband is laid off, often
his wife is able to find work (though usually at a much lower rate of
pay).

Designated group members are not only more likely to be unemployed
but also to be in underemployment. Underemployment means that people are not in jobs which fully use their skills. It is harder to document
underemployment. For instance, 14 per cent of racial minority women
and 20 per cent of racial minority men who are clerical workers in Ontario have university degrees, compared to 4 per cent of women and
7 per cent of men in the rest of Ontario's population. The analysis of
education and salary, discussed next, provides further support of underemployment.

## FIGURE A-5

### AVAILABILITY OF WOMEN IN CANADA AND IN EACH PROVINCE
Who worked in 1985 or 1986

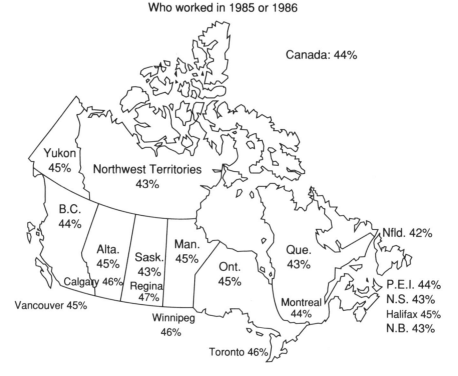

Canada: 44%

Yukon 45%

Northwest Territories 43%

B.C. 44%

Alta. 45%

Calgary 46%

Vancouver 45%

Sask. 43%

Regina 47%

Winnipeg 46%

Man. 45%

Ont. 45%

Toronto 46%

Que. 43%

Montreal 44%

Nfld. 42%

P.E.I. 44%

N.S. 43%

Halifax 45%

N.B. 43%

Source:   Adapted from 1986 Census, Employment Equity Availability Data Report, Table 3.

*Lower pay for equal qualifications.*

Table A-4 shows that all the designated group members have lower salaries than men. But this, in and of itself, does not prove disadvantage. For example, if men as a group had higher qualifications than the members of all the designated groups then these higher salaries would be justified. This assumes that education can be used as a proxy for level of qualification. Figure A-8 shows the proportion of each group which has less than secondary school, secondary school diploma, some post-secondary (which includes trades, community college, and some university) and university graduation.

## Figure A-6

### Unemployment Rates

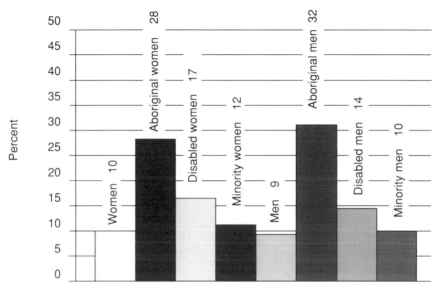

Source: Adapted from Statistics Canada, 1986 data.

## Figure A-7

### Unemployment Rates by Sex, Canada, 1975 to 1989

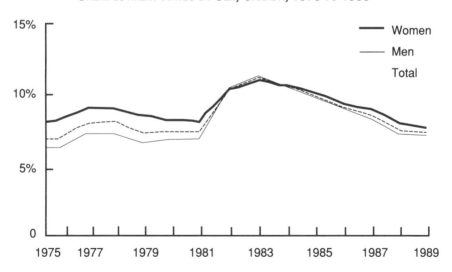

Source: Labour Canada, Women's Bureau, *Women in the Labour Force*, 1990-91 ed., p. 9. Reproduced with the permission of the Minister of Supply and Services Canada.

## TABLE A-4

### SALARIES FOR VARIOUS GROUPS IN RELATIONSHIP TO MEN

|  | Women | Men |
|---|---|---|
|  | 68%<br>($20,400) | 100%<br>($30,000) |
| Aboriginal Peoples | 56%<br>($16,800) | 76%<br>($22,800) |
| Persons with disabilities | 40%<br>($12,800) | 92%<br>($27,600) |
| Racial minorities | 66%<br>($19,800) | 97%<br>($29,100) |

Figure A-9 combines the information from Table A-4 with some of the information from Figure A-8 to show that there is no reason to believe that the higher salaries earned by men are warranted because of greater qualifications.

Figure A-9 also provides support for the contention that members of designated groups are underemployed. Figure A-9 shows the designated groups in order of the proportion who have at least obtained a secondary school diploma (*i.e.*, secondary and beyond are combined from Figure A-8). This puts the groups into the following order: racial minorities, persons with disabilities, men, women and Aboriginal Peoples.[5] The order is the same in terms of the proportion who have education beyond secondary school with one exception – persons with disabilities have the lowest level. The two lines show the salary for men and women *as a proportion of men's salary*. Men have the highest salary so it is defined as 100 per cent. By comparing the pattern of the lines (salary) to the bars (educational level) it is possible to see that some of the designated groups do not receive the return for their education enjoyed by men. Racial minorities who have the highest level of education are not paid at the same level as men – racial minority men receive 97 per cent and racial minority women only 66 per cent of the salary paid men in general, fewer of whom have as high a level of education. A higher proportion of persons with disabilities than men in general have at least a secondary school diploma; a lower proportion have gone beyond secondary school. Men who are disabled earn almost as much as men in general (92 per cent) while women earn only 40 per cent. Aboriginal men earn 76 per cent of what

## Figure A-8

### Educational Levels

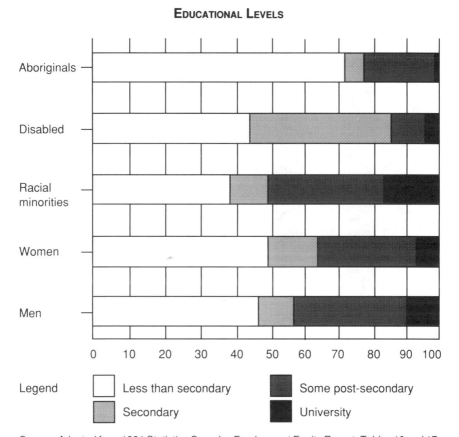

Source: Adapted from 1981 Statistics Canada, Employment Equity Report, Tables 10 and 17.

men earn while Aboriginal women earn 56 per cent. It is clear from Figure A-9 that women's salaries are significantly lower than the men's, even though the proportion at each educational level is not that different. This point is illustrated further in Table A-6 which compares the salaries of men and women with equal levels of education.

Women at each educational level earn significantly less than men with the same educational level. Women with university degrees earn $31,259 about the same as what men with some post-secondary education earn ($31,068).

### *Lower participation in positions of authority.*

The final criteria demonstrating disadvantage is lower participation in decision-making positions. The federal *Employment Equity Report* pro-

FIGURE A-9

COMPARISON OF EDUCATIONAL LEVEL AND SALARY INDEX
At Least Secondary and Beyond Secondary

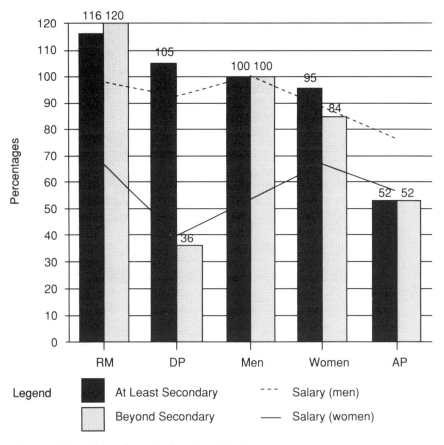

Source:  Adapted from Statistics Canada, 1991 data.

vides information on the distribution across different occupational levels for the designated groups. Two of the occupational categories are: senior management and middle and other managers. Figure A-10 shows the proportion of designated groups and white, able-bodied men comprising each of these two levels of authority. Seventy-seven per cent of upper management positions are held by white, able-bodied men who make up only 48 per cent of the labour force. White, able-bodied women hold 16 per cent of senior management jobs while comprising 38 per cent of the labour force. Members of racial minority groups hold 4 per cent of senior management jobs with 6 per cent of the total labour force. Persons with

## TABLE A-6

### AVERAGE ANNUAL EARNINGS OF FULL TIME WORKERS

| Level of education | Women | Men | Women's earnings as a % of men's |
|---|---|---|---|
| Less than grade 9 | $15,077 | $25,454 | 59% |
| High school (attend or complete) | 18,042 | 28,444 | 63% |
| Some post-secondary | 20,092 | 31,068 | 65% |
| Post-secondary certificate or diploma | 21,850 | 31,781 | 69% |
| University degree | 31,259 | 44,891 | 70% |
| TOTAL | 21,012 | 31,865 | 66% |

Source: Adapted from Earnings of Men and Women, Statistics Canada, Cat. No. 13-217, 1987.

disabilities occupy 2 per cent of upper level management positions while comprising 5 per cent of the labour force and Aboriginal Peoples hold only 1 per cent of the highest level positions of authority while comprising 2 per cent of the labour force.

The second pie chart in Figure A-10 shows the same analysis for middle and other management positions. Here white, able-bodied men hold 61 per cent of positions (48 per cent of the labour force). Thirty per cent women in middle management is approaching their 38 per cent proportion of the labour force. Racial minorities hold 4.7 per cent middle management positions (6 per cent of labour force); Aboriginal Peoples hold 1.4 per cent (2 per cent of labour force); persons with disabilities hold 3.3 per cent of middle management jobs (5 per cent of labour force). The data used to develop Figure A-10 is provided in Table A-7.

## Figure A-10

### Distribution of Various Groups in Positions of Authority (Canada, 1986)

**Upper Management Positions**

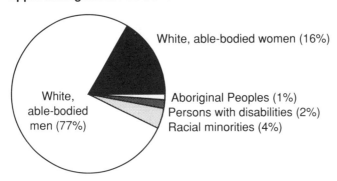

White, able-bodied women (16%)

White, able-bodied men (77%)

Aboriginal Peoples (1%)
Persons with disabilities (2%)
Racial minorities (4%)

**Middle and Other Management Positions**

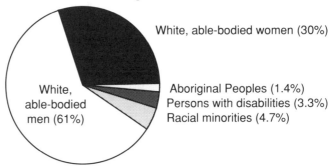

White, able-bodied women (30%)

White, able-bodied men (61%)

Aboriginal Peoples (1.4%)
Persons with disabilities (3.3%)
Racial minorities (4.7%)

Source:   Adapted from Statistics Canada, 1986 data. Combination of information from Employment Equity Availability Data Report, and Health and Activities Limitation Survey, Tables 6, 7 & 13.

*Occupational concentration for various groups.*

The lack of designated group members in positions of authority raises the issue of the kind of work most typical for the various groups. Table A-8 shows the five occupations where most members of each designated group and men work.

TABLE A-7

NUMBER AND PROPORTION OF
VARIOUS GROUPS IN POSITIONS OF AUTHORITY

| Groups | Upper level management (Total = 200,330) | | Middle and other management (Total = 975,280) | |
|---|---|---|---|---|
| | Number | Proportion | Number | Proportion |
| Aboriginal men | 2,035 | 1.0% | 7,705 | .8% |
| Aboriginal women | 855 | .4% | 6,040 | .6% |
| Men with disabilities | 3,040 | 1.5% | 23,290 | 2.4% |
| Women with disabilities | 505 | .3% | 8,490 | .9% |
| Racial minority men | 6,680 | 3.3% | 31,470 | 3.2% |
| Racial minority women | 1,520 | .8% | 14,700 | 1.5% |
| White, able-bodied men | 153,660 | 76.7% | 589,780 | 60.5% |
| White, able-bodied women | 32,035 | 16.0% | 293,805 | 30.1% |

Source:  Adapted from Statistics Canada, 1986 data.

## TABLE A-8

### OCCUPATIONAL CONCENTRATION AND DISTRIBUTION FOR VARIOUS GROUPS IN FIVE OCCUPATIONS WITH THE MOST GROUP MEMBERS

| Occupation | Number | Proportion of group within occupation (Occupational representation) | Proportion in occupation who are members of this group (Distribution) |
|---|---|---|---|
| Women (Total = 6,098,175) | | | |
| Clerical | 1,886,905 | 31% | 80% |
| Professional | 888,500 | 15% | 53% |
| Service | 847,785 | 14% | 61% |
| Other manual | 601,395 | 10% | 29% |
| Sales | 512,155 | 8% | 48% |
| Men (Total = 7,759,600) | | | |
| Other manual | 1,459,365 | 19% | 71% |
| Semi-skilled manual | 1,074,245 | 14% | 86% |
| Skilled craft & trades | 968,625 | 13% | 92% |
| Professional | 778,700 | 10% | 47% |
| Middle & other management | 652,245 | 8% | 67% |
| Aboriginal men (Total = 161,210) | | | |
| Other manual | 45,840 | 28% | 2% |
| Semi-skilled manual | 27,660 | 17% | 2% |
| Skilled craft & trades | 18,810 | 12% | 2% |
| Service | 11,810 | 7% | 1% |
| Occupations not stated | 10,970 | 7% | 2% |
| Aboriginal women (Total = 133,210) | | | |
| Clerical | 32,660 | 25% | 1% |
| Service | 27,185 | 20% | 2% |
| Other manual | 16,125 | 12% | 1% |
| Professional | 14,655 | 11% | 1% |
| Occupations not stated | 8,575 | 6% | 2% |
| Semi-professional & technical | 8,440 | 6% | 1% |

TABLE A-8 (CONT'D)

| Occupation | Number | Proportion of group within occupation (Occupational representation) | Proportion in occupation who are members of this group (Distribution) |
|---|---|---|---|
| Racial minority women (Total = 405,740) | | | |
| Clerical | 108,620 | 27% | 5% |
| Other manual | 72,725 | 18% | 4% |
| Service | 60,005 | 15% | 4% |
| Professional | 53,755 | 13% | 3% |
| Sales | 21,635 | 5% | 2% |
| Racial minority men (Total = 466,955) | | | |
| Other manual | 91,000 | 20% | 4% |
| Professional | 65,240 | 14% | 4% |
| Service | 55,385 | 12% | 4% |
| Semi-skilled manual | 48,405 | 10% | 4% |
| Clerical | 38,125 | 8% | 2% |
| Women with disabilities (Total = 314,355) | | | |
| Clerical | 71,335 | 23% | 3% |
| Service | 58,695 | 19% | 4% |
| Other manual | 47,125 | 15% | 2% |
| Professional | 33,355 | 11% | 2% |
| Sales | 24,910 | 8% | 2% |
| Men with disabilities (Total = 438,635) | | | |
| Other manual | 102,975 | 24% | 5% |
| Semi-skilled manual | 90,205 | 21% | 7% |
| Skilled craft & trades | 61,645 | 14% | 6% |
| Service | 30,020 | 7% | 2% |
| Clerical | 27,035 | 6% | 1% |
| Sales | 26,765 | 6% | 3% |

Source: Adapted from Employment Equity Report, Tables 6 and 13; 1986 Census and Health and Limitation Survey.

## NOTES

1. This is 1986 data. 1991 data in Figure 1-5 shows that male LFPR dropped to 75 per cent; while female LFPR increased from 55 per cent to 58 per cent.
2. Labour force participation rates and unemployment rates differ greatly for Aboriginal Peoples living on-reserve versus off-reserve, as shown in the table below.

TABLE A-3

|  | Labour force participation rate | Unemployed |
|---|---|---|
| On-reserve | 43.2% | 34.9% |
| Off-reserve | 65.1% | 20.5% |
| Canadian population | 66.5% | 10.3% |

Source: Adapted from "A Profile of the Aboriginal Population Residing in Selected Off Reserve Areas" prepared by Statistics Canada for Aboriginal Data and Native Issues Unit of the Housing, Family and Social Statistics Division, February 1990.

3. This data is not based on the working age population nor on the labour force but, rather, on those over 15 years of age who worked in 1985 or 1986 and so is more conservative than availability data reflected for labour force.
4. *Supra* note 2.
5. The educational attainment of on-reserve and off-reserve Aboriginal Peoples differs greatly. For those who live off the reserve the educational level falls between non-Aboriginals and those who live on the reserve.

TABLE A-5

HIGHEST LEVEL OF EDUCATION
For those aged 15 years and older

| Level of education | On-reserve | Off-reserve | Canadian population |
|---|---|---|---|
| Less than grade 9 | 43.6% | 21.0% | 17.3% |
| Grades 9-13 | 34.5% | 34.3% | 27.1% |
| High school degree | 3.8% | 9.3% | 12.8% |
| Post-secondary education | 18.1% | 35.4% | 42.8% |

Source: Adapted from "A Profile of the Aboriginal Population Residing in Selected Off Reserve Areas" prepared by Statistics Canada for Aboriginal Data and Native Issues Unit of the Housing, Family and Social Statistics Division, February 1990.

# APPENDIX B

# Data Collection Form
# Required by the Federal Government
# under the
# *Employment Equity Act*

Reproduced with permission of The Director-General, Employment Equity,
Employment and Immigration Canada.

Employment and Immigration Canada    Emploi et Immigration Canada

**OCCUPATIONAL GROUPS : PERMANENT FULL-TIME EMPLOYEES\***
*CATÉGORIES PROFESSIONNELLES : SALARIÉS PERMANENTS À TEMPS PLEIN\**

NOTE: See instructions
*NOTA: Voir instructions*

Form **2** Part A, Page 1
*Formulaire   Partie A,*

Name of Business:
*Nom de l'entreprise:*

Reporting Period:
*Période de rapport:*  19___

Industrial Sector:
*Branche d'activité:*

☐ National (Canada)
   *National (Canada)*

☐ Province / Territory (specify)
   *Province / territoire (préciser)*

☐ Designated CMA (specify)
   *RMR désignée (préciser)*

Location-Endroit

| Occupational Groups *Catégories professionnelles* | Top and bottom of salary range *Maximum et minimum de l'échelle de rémunération* | ** Quarter *Quart* | All Employees *Tous les salariés* | | | Aboriginal Peoples *Autochtones* | | | Persons with Disabilities *Personnes handicapées* | | | Members of Visible Minorities *Membres des minorités visibles* | | |
|---|---|---|---|---|---|---|---|---|---|---|---|---|---|---|
| | | | Total Number *Nombre total* | Men *Hommes* | Women *Femmes* | Total Number *Nombre total* | Men *Hommes* | Women *Femmes* | Total Number *Nombre total* | Men *Hommes* | Women *Femmes* | Total Number *Nombre total* | Men *Hommes* | Women *Femmes* |
| | Col. 1 | | Col. 2 | Col. 3 | Col. 4 | Col. 5 | Col. 6 | Col. 7 | Col. 8 | Col. 9 | Col. 10 | Col. 11 | Col. 12 | Col. 13 |
| Upper-level managers *Cadres supérieurs* | | 4. 3. 2. 1. | | | | | | | | | | | | |
| Middle or other managers *Cadres intermediaires et autres cadres* | | 4. 3. 2. 1. | | | | | | | | | | | | |
| Professionals *Professionnels* | | 4. 3. 2. 1. | | | | | | | | | | | | |
| Semi-professionals and technicians *Semi-professionnels et techniciens* | | 4. 3. 2. 1. | | | | | | | | | | | | |
| Supervisors *Surveillants* | | 4. 3. 2. 1. | | | | | | | | | | | | |
| Foremen / women *Contremaîtres* | | 4. 3. 2. 1. | | | | | | | | | | | | |

\* Use separate Parts for permanent part-time and temporary employees
  *Utiliser les autres parties pour les salariés permanents à temps partiel et les salariés temporaires*

\*\* † refers to the lowest salary quarter; 4 refers to the highest salary quarter /
   *† représente les salaires du quart le moins élevé; 4 représente les salaires du quart le plus élevé*

I MP 38/1 (7-86)

Canada

302

NOTE: See instructions
NOTA: Voir instructions

Form **2** Part A, Page 2
Formulaire Partie A,

| Occupational Groups / Catégories professionnelles | Top and bottom of salary range / Maximum et minimum de l'échelle de rémunération Col. 1 | ** Quarter / Quart | All Employees / Tous les salariés | | | | Aboriginal Peoples / Autochtones | | | | Persons with Disabilities / Personnes handicapées | | | | Members of Visible Minorities / Membres des minorités visibles | | |
|---|---|---|---|---|---|---|---|---|---|---|---|---|---|---|---|---|---|
| | | | Total Number / Nombre total Col. 2 | Men / Hommes Col. 3 | Women / Femmes Col. 4 | | Total Number / Nombre total Col. 5 | Men / Hommes Col. 6 | Women / Femmes Col. 7 | | Total Number / Nombre total Col. 8 | Men / Hommes Col. 9 | Women / Femmes Col. 10 | | Total Number / Nombre total Col. 11 | Men / Hommes Col. 12 | Women / Femmes Col. 13 |
| Clerical workers / Employés de bureau | | 4 3 2 1 | | | | | | | | | | | | | | | |
| Sales workers / Employés du secteur de la vente | | 4 3 2 1 | | | | | | | | | | | | | | | |
| Service workers / Employés du secteur des services | | 4 3 2 1 | | | | | | | | | | | | | | | |
| Skilled crafts and trades workers / Travailleurs qualifiés et artisans | | 4 3 2 1 | | | | | | | | | | | | | | | |
| Semi-skilled manual workers / Travailleurs manuels spécialisés | | 4 3 2 1 | | | | | | | | | | | | | | | |
| Other manual workers / Autres travailleurs manuels | | 4 3 2 1 | | | | | | | | | | | | | | | |
| TOTAL NUMBER OF EMPLOYEES / NOMBRE TOTAL DES SALARIÉS | | 1 | | | | | | | | | | | | | | | |

** 1 refers to the lowest salary quarter; 4 refers to the highest salary quarter /
1 représente les salaires du quart le moins élevé; 4 représente les salaires du quart le plus élevé

# APPENDIX C

# Data Collection Forms
# Required in Quebec

## Données 2.1 — sur les emplois

Nom de l'organisation: _____

Complété le: _____

Ligne de progression: _____

Page ___ de ___

| no | EMPLOIS et unité (s) administrative(s) | CLASSIFICATION ET ÉCHELLE SALARIALE | FORMATION : - niveau - spécialité - équivalence (s) | EXPÉRIENCE (emploi d'accès) | ZONE | CODE(S) CTP DE L'EMPLOI | CODE(S) CTP DES EMPLOIS D'ACCÈS | EFFECTIFS | | | | | | |
|---|---|---|---|---|---|---|---|---|---|---|---|---|---|---|
| | | | | | | | | TOTAL | GROUPE CIBLE | | | | | |
| | | | | | | | | | nb | % | nb | % | nb | % |
| ① | ④ | ⑤ | ⑥ | ⑦ | ⑧ | ⑨ | ⑩ | | | | | | | |

COMMISSION DES DROITS DE LA PERSONNE DU QUÉBEC — NOVEMBRE 1988

Complété le: _____
Données valables en date du: _____

● Ligne de progression: _____

Page ____ de ____

Groupe cible _____

**Analyse des effectifs** 2.2

| ● no | ● EMPLOIS | ❶ PERMANENTS à temps plein | | | ❷ PERMANENTS à temps partiel | | | ❸ PERMANENTS TOTAL | | | ❹ TEMPORAIRES | | |
|---|---|---|---|---|---|---|---|---|---|---|---|---|---|
| | | TOTAL | GROUPE CIBLE | | TOTAL | GROUPE CIBLE | | TOTAL | GROUPE CIBLE | | TOTAL | GROUPE CIBLE | |
| | | | nb | % | | nb | % | | nb | % | | nb | % |
| | | | | | | | | | | | | | |

COMMISSION DES DROITS DE LA PERSONNE DU QUÉBEC — NOVEMBRE 1988

**Analyse de disponibilité** 2.3

Complété le: _____

Page ___ de ___

Groupe cible _____

● Ligne de progression: _____

**CALCUL DE LA DISPONIBILITÉ: PHASE DU DIAGNOSTIC**

**CALCUL DES OBJECTIFS QUANTITATIFS**

| ● no | EMPLOIS | ● ZONE | ❶ Sources des statistiques | ❷ Actualisation | ❸ Total | ❹ Groupe cible | Personnes en cours de formation ❺ Sources des statistiques | ❻ Total | ❼ Groupe cible | Objectifs quantitatifs ❽ Total | ❾ Groupe cible |
|---|---|---|---|---|---|---|---|---|---|---|---|
| | | | | | TAUX | | | | | TAUX | |
| | | | | | TAUX | | | | | TAUX | |
| | | | | | TAUX | | | | | TAUX | |
| | | | | | TAUX | | | | | TAUX | |

COMMISSION DES DROITS DE LA PERSONNE DU QUÉBEC — NOVEMBRE 1988

## Calcul de la disponibilité pour un groupement d'emplois  2.4

Complété le : _____

Groupement : _____

Page ____ de ____

Groupe cible _____

| no | EMPLOIS | EFFECTIFS | | DISPONIBILITÉ | | PONDÉRATION | |
|----|---------|-----------|--|---------------|--|-------------|--|
| | | ❷ TOTAL | ❸ GROUPE CIBLE | ❹ Diagnostic | ❺ Objectifs | ❻ Diagnostic | ❼ Objectifs |
| | | A = | B = | | | C¹ = | C² = |

❻ TAUX DE DISPONIBILITÉ :

$$D = \frac{C^1}{A} = \underline{\quad} = \underline{\quad} \%$$

❽ POURCENTAGE DU GROUPE CIBLE DANS LES EFFECTIFS

$$E = \frac{B}{A} = \underline{\quad} = \underline{\quad} \%$$

❾ SOUS-UTILISATION :

(en pourcentage) $F = (D) \underline{\quad} - (E) \underline{\quad} = \underline{\quad} \%$

(en nombre) $G = (A) \underline{\quad} \times (F) \underline{\quad} = \underline{\quad}$

❿ OBJECTIF POUR LE GROUPEMENT

(en pourcentage) $H = \frac{C^2}{A} = \underline{\quad} = \underline{\quad} \%$

COMMISSION DES DROITS DE LA PERSONNE DU QUÉBEC — NOVEMBRE 1988

## Synthèse des résultats 2.5

Complété le: _____
Données valables en date du: _____

Ligne de progression: _____

Page ___ de ___
Groupe cible _____

| EMPLOIS | | EFFECTIFS | | | DISPONIBILITÉ (diagnostic) | SOUS-UTILISATION | | OBJECTIFS QUANTITATIFS | |
|---------|---|-----------|---|---|---------------------------|------------------|---|------------------------|---|
| no | | TOTAL | GROUPE CIBLE | | GROUPE CIBLE | GROUPE CIBLE | | GROUPE CIBLE | |
| | | | nb | % | % | % | nb | % | nb |

COMMISSION DES DROITS DE LA PERSONNE DU QUÉBEC — NOVEMBRE 1988

**Analyse du système d'emploi** 3.1

Complété le : _____
Catégorie d'emplois : _____
Statut d'employé : _____
Emploi(s) : _____

Page _____ de _____

Unité(s) administrative(s) _____
(s'il y a lieu)

Groupe cible _____

Sous-système : _____

| ❶ SUJETS OU ACTIVITÉS ** | ❷ SOURCES D'INFORMATION (documents et personnes ressources) | ❸ DESCRIPTION DES RÈGLES ET PRATIQUES | ❹ RISQUES D'EXCLUSION OU DE TRAITEMENTS DÉFAVORABLES PAR DISCRIMINATION | ❺ RÉSULTATS DES MESURES (s'il y a lieu) | ❻ INVENTAIRE DES CORRECTIFS POSSIBLES |
|---|---|---|---|---|---|
| | | | | | |

* L'analyse s'effectue par emploi ou par groupe d'emplois, dans la mesure ou tous les emplois du groupe sont régis par les mêmes règles ou pratiques
** Suivant l'ordre proposé dans le présent cahier portant sur l'analyse du système d'emploi

COMMISSION DES DROITS DE LA PERSONNE DU QUÉBEC — NOVEMBRE 1988

## Correction de la sous-utilisation 4.1

Complété le: _____

Page _____ de _____

Groupe cible _____

❶ Objectif _____ %

Emploi ou groupement d'emplois: _____

| ❷ Périodes | ❸ Effectifs totaux en fin de période | ❹ Objectif de représentation du G.C. en nb | ❺ Effectifs ajustés des membres du G.C. | ❻ Nominations de membres du G.C. | ❼ Postes à combler | ❽ Taux de nomination des membres du G.C. | Résultats escomptés | | | Résultats obtenus | | |
|---|---|---|---|---|---|---|---|---|---|---|---|---|
| | | | | | | | ❾ Nominations | ❿ NB total | ⓫ % fin de période | ⓬ Nominations | ⓭ NB total | ⓮ % fin de période |
| de à | | | | | | | | | | | | |
| 1 ............... | | | | | | | | | | | | |
| 2 ............... | | | | | | | | | | | | |
| 3 ............... | | | | | | | | | | | | |
| 4 ............... | | | | | | | | | | | | |
| 5 ............... | | | | | | | | | | | | |

❼ CONDITIONS REQUISES

❽ DÉLAIS REQUIS

❾ RÉSULTATS OBTENUS

❿ EFFETS ATTENDUS

⓫ MESURES DE REDRESSEMENT

COMMISSION DES DROITS DE LA PERSONNE DU QUÉBEC — NI-XI MIHI  1988

Complété le : _____

Page _____ de _____

Groupe cible : _____

## Prévision des mouvements de personnel  4.2

Emploi ou groupement d'emplois : _____

| Périodes de — à | Effectifs totaux en début de période | Postes vacants en début de période | Départs | | Promotions et mutations | | Retraites | | Créations | Abolitions | Postes vacants en fin de période | Postes à combler | Effectifs totaux en fin de période |
|---|---|---|---|---|---|---|---|---|---|---|---|---|---|
| | | | G.C. | Autres | G.C. | Autres | G.C. | Autres | | | | | |
| 1 | | | | | | | | | | | | | |
| 2 | | | | | | | | | | | | | |
| 3 | | | | | | | | | | | | | |
| 4 | | | | | | | | | | | | | |
| 5 | | | | | | | | | | | | | |

Emploi ou groupement d'emplois : _____

| | | | | | | | | | | | | | |
|---|---|---|---|---|---|---|---|---|---|---|---|---|---|
| 1 | | | | | | | | | | | | | |
| 2 | | | | | | | | | | | | | |
| 3 | | | | | | | | | | | | | |
| 4 | | | | | | | | | | | | | |
| 5 | | | | | | | | | | | | | |

COMMISSION DES DROITS DE LA PERSONNE DU QUÉBEC — NOVEMBRE 1988

# Correction du système d'emploi  4.3

Complété le: _____
Catégorie d'emplois: _____
Statut d'emploi: _____
Emploi (s): _____

Page ____ de ____

Unité (s) administrative(s) _____
(s'il y a lieu)

Groupe cible _____

Sous-système: _____

| ❶ RÈGLES OU PRATIQUES NÉCESSITANT UN CORRECTIF | ❷ MESURES D'ÉGALITÉ DE CHANCES | ❸ OBJECTIFS QUALITATIFS | ❹ CONDITIONS REQUISES | ❺ DÉLAIS REQUIS | ❻ RÉSULTATS OBTENUS |
|---|---|---|---|---|---|
| | | | | | |

COMMISSION DES DROITS DE LA PERSONNE DU QUEBEC — NOVEMBRE 1986

Complété le: _____

Page ___ de ___

**Mesures
de soutien** 4.4

| PROBLÈMES IDENTIFIÉS | MESURES DE SOUTIEN | EFFETS ATTENDUS | CONDITIONS REQUISES | DÉLAIS REQUIS | RÉSULTATS OBTENUS |
|---|---|---|---|---|---|
| | | | | | |

COMMISSION DES DROITS DE LA PERSONNE DU QUÉBEC — NOVEMBRE 1988

# Data Collection Forms
# Required in Ontario

# DATA COLLECTION IN ONTARIO

(This is not an official form, but is based on the draft regulations released June 16, 1993)

For small employers:
    Private sector employers with fewer than 100 employees
    Broader public sector employers with fewer than 50 employees

Any cell with less than 5 data points does not have to be reported.

| Plan period | Men | Women | Aboriginal Peoples | | Persons with disabilities | | Racial minorities | | Non-designated group employees | Total employees |
|---|---|---|---|---|---|---|---|---|---|---|
| | | | Men | Women | Men | Women | Men | Women | | |
| Beginning | | | | | | | | | | |
| End | | | | | | | | | | |

## DATA COLLECTION IN ONTARIO

Medium sized employers include two groups of employers:

*private sector* employers with between 100 and 500 employees;
*broader public sector* employers with between 50 and 500 employees

Report

- for each geographic area, and
- by employment status (permanent full-time, permanent part-time, term, and seasonal)

Any cell with less than 5 data points does not have to be reported.

| Occupations | Plan period | Men | Women | Aboriginal Peoples | | Persons with disabilities | | Racial minorities | | Non-designated group employees | Total employees |
| --- | --- | --- | --- | --- | --- | --- | --- | --- | --- | --- | --- |
| | | | | Men | Women | Men | Women | Men | Women | | |
| Senior Managers | Beginning | | | | | | | | | | |
| | End | | | | | | | | | | |
| Middle & other managers | Beginning | | | | | | | | | | |
| | End | | | | | | | | | | |
| Professionals | Beginning | | | | | | | | | | |
| | End | | | | | | | | | | |
| Semi-professionals & technicians | Beginning | | | | | | | | | | |
| | End | | | | | | | | | | |
| Supervisors | Beginning | | | | | | | | | | |
| | End | | | | | | | | | | |

| Occupations | Plan period | Men | Women | Aboriginal Peoples | | Persons with disabilities | | Racial minorities | | Non-designated group employees | Total employees |
|---|---|---|---|---|---|---|---|---|---|---|---|
| | | | | Men | Women | Men | Women | Men | Women | | |
| Foremen Forewomen | Beginning | | | | | | | | | | |
| | End | | | | | | | | | | |
| Administrative & senior clerical | Beginning | | | | | | | | | | |
| | End | | | | | | | | | | |
| Sales & service (Skill level III) | Beginning | | | | | | | | | | |
| | End | | | | | | | | | | |
| Skilled crafts & trades | Beginning | | | | | | | | | | |
| | End | | | | | | | | | | |
| Clerical | Beginning | | | | | | | | | | |
| | End | | | | | | | | | | |
| Sales & service (skill level II) | Beginning | | | | | | | | | | |
| | End | | | | | | | | | | |
| Semi-skilled manual workers | Beginning | | | | | | | | | | |
| | End | | | | | | | | | | |
| Sales & service (skill level I) | Beginning | | | | | | | | | | |
| | End | | | | | | | | | | |
| Other manual workers | Beginning | | | | | | | | | | |
| | End | | | | | | | | | | |

# DATA COLLECTION IN ONTARIO

For large employers:
employers with more than 500 employees

Report

- for each geographic area, and
- by employment status (permanent full-time, permanent part-time, term, and seasonal)

Any cell with less than 5 data points does not have to be reported.

Plan period _____ (Complete one form at beginning and one at end of plan period.)

| Occupations | Salary* quartiles | Men | Women | Aboriginal Peoples | | Persons with disabilities | | Racial minorities | | Non-designated group employees | Total employees |
|---|---|---|---|---|---|---|---|---|---|---|---|
| | | | | Men | Women | Men | Women | Men | Women | | |
| Senior Managers | 4th | | | | | | | | | | |
| | 3rd | | | | | | | | | | |
| | 2nd | | | | | | | | | | |
| | 1st | | | | | | | | | | |
| Middle & other managers | 4th | | | | | | | | | | |
| | 3rd | | | | | | | | | | |
| | 2nd | | | | | | | | | | |
| | 1st | | | | | | | | | | |
| Professionals | 4th | | | | | | | | | | |
| | 3rd | | | | | | | | | | |
| | 2nd | | | | | | | | | | |
| | 1st | | | | | | | | | | |

*Salary includes benefits.

| Occupations | Salary* quartiles | Men | Women | Aboriginal Peoples | | Persons with disabilities | | Racial minorities | | Non-designated group employees | Total employees |
|---|---|---|---|---|---|---|---|---|---|---|---|
| | | | | Men | Women | Men | Women | Men | Women | | |
| Semi-professionals & technicians | 4th | | | | | | | | | | |
| | 3rd | | | | | | | | | | |
| | 2nd | | | | | | | | | | |
| | 1st | | | | | | | | | | |
| Supervisors | 4th | | | | | | | | | | |
| | 3rd | | | | | | | | | | |
| | 2nd | | | | | | | | | | |
| | 1st | | | | | | | | | | |
| Foremen Forewomen | 4th | | | | | | | | | | |
| | 3rd | | | | | | | | | | |
| | 2nd | | | | | | | | | | |
| | 1st | | | | | | | | | | |
| Administrative & senior clerical | 4th | | | | | | | | | | |
| | 3rd | | | | | | | | | | |
| | 2nd | | | | | | | | | | |
| | 1st | | | | | | | | | | |
| Sales & service (skill level III) | 4th | | | | | | | | | | |
| | 3rd | | | | | | | | | | |
| | 2nd | | | | | | | | | | |
| | 1st | | | | | | | | | | |

*Salary includes benefits...

| Occupations | Salary* quartiles | Men | Women | Aboriginal Peoples | | Persons with disabilities | | Racial minorities | | Non-designated group employees | Total employees |
|---|---|---|---|---|---|---|---|---|---|---|---|
| | | | | Men | Women | Men | Women | Men | Women | | |
| Skilled crafts & trades | 4th | | | | | | | | | | |
| | 3rd | | | | | | | | | | |
| | 2nd | | | | | | | | | | |
| | 1st | | | | | | | | | | |
| Clerical | 4th | | | | | | | | | | |
| | 3rd | | | | | | | | | | |
| | 2nd | | | | | | | | | | |
| | 1st | | | | | | | | | | |
| Sales & service (skill level II) | 4th | | | | | | | | | | |
| | 3rd | | | | | | | | | | |
| | 2nd | | | | | | | | | | |
| | 1st | | | | | | | | | | |
| Semi-skilled manual workers | 4th | | | | | | | | | | |
| | 3rd | | | | | | | | | | |
| | 2nd | | | | | | | | | | |
| | 1st | | | | | | | | | | |
| Sales & service (skill level I) | 4th | | | | | | | | | | |
| | 3rd | | | | | | | | | | |
| | 2nd | | | | | | | | | | |
| | 1st | | | | | | | | | | |

*Salary includes benefits.

| Occupations | Salary* quartiles | Men | Women | Aboriginal Peoples | | Persons with disabilities | | Racial minorities | | Non-designated group employees | Total employees |
|---|---|---|---|---|---|---|---|---|---|---|---|
| | | | | Men | Women | Men | Women | Men | Women | | |
| Other manual workers | 4th | | | | | | | | | | |
| | 3rd | | | | | | | | | | |
| | 2nd | | | | | | | | | | |
| | 1st | | | | | | | | | | |

*Salary includes benefits.

# Glossary

**Able-bodiedism:** The belief that only able-bodied people are talented and able to work.

**Aboriginal Peoples:** The original people in Canada including status and non-status "Indians", Inuit, Denes, and Métis. Also referred to as First Nations or Native peoples.

**Accommodation:** Employment practices, systems and support mechanisms designed to accommodate differences so that no individual experiences reduced access to employment opportunities or benefits because of their sex, race, colour or disability status.

**Adverse impact:** The effect of an employment practice or process which disproportionately excludes members of designated groups (and which cannot be shown to be job-related).

**Barrier elimination measures:** Permanent changes to employment systems and practices which are identified as systemically (or intentionally) discriminating.

**Barriers:** Hindrances which block members of designated groups from having equality or opportunity in employment.

**Census agglomeration (CA):** See **Geographic areas**.

**Census metropolitan area:** see **Geographic areas**.

**Concentration:** A disproportionately high ratio of any one group of workers to other employees in a specific type of job, work unit, organizational level, or occupational group.

**Corrective measures:** Term used in Quebec to refer to positive measures.

**Credentialism:** Use of criteria such as diplomas, university degrees, training certificates and other formal criteria not justified by the needs of the job.

**Designated groups:** Groups which are disadvantaged because of systemic discrimination and require EE initiatives. Currently the groups are: Aboriginal Peoples, persons with disabilities, racial minorities and women.

**Direct discrimination:** Deliberately excluding members of a particular group because of prejudice or ill will. Direct discrimination does not have to be malicious.

**Disabled:** The World Health Organization's definition is: "any restriction or lack (resulting from impairment) of ability to perform an activity in the manner or within the range considered normal for a human being".

**Disadvantaged groups:** Groups which require EE initiatives because they suffer from higher levels of unemployment, lower pay relative to their abilities and little participation in positions of authority.

**Distribution:** Work-force analysis which assesses the proportion of designated group members found across various occupational groupings. The formula used to calculate is: Designated group members in an occupation ÷ Total number of designated group members.

**Duty to accommodate:** The requirement, recognized by Supreme Court of Canada, that under human rights legislation, whether stated explicitly or not, that employers must accommodate employees in groups protected by human rights legislation. See **Accommodation**.

**Employment equity:** A pro-active set of initiatives or activities designed to ensure fair representation and employment systems throughout organizations by removing systemic discrimination.

**Employment systems:** The policies and practices by which an organization attracts, selects, trains, promotes and compensates employees, establishes and defines the jobs, and determines the conditions of employment at the workplace.

**Employment systems review:** Review of employment systems to identify and eliminate all existing discriminatory practices, both formal and informal. Systemic discrimination works through the normal operations of employment systems which are not designed to discriminate – but which do. A review is necessary to remove the unintentional adverse impact of these systems.

**First Nations peoples:** See **Aboriginal Peoples**.

**Flow data:** Information on the flow of people through an organization due to hires, transfers, demotions, and promotions. Flow data is also called transaction data because it is based on various human resource transactions.

**Geographic areas** (as defined in draft regulations for Ontario *Employment Equity Act*):

(a) Each census metropolitan area or census agglomeration in which one or more workplaces of the employer are located; or
(b) For those workplaces that are not located in a census metropolitan area or census agglomeration, each upper tier municipality in which one or more workplaces of the employer are located.

*Census agglomeration* (CA) and *Census metropolitan area* (CMA) (as defined Statistics Canada):

A large urban area, together with adjacent urban and rural areas which have a high degree of economic and social integration with that urban area. If the population is at least 10,000 based on the last census then it is a census agglomeration. If the population is at least 100,000 based on the last census it is a census metropolitan area; once an area is defined as a CMA it remains so, even if the population drops below 100,000.

There are 246 urban areas, 32 CAs and 10 CMAs. (Statistics Canada, *1991 Census Dictionary (Reference)*. Catalogue No. 92-301E, pp. 178-79 and 182-84). Reproduced with the permission of the Minister of Industry, Science and Technology, 1993.

**Upper tier municipality** (as defined by the Ontario government): Upper tier municipality means a territorial district, a country or a regional district, or metropolitan municipality but does not include a regional or district municipality that is located in a territorial district.

**Goals:** Can be used to refer to the ultimate goal of EE – to have a representative work-force and to have employment systems which work for all employees. Alternatively, refers to the annual plans set to bring about these ultimate goals.

**Intentional discrimination:** See **Direct discrimination**.

**Job relatedness:** Refers to the suitability of employment systems or job qualifications to what is truly required to accomplish the job. For example, it may be found that a job can be satisfactorily accomplished in more than one way.

**Labour force:** The labour force is comprised of two groups of people over the age of 15: (1) those who are employed, and (2) those who are unemployed. Unemployed persons are ready and available to work and are looking for work. Those who are outside of the labour force are groups that are not available for work such as those who are retired, students, persons in institutions (*e.g.*, prisons), homemakers.

**Labour shortage:** A labour shortage occurs when there are not enough people available for jobs.

**Mainstream:** Majority or dominant group or culture, such as Whites, the able-bodied and men in Canada.

**Minority:** Any group which has limited access to the scarce resources of wealth, status and power.

**Native Peoples:** See **Aboriginal Peoples.**

**Numerical goals:** See **Quantitative goals**.

**Occupational representation:** Work-force analysis which examines the proportion of occupational groups held by members of the various designated groups. The formula used to calculate is: Designated group members within an occupation ÷ Total in the occupation.

**Occupational segregation:** The tendency to stereotype jobs, according to sex or race, so that some occupations become known as "women's jobs" or are typically expected to be held by members of a particular racial group.

**Pay equity:** A means of removing systemic discrimination from the wage determination system to ensure equal pay for work of equal value for jobs traditionally performed by women, compared to jobs traditionally performed by men.

**Persons with disabilities:** Persons who have a persistent physical, mental, psychiatric, sensory, or learning impairment and who consider or believe that an employer would consider that there is a disadvantage in employment by reason of the impairment.

**Positive measures:** Pro-active, temporary measures designed to remedy the effects of past discrimination against members of the designated groups. Positive measures speed up the rate of change within the workplace creating a critical mass which further helps the process of overcoming discrimination.

**Qualitative goals:** Non-numerical or non-quantitative goals. These goals focus on changing employment systems or the organizational environment. Also referred to as qualitative measures.

**Quantitative goals:** Goals which focus on changing the number of designated group members within one or more jobs. Same as numerical goals.

**Racial minorities:** Persons who are visibly different from the dominant group and are non-white in colour/or non-caucasian in race. Same as visible minorities.

**Racism:** Any action or institutional practice, backed by institutional power, that subordinates people because of their race or colour. Racism is the assumption of the superiority of one racial group over another and the power to act on this arrogance.

**Reasonable accommodation:** See **Accommodation**.

**Reciprocal:** The complementary or opposite. The reciprocal of racial minorities is Whites, of Aboriginal Peoples is those who are not of First Nations ancestry, of persons with disabilities is persons who are able-bodied, of women is men.

**Remedial measures:** A term used in Quebec, see **Positive measures.**

**Representation:** Representation measures the proportion of each designated group found in the total organizational work-force.

**Self-identification:** An employee's specification of her/his characteristics in terms of each of the four designated groups.

**Skill shortage:** People available to work lack the skills required by the jobs. It is possible for a skill shortage to exist for some jobs at the same time that large numbers of people are unemployed.

**Special measures:** Go beyond just elimination of discrimination. Redress lasting effects of past discrimination. Special measures include: positive and supportive measures. Such programs are not discriminatory under human rights laws and the *Canadian Charter of Rights and Freedoms* when they are used to redress discrimination (for instance, where there is an under-representation of one or more of the designated groups within a job).

**Stock data:** A snapshot of designated group member status for an organization's employees at one point in time.

**Supportive measures:** Pro-active measures to remove barriers which have a greater impact on designated group members but typically affect others as well. Such measures foster a work environment beneficial to all employees and generally improve the quality of the workplace.

**Systemic discrimination:** Adverse impact which disadvantages certain groups through the normal operation of employment systems which unintentionally discriminate.

**Systems review:** See **Employment systems review**.

**Target:** Ultimate desired outcome of EE – representative work-force and employment systems which work for all employees.

**Target groups:** See **Designated groups**.

**Third party identification:** Someone other than the employee is asked to specify each employee's characteristics in terms of each of the four designated groups. That person is usually the supervisor or someone in human resources. Third party identification can also be done with verification. This means that someone other than the employee specifies the designated group characteristics and this information is then given to the employee for her/his verification.

**Timetable:** Schedule for completion of EE goals.

**Transaction data:** Information on the flow of people through the organization due to hires, transfers, demotions, and promotions. Flow data is also called transaction data because it is based on various human resource transactions.

**Underrepresentation:** A disproportionately lower level of designated group workers within an occupational category, organizational level or within a job than is warranted, given availability. Where underrepresentation exists EE initiatives are needed.

**Upper tier municipality**: see **Geographic areas**.

**Visible minorities:** See **Racial minorities**.

**Work-force analysis:** Collecting and analyzing data on current employees (and new hires) as to their designated group status. This data is used in identifying problem areas where EE initiatives are needed, in setting numerical goals and timetables and in assessing when a representative work-force has been achieved for each designated group.

**Working age population:** All those in the population over the age of 15. The population is comprised of those who are in the labour force (employed or unemployed) and those not in the labour force. Among the latter may be those who are discouraged workers and those who do not wish to be in the labour force at the time. Discouraged workers are those who want to work but are not looking for work because of discouragement in finding work at a previous point in time. Those who do not wish to be in the labour force include retirees, students and homemakers.

# INDEX

women, percentage of, 124
Legislation
*Canadian Charter of Rights and Freedoms*
equality section, 39
general relevance to employment equity, 38-39
limit on equality, 40
designated groups, definitions under, 31
federal coverage, 21-22
federal *Employment Equity Act*
mechanics of, 25
origin of, 25
proposed changes to, 26-27
human rights. *See* Human rights legislation
human rights codes, 23
Ontario *Employment Equity Act*
communication with commission, 29
compatibility with other legislation, 32
coverage of, 28
enforcement, 32
implementation timetable, 30
information to be provided to employees, 93
preparation for, 27-28
regulations under, 30
requirements of, 28-29
seniority rights, 30
standards of judgment, 29
union/management responsibility, 29
pay equity. *See* Pay equity legislation
provincial coverage, 22
Quebec *Charter of Human Rights and Freedoms*
generally, 32-33
guidelines for developing programs, 33-34
workplace equality. *See* Workplace equality legislation

**M**

Metis. *See* Aboriginal Peoples
Monitoring and evaluation
components of, 269-73
assessing accomplishments, 270-72
collecting information on

initiatives and activities, 270
communicating information of progress, 272
deciding on future activities, 272
establishing future goals and timetables, 273
reviewing goals and timetables, 270
pitfalls, 278-79

**N**

Non-sexist language chart, 58

**O**

Ontario. *See* Legislation

**P**

Pay equity legislation
employment equity
compared to, 41-45
implementation conflicts with, 44-45
income comparison charts, 43-44
occupational segregation, 42
purpose of, 40
Persons with disabilities
disability categories, 52
duty to accommodate, 196-97
employment barriers to
accessibility problems, 67
discomfort/embarrassment feelings, 65-66
generalization of inability, 65
need to accommodate, fear of, 66-67
over-protectiveness, 66
poor employee presumption, 67
evolution of view of, 64
numbers in households, 55
percentage of population by province, 286
preferred terminology, 53
staffing selection considerations, 230-35
Physical demands analysis, 232-35

**Q**

Qualifications. *See* Staffing
Quebec. *See* Legislation